REVOLT!

REVOLT!

How to Defeat Obama and Repeal His Socialist Programs— A Patriot's Guide

DICK MORRIS
and EILEEN McGANN

An Imprint of HarperCollinsPublishers
www.harpercollins.com

HarperCollins books may be purchased for educational, business, or sales promotional use. For information, please write: Special Markets Department, HarperCollins Publishers, 10 East 53rd Street, New York, NY 10022.

FIRST EDITION

Library of Congress Cataloging-in-Publication Data is available upon request.

ISBN: 978-0-06-207330-3
ISBN: 978-0-06-208948-9 (B & N edition)

11   12   13   14   15   DIX/RRD   10   9   8   7   6   5   4   3   2   1

To the memory of Eugene J. Morris
(1910–2010), and

To the millions of patriots who joined
the Tea Party movement to save our
country from socialism

CONTENTS

INTRODUCTION: A LABOR OF NECESSITY

On December 6, 2010, President Barack Obama publicly surrendered.

And although the red, white, and blue flag still furled over the White House on that wintry day, it might as well have been all white.

Because when Obama ditched his seminal campaign pledge—to allow the Bush tax cuts to expire and to raise taxes on families making more than $250,000 a year—he acknowledged that the game had changed.

For him and for us.

It was a humbling moment and a stunning admission. Only two years into his term, Obama was in retreat on the very cornerstone of his presidency—a massive and audacious income redistribution scheme to be achieved by increasing taxes on the wealthy (families making over $250,000) to pay for expansive programs to benefit the poor.

Americans never supported it and Republicans blocked it. Left with no other choice, Obama capitulated.

The White House called it a "compromise." But Barack Obama's "compromise" with the Republicans was no more of a compromise than the deal that Japan's Emperor Hirohito cut with General Douglas MacArthur on the deck of the battleship *Missouri* after the atomic bombing of Hiroshima and Nagasaki. It was an abject surrender, not a compromise; an utter submission, not triangulation.

There's a big difference.

Obama was not making a calculated, voluntary move to the center, as some have suggested. Not at all. Those who think he was are altogether mistaken.

Moving to the center is not just a two-dimensional process of taking the best from the left and the right and synthesizing it all into a new paradigm that is palatable to some of the left and some of the right. That's the essence of it, but there's more to it—an additional third dimension that reflects the difference between arriving there from a position of strength or from a position of weakness.

In the course of coming in from the cold of his extreme far-left positions, the president looked like a wimp, openly abandoning his long-held fervent views in the face of electoral defeats, adverse court rulings, recalcitrant Democrats, and strong, united Republican opposition.

It was not courage that propelled him to change his position; it was weakness that forced him to back down. And the future will only bring more and more surrenders.

The game change for us is that he is vulnerable; he can be beaten. Weak presidents don't get reelected.

But he's hasn't been knocked out yet. We have work to do.

The liberal media tried to spin Obama's successes in the lame duck session of Congress—held right after the election—as major achievements. But how could he fail with a Congress filled with defeated Democrats who were no longer even marginally accountable to us?

The fact is that Obama blinked in the tax cut fight and he will blink again and again and again if we confront him and stand firm.

Stay tuned.

Now is the time for us to force him to back down over and over, until he backs out of the White House on January 20, 2013!

But that's just part of what we need to accomplish. It's not just Obama who must be defeated. For the next two years, we have our work cut out for us—rolling back Obama's disastrous programs, sending his Democratic cronies back home, capturing the Senate, and building bigger Republican majorities in the House.

We need to revolt.

This is a labor of necessity that we cannot turn our backs on.

Because we've all had enough. Enough ObamaCare, enough corporate bailouts, enough repeated attempts to raise our taxes, enough failed economic policies that generate class warfare and pit neighbor against neighbor. Enough of Congress and the White House ignoring us.

It's time to fight back, time to rebel, time to say "No more." Time to remind Obama and the Democrats that this is our country, our lives, our families that they are endangering with their drastic policies. We won't stand for it any longer.

And we don't have to.

Because the astonishing events that started with the Tea Party Patriots and culminated in the voting booths across America on Tuesday, November 2, 2010, were only the first phase in a long and unavoidable journey that lies ahead of us for the next two years.

A journey of necessity that we must complete; a journey of necessity that we must start today.

The new Republican majority in the House of Representatives and the diminished power of the Democratic establishment in the Senate have given us the means, the motive, and the opportunity to reject the Obama agenda, repeal his ill-advised programs, and show him the door out of the White House.

That is our mandate: to save us all from the socialist ideas of Obama and his Democratic cronies.

These ideas, if realized, will transform our country, our culture, and our economy into an unrecognizable society and will obliterate the values that have been inherent in these United States for more than two hundred years and are the very basis of our liberty and freedom.

Most Americans don't agree with the ideas this administration is trying to force on us.

Ideas that are naive and don't work.

Ideas that must be rejected.

Let's not mince words. Barack Obama is a socialist! He wants to expand the role of the government until it mirrors the bloated size of modern Europe. He wants universal, government-controlled health care. He wants banks under direct federal control, subservient to the government's economic directives. He wants indirect government control over manufacturing. By controlling what comes out the smokestack, he realizes, he can control what gets made in the factory. He wants to ban the use of coal no matter how much it makes us dependent on foreign oil. He seeks to change our tax laws into a massive scheme for income redistribution. And he wants the poor to have upward mobility, not through hard work and education, but through increasing government handouts, aid paid for by outvoted rich people.

That's what Barack Obama wants. But we can—and must—stop his plans to transform our country into a European socialist nanny-state with an oversize government that dictates just about everything that we do. We can't afford not to.

We can—and must—stop Obama's health care debacle that will inevitably lead to the intentional rationing of critical health care to the sickest and most vulnerable, while costs skyrocket. We owe it to our parents and to those who have no one to fight for them.

We can—and must—stop Obama's madcap economic policies, which are just plain wrong. Simply look around. He's on the brink of destroying everything that we've worked for. He's given us no choice.

We can—and must—stop him from raising taxes on the very people who create jobs and lift the economy.

We can—and must—stop him from implementing endless federal regulations that will paralyze our ability to do business or to live our lives without constant government intrusion.

And, finally, we can—and must—stop his unprecedented and astronomical spending, which is driving the deficit through the roof and bankrupting our future.

How can we do these things?

By continuing the Revolt that started in November 2010; by continuing our expression of vigorous dissent.

This book is a guide to beating Obama's policies over the next two years so that we can beat him in the next presidential election and, ultimately, increase the Republican majority in Congress so that we can get America back on the right track.

We can do it. Join us in this labor of necessity.

Think about it: Obama is checkmated as long as Republicans hold firm, challenge him on solid grounds anchored in public opinion, and remain united. He can either lose the election of 2012 because he is an obstinate ideologue who won't compromise and won't abandon his socialist principles or he can lose it because he totally surrenders and is too weak to be president.

He does not have a third option—winning the budget fights and winning reelection—as long as the Republicans properly mount their challenge, because public opinion, the essential element for victory, is not with him.

- Americans want spending cuts, not tax increases.

- Americans believe that cutting spending is more important even than cutting the deficit.

- Americans oppose ObamaCare.

- Americans are against letting the EPA impose carbon dioxide restrictions without consulting Congress.

- Americans are against an administrative fiat by the NLRB to eliminate the secret ballot in union elections.

- Americans oppose earmarks.

- Americans do not want the FCC to limit or censor talk radio or to control the Internet.

These are the battlegrounds for 2011–2012. It is on this turf that the Republican House majority must fight. The fearful "moderate" Democratic senators will cave in. And then Obama will be forced to surrender because the Force—public opinion—is not with him. In 2009 and 2010, Obama could ignore the opinions of the majority of Americans because his Congressional majority was so overwhelming that he could ram through anything he wanted. Now he has lost his majority and he will have to back down when the public turns against him.

And with each surrender—over his desire to raise the debt limit without mandated spending cuts, over his support for bailing out states in trouble, and over his demand to raise taxes in the 2012 budget, Obama will get weaker and weaker.

His inability to fight and win the war on terror and his choice to become mired in Afghanistan with no real plan for winning will contribute to the image of weakness.

In 2012 he will face America, denuded of all the programs he passed in 2009–2010, with an economy still struggling with 7–8% unemployment, and with a manifest inability to measure up to the job of president.

Former British prime minister Tony Blair said it best in his new memoir, *A Journey: My Political Life*. He described how voters can bring down a politician: ". . . once public opinion had gone sour it didn't seem to matter whether what [the government] did was right or wrong; and that once the mood had turned from the government and embraced us [the opposition], the mood was merciless in its pursuit, indifferent to anything other than satisfying itself."[1]

Now it is up to us.

Obama's surrender on the extension of the Bush tax cuts at the end of last year is a case study of what can—and must—be done in the next two years. We don't have to cave in—he does!

We learned in November 2010 that we can win, we can prevail. And we will. But we have a lot more to do in 2011 and 2012.

Now we need to work together to vigorously reject Obama's fanatical agenda, repeal his reckless legislative follies, and replace him as president.

We have no choice.

It's that serious. Because it is our obligation, our duty, to save America.

By continuing the Revolt that started in November 2010.

This book is a guide to beating Obama's policies over the next two years so that we can ultimately beat him in the next presidential election.

Join us in this labor of necessity.

**Author's Note: As of the date *Revolt!* went to press,
all the information in this book was current and accurate.**

PART ONE

DEFEATING OBAMA

There is only one way to defeat Obama's misguided and dangerous socialist agenda for America, and that is to resoundingly and categorically defeat Barack Obama.

It's that simple: He and his fanatical policies have got to go.

We know that. We've already started the process by taking over the House of Representatives. With the leadership of courageous Tea Party members and other activists across the country, along with the support of so many disgusted and alienated voters, we threw out a large number of arrogant and self-serving congressmen, who deserved exactly what they got. We also sent Obama a message about our plans for him.

In case there's any doubt about it, we're planning to send him back to Illinois. For good.

Accomplishing this will require a disciplined twofold strategy: First we have to block him in Congress by repealing his most offensive programs and impeding any new catastrophic legislation. Then we need to rout him in the voting booth.

And we can—and must—do both.

Let's start with Congress first. During the next two years, we have to capitalize on our control of the House in order to systematically undo the damage that Obama and his naive policies have already done. That includes using the budget to defund health care "reform" and his other extravagant follies, and doing whatever else it takes to reject and repeal his colossal blunders.

At the same time, we have to thwart any fresh attempts by Obama to further devastate our fragile economy. There's no doubt about it, he'll be back with more and more outlandish legislative schemes to implement his radical dreams. That's why we have to be both vigilant in recognizing what he is up to and rigorous in stopping him. Each and every time one of his wacky and expensive programs comes up for a vote, we need to beat him.

But it won't be enough just to thrash his initiatives and reverse his mistakes. We also need to trounce him in the voting booth and get him out of the White House. So, our next step, on November 6, 2012, is to vote him out of office.

We'll gladly give him a one-way ticket back home.

Let's face it. Defeating an incumbent president, even an unpopular one, is not an easy task. A sitting president has an amazing arsenal of tools available to woo the voters that a challenger can never match. And, in fact, most presidents are reelected. Of the ten presidents since World War II, seven were reelected: Harry Truman, Dwight Eisenhower, Lyndon Johnson, Richard Nixon, Ronald Reagan, Bill Clinton, and George Bush 43. Only Gerald Ford, Jimmy Carter, and George Bush 41 were not.

But when a president loses badly in the Congressional elections after only two years in office, it becomes a lot harder for him to bounce back. Only Eisenhower and Clinton won a second term after losing control of Congress during their first midterm election. And, in Ike's case, the magnitude of the swing in opposition seats was not very great and he personally remained a very popular and likable figure. In Bill Clinton's case, he moved deliberately and significantly to the center and enthusiastically embraced conservative policies that attracted swing voters.

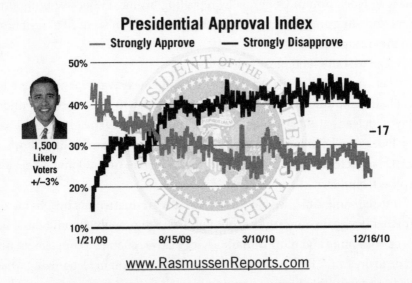

Presidential Approval Index

— Strongly Approve   — Strongly Disapprove

That's not likely to happen with Obama. After the cataclysmic Congressional elections, he did not seem to have even considered a voluntary change in his political direction. And he won't. When he finally realized that he did not have the support in Congress to limit the extension of the Bush tax cuts, he surrendered, while petulantly lashing out at the Republicans.

Obama is vulnerable and we can defeat him. To borrow his own words, "Yes, we can!"

Consider how far and how fast he has fallen. When he took office, he was riding high. His favorability and job approval were stratospheric. Now they have plunged sharply; each week seems to bring him to a new low! [1]

The Zogby poll shows Obama even lower with his approval dipping below 40%! [2]

What happened?

- Obama reached the height of his surge in popularity after his victories in the early caucuses and primaries. In the later primaries, he mostly lost the large, industrial states like Michigan, Pennsylvania, and Ohio to Hillary, in part due to the Rev. Wright tapes. He won the nomination anyway because his early victories, many in sparsely populated caucus states, had given him enough delegates to prevail.

- McCain had surged to a lead over Obama after the conventions, and the Democrat only moved ahead because of the sudden economic collapse and McCain's inability to seize the moment by opposing TARP. So Obama was fading at the finish line.

- Doubts about Obama surfaced right before the election in the Joe the Plumber flap, where he explicitly embraced income redistribution.

- On taking office, he overpromised on what his stimulus package could deliver, claiming it would stop the recession and lower unemployment.

- His health care bill was a vast overreach. And when he failed to sell it to the people, he pushed it anyway. Even when the most liberal state in the nation—Massachusetts—voted for a Republican senator,

Scott Brown, to protest the proposal, he used parliamentary tricks to push it through anyway.

• As unemployment soared up to nearly 10% and stayed there for his entire first two years as president, public patience wore thinner and thinner. More and more people began to realize that, at best, Obama had no clue as to what to do and that, at worst, his policies were causing things to get worse.

• Obama's takeover of GM and Chrysler illustrated the lengths he will go to socialize our economy. His vast expansion of federal regulatory powers over banks and his huge financial bailouts of the states underscored that he was a big-spending, big-government man, out of control.

• The British Petroleum oil spill began to create an image of incompetence. As the facts of his late and tepid response came out, we began to suspect that he would rather spend his time using the spill to stick it to the oil companies than figuring out how to mitigate the environmental damage. As BP scrambled to contain the spill and Obama looked on passively, he seemed like a president out of touch and out of answers.

• Terror attacks began again after a seven-year hiatus under Bush after 9/11. At Fort Hood, a gunman massacred our troops, and a terrorist was only seconds away from detonating a bomb in a plane over Detroit before alert passengers wrestled him to the ground. Mayhem was only narrowly averted in Times Square in the heart of New York City when a terrorist failed to set off his bomb amid a crowded street.

• The war in Afghanistan grew hotter and seems to have no end in sight. This peace candidate has failed to end the war and has only escalated it.

Then came his "shellacking"[3] at the polls on November 2, 2010. His losses showed the country how weak he was and how much his citizens disapproved of his presidency. When he caved in and backed the Republicans on extending the Bush tax cuts, voters gave him credit for compromise, but the affair reinforced his image of weakness.

Now it is up to us to finish the job.

FIRST ORDER OF BUSINESS: BARACK OBAMA

How do we defeat Obama?

There's only one way: by running front and center against his deplorable policies and programs. Our message is very simple: Obama's big picture for our country will bankrupt us and transform the America that we love into a superbureaucracy that controls every aspect of our lives and businesses. That's his plan; that's his passion; that's his ideal.

It's not ours. That's why we have to stop him. It's not too late. But we can't waste any time. Starting today, we have a burning mission: to incessantly remind our fellow voters that Obama is the archetype of a zealous tax and spend liberal. That's truly what he is. That's truly what he believes in.

This is not simply a call to obstruct everything that Obama proposes. If, by chance, he suddenly introduces initiatives that make sense, we should support them. This is not a call for a knee-jerk opposition to everything he calls for.

It is, however, a call to systematically reverse his calamitous signature achievements, such as health care and deficit spending, and to stop him from any further disasters.

It's important not to forget just how dangerous his ideas are. We need to remind voters about the real Obama. To do that, we need to repeatedly call attention to his history: the genuinely frightening implications of his health care "reform," his commitment to class warfare and the redistribution of wealth, his nonstop plans to raise more and more taxes, his utter failure to create jobs, and his over-the-top spending. In short, we need to use his dismal record and his frightening delusions to beat him.

To do otherwise and run a campaign that attacks him personally would only help him win reelection. It might be tempting to some, but that kind of strategy would take us down a dangerous and futile road. We have to take the high road. Voters like Obama, even if they don't believe that he is particularly competent. So personal attacks just won't work.

Pollsters routinely rate presidents according to two different measures: personal favorability and job approval. The former measures the public's opinion of the politician as a person, while the latter gauges how people feel he is doing his job as president.

Most modern presidents score better on personal favorability than on job approval. Americans like their presidents. So, at times, even though our economy may be falling apart or casualties in a foreign war may be mounting so high that we express disapproval of a president's policies, we still like the guy.

Here's an average of post–World War II presidents and their ratings compiled by Gallup. Notice how their personal favorability is usually higher than their job approval.

COMPARISON OF FAVORABLE PERSONAL RATINGS AND JOB APPROVAL RATINGS OF PRESIDENTS: EISENHOWER TO BUSH

President	Average Favorable Personal Rating	Average Favorable Job Approval Rating
Eisenhower	84%	65%
Kennedy	88%	70%
Johnson	77%	55%
Nixon	80%	49%
Ford	73%	47%
Carter	70%	45%
Reagan	70%	53%
George H. W. Bush	73%	61%
Clinton	56%	55%
George W. Bush	67%	68%

Source: Gallup, http://www.gallup.com/poll/8938/historical-favorability-ratings-presidents.aspx[4]

Recently Bill Clinton and George W. Bush have had favorability and job approval ratings that were more equal. Clinton's scandal with Monica Lewinsky and his impeachment diminished his popularity, while unhappiness about President Bush's handling of Iraq and the failure to find weapons of mass destruction in Iraq slashed Bush 43rd's previously high favorability ratings.

But Obama has picked up the old pattern of higher personal favorability than job approval. Because Americans genuinely admire Obama's personal journey and because of what his election as president represents for America, Obama's personal favorability has run much higher than his job approval. Pollster John Zogby says that the gap between them has averaged 7 to 8 points during his first two years in office.[5]

This means that in working to defeat Obama, we must be especially careful to take on the president, not the man. Our attacks must never go to his motivations, character, veracity, integrity, personal life, middle name, or intellect. That won't work. Americans may wonder if Obama knows how to handle the economy, and most think his ideas about health care are cockeyed, but they still admire him personally. It's important not to forget that.

Some may have come to feel that he is a liar and a faker. Even in that case, it would be best for those who do to keep their opinions to themselves and their eyes on the ball. We want to defeat him! It might feel temporarily good to criticize him personally, but those who do so are helping him. Those who criticize what he has done in office, his initiatives and his programs, are hurting him.

HOW TO BEAT OBAMA

To understand how to defeat Obama in 2012, it's important to examine what brought his party down in 2010. There are three theories:

The first is the *Gospel According to Obama*, which claims that the Democrats lost because he failed to end the bitter partisan tone in Washington.

The president is fond of saying that he simply did not communicate his message well and that he was so intent on getting the policy right that he neglected to explain it adequately. "I neglected some things that matter a lot to people, and rightly so: maintaining a bipartisan tone in Washington . . .

I'm going to redouble my efforts to go back to some of those first principles."[6]

Of course, this apologia for the election defeat is pure self-serving nonsense. There's no evidence that Obama didn't tell us enough about health
care or the bank bailouts. He did. The problem isn't that we didn't understand him, it's that Americans fundamentally disagree with him. His tone
or communications style is not the issue. In fact, most of us like his cool-
ness, his calm and dispassionate reason. We find his speaking style attractive (even if he does have to drag a teleprompter everywhere he goes). And,
when he gets going, we sometimes even forget how much we disagree with
him and find ourselves attracted to his enthusiasm. Although MSNBC an-
chor Chris Matthews seems to be the only one who feels a tingle going up
his leg when the president speaks.

But it's not like we don't understand him. We do.

We get it. But we don't like it.

We don't like partisan rancor, but if the alternative is to follow Obama's
misguided policies, we would rather hear the noise of debate in Washington than the sound of boots marching in lockstep in the wrong direction,
as they did when ObamaCare passed through Congress.

There's nothing that Obama could do to improve communications
about that. Nothing at all.

Then there's the *Establishment Gospel*, which posits that the Democrats
lost simply because the economy was in the tank. According to this line
of reasoning, the Congressional defeats were directly linked to the unemployment rate and slow—almost nonexistent—economic growth. With
foreclosures and For Sale signs all around us, we are constantly reminded
of how dire the economic situation has become. And it touches all of us. A
McLaughlin & Associates poll reports that 84% of us know someone who
has lost their job.[7]

The implication, of course, is that Obama's success or failure is totally
dependent on the economy's improvement or decline. If the numbers get
better, he'll win. If not, he'll be a one-term president. Under this theory, it's
out of our hands. It doesn't matter how the campaigns go. If the Federal
Reserve and the Treasury and the global economy pull us out of the recession, Obama is in for eight years.

But history doesn't bear this argument out. Bush 41 lost in 1992 despite improving economic numbers. The recession ended in March of 1991—a year and a half before he was defeated,[8] and the fourth quarter of 1992, when the ballots were counted, featured an astounding 4.3% growth rate.[9] And, in 1994, a recovering economy did not save Clinton's Democrats when they went down to massive defeat, losing both Congressional houses.

It takes time for good economic news to filter down to the voters. The economists may be euphoric, but the public barely notices when unemployment drops a bit or growth rises. It takes a while for people to see any change in their own lives and for the word to get around.

And things are so bad right now, even a modest improvement will still leave us in dire straits. If unemployment drops to, say, 7%, there won't be any celebrations. To have the truly massive recovery that a president needs to buoy his chances for reelection, the turnaround must be long lasting and massive.

When Clinton was reelected in 1996, aided by a robust recovery, the reversal in our national fortunes had been going on for five years. An amazing 11.5 million new jobs[10] had been created since he took office. That is the kind of economic performance a president needs to get a second term. A few good numbers or a couple of quarters of positive news didn't do much. It was only a real economic sea change that helped to boost his fortunes.

What about Ronald Reagan, who also lost ground due to a bad economy, during the midterm elections of 1982, but was able to win two years later, proclaiming "It's morning again in America"? But remember that Reagan's reverses in the midterm elections of 1982 were comparatively minor. He lost only twenty-seven seats in the House and none in the Senate. Though he fell further behind in the House, the Republican Party kept control of the upper chamber. The recession, which ended in late 1982, was followed by a robust recovery, the sort Obama can only dream about. In 1983, economic growth was 4.5%, and in the reelection year of 1984 it soared to 7.2%. Obama might post numbers like these and cruise to reelection, but don't bet on it.

Finally, there's the *Conservative Gospel*, which correlates the 2010 Congressional losses to the fact that Americans fundamentally disagree with Obama's policies. According to the Rasmussen Reports' Daily Presidential Tracking Polls, 57% of American voters oppose his health care reform legislation and want it repealed, while only 39% oppose repeal.[11] Americans think government spending has gotten too big and that the deficit is out of control. They are basically in sharp disagreement with their president.

That's why the Democrats lost so dramatically, and that's why the voters repudiated the president's programs. This is the only explanation that fits the facts of the 2010 election. According to the McLaughlin Poll, there has been a marked shift to the right among the American people, and almost half now describe themselves as "conservative."

IDEOLOGY OF AMERICAN VOTERS

	Nov. 2008	Nov. 2010
Conservative	40%	49%
Moderate	35%	28%
Liberal	21%	21%

Source: McLaughlin & Associates [12]

Obama has made us conservative. We get it. He doesn't.

So, to beat Obama, we must focus intently on his policies and programs.

Obama's obvious weakness is his total failure to create jobs. At this writing, we have already lost 9 million of them since he took power. Next to Herbert Hoover, Barack Obama has the all-time worst jobs record of any president in history.

Republicans need to make the nation understand that Obama's policies are holding our economy down. That is our mission for the next two years.

People need to realize that his threatened tax increases are deterring consumer spending. Americans are afraid to spend money when they don't know whether their taxes will suddenly rise dramatically—both as individuals and as business owners.

We need to make people recognize that it is ObamaCare that has stopped job creation in the health care sector and raised insurance rates. His bank overregulation, particularly of community banks, is strangling loans to small businesses. The threat of a carbon tax and forced unionization is paralyzing manufacturing. Who can grow and expand with the federal government's tax policy in limbo? What will be deductible? What will capital gains taxes be? Will rates go up? Will the ceiling on Social Security taxes be lifted? Will the deficit block new lending? Who knows? So who can plan? Who can add new jobs?

We can't have a recovery with this widespread fear and uncertainty.

Obama doubtless hopes that these issues will be ancient history by November 2012. His political people want us to forget our fears about his health care changes—that's why it is slated to take full effect only after the presidential election. They hope that the failure of the stimulus package will fade from memory by the time Obama seeks a second term.

After all, when the presidential race came around in 1996, who remembered Bill Clinton's 1993 tax increases or Hillary's 1994 health care proposals?

Obama is right: unless the Republican House keeps those issues front and center, they will fade from memory. And we must not let that happen!

Having battled to defeat Obama's socialist agenda throughout '09 and '10, conservatives must now fight to defund and repeal it in '11 and '12. And we know that even if our bills pass the Democratic Senate, Obama will undoubtedly veto them.

Our only choice is to wrap our proposals to defund ObamaCare into the two pieces of legislation that have to pass for the government to keep operating: the increase in the debt limit, which we will need this spring, and the 2012 budget, which will have to pass by October 1, 2011. We have to stop his program before it starts. Before they will approve a debt limit increase or a new federal budget, Republicans must demand that Obama's expensive and intrusive programs be cut. They must hold firm despite the chaos that will ensue. Obama will refuse to sign a debt limit increase or a new federal budget without his programs. The great budget battle lines will be drawn.

As we fight these battles we will be keeping the issues Obama wants to go away alive. We are assuring that they will remain front and center in the 2012 elections.

Not so if the GOP folds and accepts compromises with Obama. If we settle for some improvements in his health care proposal—a weakening here, a dilution there—conservatives will be unable to make these issues central to the 2012 election. If we compromise in '11 and '12, we will have to live with Obama as president for four more long years.

It's that simple.

We must use the battles over the debt limit and the federal budget for fiscal year 2012 to replay and relitigate all the issues that made Obama so unpopular that he lost control of the House.

Start with blocking tax increases.

Higher taxes are Obama's central goal. He sees them not as vehicles to raise money, much less as necessary steps toward lowering the deficit. To him, they are instruments to redistribute income and promote what he calls "social justice." His goal is economic leveling, which entails soaking the rich with ever higher taxes and using the money to fund a permanently enhanced public sector that placates and pacifies voters with subsidies. Capital flows from private hands to the government, and socialism sets in.

That's what he wants.

But when he took office, Obama realized that he could not raise taxes, especially not right in the middle of a massive recession. His party wouldn't have passed it, no matter how overwhelming his majorities, and he would not have gotten any Republican support.

So Obama decided instead to raise spending to incredible heights and borrow the money, making the deficit totally unmanageable. By incurring a massive debt and building up a huge deficit, Obama assured that the cry for an American tax increase would swell and sweep around the world. He knew that the pressure to close the deficit he had created would be irresistible. Central to his political strategy was the assumption that the forces of fiscal responsibility would make Republicans join in voting for higher taxes.

But he thought wrong.

Republicans must, instead, pass a debt limit bill and a budget that brings down the deficit dramatically and ratchets back his big spending policies—but does it with no tax increase.

In the next chapter, you'll find out just how to accomplish this. Surprisingly, it's not that hard, even with an extension of the Bush tax cuts and an end to the alternative minimum tax (AMT) hikes.

All you have to do is to roll back the massive, unbelievable spending increases that Obama pushed through in the opening months of his presidency: the so-called stimulus package. Under his leadership, the government spent money on all kinds of junk. Every useless program that had been kicking around for years, every congressman's dream pork barrel appropriation got money.

To bring down the deficit to about 3% of our economy (the level economists aim at) you have to get rid of all of that new spending. The way budget mavens put it is, you have to freeze domestic discretionary spending at 2008 levels for three years. That's not so hard to do. After all, the federal government wasn't exactly starved for funds in 2008. We just had not yet gone on the wild spending spree of the Obama years.

We also need to stop the crazy growth of Medicaid spending, which has doubled in the past ten years, and cancel Obama's plans to add 16 million people to the rolls as part of ObamaCare.

Then we just have to commit to bringing our troops home by 2015, leaving only 60,000 in Iraq and Afghanistan.

And you're there! The deficit will be down to a reasonable size by 2014.

No need to cut Medicare or Social Security . . . and no need to raise taxes. The numbers work just fine without higher taxes.

This is important: Republicans must not be dragged by our idealism into battles we cannot win and that, if we wage, will cost us the White House in 2012. It is vital for the long term that we reform Medicare and Social Security. But we'll do that after we win in 2012. Not before! Don't sacrifice our chances by wading into those thickets. We will have our hands full with the essential fights we must win.

Then, Republicans must use the debt limit and budget battles to defund ObamaCare. The program he jammed through Congress is massively unpopular. More than any other factor, it was what led to his defeat in the 2010 elections.

Republicans cannot actually repeal ObamaCare until we retake the White House and win a Senate majority. But there's a lot we can do to stop it cold in the meantime. We can take away the money to implement it. We can refuse to appropriate money to the IRS to hire the 16,500 new agents the Congressional Budget Office (CBO) says it will need to enforce the requirement that everybody buy health insurance and that employers provide it.[13] And we can stop funds from going to the Department of Health and Human Services (HHS) that would be used to implement Medicare cuts or to gather data on which to base health care rationing. Zero funding!

The courts may help us out in stopping ObamaCare. As we said in our previous book, *2010: Take Back America—A Battle Plan*, ObamaCare is unconstitutional. Now a Virginia District Court has found that the individual insurance mandate to buy insurance violates the Constitution. If the Supreme Court agrees, we may kill ObamaCare even before the 2012 elections. But we can't take that for granted. We must paralyze ObamaCare by defunding it now.

The Republican House can also stop Obama from using his control over the executive branch to attempt an end run around Congress to enact his most controversial proposals without even asking for legislative approval. In two areas where Congress has rejected his bills (even with his overwhelming Democratic majority), the president has moved to implement them by executive action.

Congress turned down his cap and trade proposal to combat global climate change. So Obama is getting the federal Environmental Protection Agency (EPA) to require businesses and industries to buy permits to emit carbon dioxide, using what it claims is its power under the Clean Air Act, passed in 1970. Carbon dioxide, of course, is not a health risk like the particulates, sulfur dioxide, or nitrous oxides, which are the targets of the statute. We all breathe carbon dioxide with each breath. But because he says it contributes to global climate change, Obama wants the EPA to limit CO_2 emissions.

Meanwhile, the National Labor Relations Board (NLRB) is moving to impose Obama's card check legislation (the so-called Employee Free Choice Act) on the nation's business. Currently, when workers want to form a union, a majority of them have to check off cards asking for one and then the issue is put to a referendum—by secret ballot. Obama tried to get Congress to eliminate the secret ballot and let the card checkoffs alone determine the workers' wishes. But much of the time, the referenda result in a rejection of the union, even though a majority have signed cards asking for one. The workers say one thing when their union rep is peering over their shoulder and another when the ballot is confidential. Congress rejected the proposal. But now the NLRB, by a 3–2 party line vote, is planning to ban the secret ballot and just use card checks.

The pollution tax and the card check law are both job killers and Americans overwhelmingly oppose them.

According to the Rasmussen Reports, 61% of voters think "it's fair to require a secret ballot vote if workers want a union. Only 18% disagree."[14]

Voters break even on whether or not carbon dioxide and other greenhouse gas emissions should be regulated. Rasmussen Reports found them splitting 41–41 on the question. But when asked if the EPA should be able to impose these regulations without consulting with Congress, voters said no by 53–24.[15]

So the Republican House must amend the EPA and NLRB budgets to prohibit these agencies from using any of the money it appropriates to implement a carbon tax or card check regulations.

No sooner did the election results come in last year than Obama's Federal Communications Commission (FCC) came up with new ways to squelch talk radio and control the Internet. We must block this devious attack on free speech launched in the names of "localism," "fairness," and "net neutrality." Republicans should insert language into the FCC appropriation prohibiting the proposed changes.

Finally, Republicans need to put an end to budget earmarks once and for all. GOP congressmen and senators have just voted to do so. In the House, that will, of course, be binding on the Democrats whether they like it or not. But we don't have the majority in the Senate, and know that the Democrats—particularly those running for reelection—will jam up the budget with earmarks.

They will say the earmarks are to create jobs in their home states, but don't believe it. They are really devices to generate campaign cash for themselves. Democratic senators such as Robert Casey (PA), Robert Menendez (NJ), Bill Nelson (FL), Jim Webb (VA), Debbie Stabenow (MI), Sherrod Brown (OH), Jeff Bingaman (NM), and Jon Tester (MT)—who are all up for reelection—receive between a quarter and a third of their total campaign war chest from lobbyists for whose clients they have secured earmarks. (Go to Part IV, The Democrats We Must Defeat, to see who is funding their campaigns with donations, and in return for earmarks.)

Without the earmarks, would the campaign funds still flow? We doubt it. These Democrats are hanging on to their earmarks so that they can use them as a legal form of bribery to get campaign donations in return.

We have to put an end to this little shell game! We must stop any earmarks from making their way into the budget for 2012!

Finally, we need to force changes in the new regulations that Obama imposed on small community banks. The big boys on Wall Street need more regulating. But we need to free local banks from the shackles that Obama's federal bureaucracy imposed on them. These restraints, more than anything else, are impeding our economic growth. Banks must be freed to make loans to create jobs or jobs won't be created!

We need to bring all these issues into the debt limit and the budget battles. We must wage the fight on nine fronts:

1. Stop any increase in taxes
2. Roll back Obama's outrageous spending
3. Cut the deficit to 3% of GDP
4. Defund ObamaCare
5. Block the EPA from imposing a carbon tax
6. Halt NLRB efforts to ban secret ballots in union elections
7. Kill all earmarks in the budget
8. Block the FCC from curtailing free speech
9. Free community banks to lend, thus creating jobs

In effect, we must use the debt limit and the budget debates throughout 2011 to revive, relive, refight—and win—the Greatest Hits of 2010!

Obama will veto the debt limit extension and the budget as long as our amendments are attached. He will demand clean bills that preserve his programs and his spending. But the Republican House must not give in. We need to battle through the stalemate that follows. Don't blink. Don't cave. Even if a government shutdown results. Don't compromise. Just fight and win.

In American politics, it is the president who sets the agenda, not Congress. And the president will want to move on. He won't want a Republican House to pick through the budget increases he got passed in 2009 or the new laws he enacted in 2010 or the executive orders now coming down the pike. He will want to move on to new turf.

But the Republican House and the American people cannot let him change the subject. We need to review all that he has pushed through and defund it, cut it, and block it. In that sense, the president will still be setting the agenda, but it will be the agenda he set in his first two years, not the new agenda he would like to focus on.

The nation will be watching this Armageddon-like battle very, very closely. Just as we hung in suspense on every vote as Obama passed his health care program, over our objections, in 2010, we will be riveted to the television (FoxNews, we hope!) as the 2011 confrontation over the debt limit and the budget unfolds. Obama will fight with every ounce of his strength as the 2012 elections approach. The issues of 2010 will be the issues of 2012. And then, we've got him!

Some ask if Obama will move to the center. Will he emulate Bill Clinton and his strategy of 1995 and 1996?

He won't, because there is no center. Either you raise taxes or you don't. No matter how Obama may try to dress up or conceal a tax hike by claiming that he is also cutting spending, it will still be a tax increase. Obama won't get credit for the spending cuts, and the debate will quickly move to his tax proposals.

The other issues Republicans will insert in the budget debate also do not admit of compromise. Either you let the IRS go after people who don't have health coverage or you don't. The budget either permits Medicare cuts and rationing or it doesn't. Either it bans a carbon tax or allows it; either allows a secret ballot in union elections or doesn't.

There is no compromise. There is no center ground. If Obama proposes to phase in his programs more gradually or to adjust them to make them more palatable, that won't help much. The heart of his proposals will remain unpopular.

Obama may well try to disguise his defeats as compromises. His cave-in during the lame duck session of Congress in December 2010, when he agreed to extend the Bush tax cuts, for example, was portrayed as a bipartisan compromise, a concession to lower the intensity of the partisan debate. But America was not deceived. We saw it for what it was—a Republican victory and a defeat for Obama. We could tell the difference between compromise and surrender.

And even if Obama is able to moderate the liberal, dogmatic, obstinate image he acquired during his first two years, by gracefully conceding fights he is losing and making a virtue out of surrender, it will still hurt him. He cannot escape being increasingly seen as weak, or Carteresque. His inability to stand firm on foreign policy and his continuing defeats at the hands of the Republican House will lead voters to conclude that he is not up to the demands of the presidency. The bad economy—even if there is a slight lowering of unemployment—will reinforce the impression of a president who is in over his head.

Obama will have to choose between a rock and a hard place. Either stand up to the Republican House, battle tenaciously, and try to win, at the price of looking doctrinaire, liberal, and dogmatic. Or give in and make concessions and look weak and inept. Either way, we have him. Once we fight—and if we hold firm—we've got him!

But won't Obama have all the money he needs to win? Won't he be flush with campaign funds? Won't his union buddies hand over the keys to their treasure chests to keep their man in office?

Of course an incumbent president will have a big financial advantage. But money doesn't always determine elections. At the start of the 2010 election, Congressional Democrats in both chambers enjoyed a huge financial advantage. Since they were in power and solidly controlled both houses, they outraised the House and Senate Republicans dramatically.

But, as the likelihood of a Republican victory loomed larger, the GOP began to catch up and raised more than their rivals did in the crucial months before the election. Obama will, indeed, have an early financial edge, but, by Election Day, it is likely to have eroded.

Nor can Obama ignore the rising discontent on his left flank. Democrats were outraged when he conceded the fundamental issue of the 2008 campaign and did not raise taxes on the wealthy. He has not closed the Guantánamo Bay detention center. He failed to get a public option on health care (i.e., a government-owned insurance company). And his job creation record is dismal.

Will all this discontent lead to a Democratic primary challenge? It very well might. Perhaps someone like former senator Russ Feingold (D-WI) or radical congressman Dennis (the Menace) Kucinich (D-OH) might mount a challenge. If they do well in the polls, that might open the door for Hillary Clinton to run. It's too early to tell. But the more Obama concedes to the Republicans in the House, the more he catalyzes a primary on the left. And let's all remember history: the three presidents who faced serious primary challenges—Johnson, Ford, and Carter—saw their party defeated in the ensuing general election.

Of course, you can't beat somebody with nobody. Whom will the GOP run? Whom should we nominate?

AND THE REPUBLICAN CONTENDER IS . . . ?

The Republican victories of 2010 were based on national issues, but there were no national leaders.

In 1994, when the GOP took Congress, it was clear that Newt Gingrich was the leader. He had been planning for the 1994 takeover for much of his adult life. It was he who worked for years through GOPAC (Grand Old Party Political Action Committee) to fund state legislative races around the country to groom and advance local Republicans for the day when they would be able to topple their Democratic congressmen. It was he who uncovered the dozens of Democrats who bounced checks to the House Bank.

But the GOP victories of 2010 had no leaders. Incoming House Speaker John Boehner (R-OH), Senate Minority Leader Mitch McConnell (R-KY), and Republican National Committee Chair Michael Steele all worked hard to win, but none of them was really the leader. Most Republican voters were only dimly aware of who they were.

The real hero was the Tea Party movement, which engineered a massive grassroots rebellion against Obama's policies, spearheaded by people like Tea Party Patriots leaders Jenny Beth Martin and Mark Meckler, Americans for Prosperity director Tim Phillips, and billionaires David and Charles Koch. FoxNews' Glenn Beck and Sean Hannity, and 60 Plus Association leader Jim Martin were the spark plugs that catalyzed the win, but they were unknown. (See Part VI, The New Leaders, for brief sketches of them.)

Sarah Palin's endorsements and active campaigning contributed mightily to the victory—far more than any other politician's—but the 2010 elections were dominated by the grass roots. It was the millions of Tea Party activists who impelled the Republican Party to victory.

So the Republican Party is leaderless. Who will emerge as its candidate in 2012?

First let's understand how the candidate will be nominated. The process will fundamentally change this year. In fact, it will be the opposite of what we are used to.

Since the procedural reforms initiated by Democrat George McGovern in 1973, which carried over into the Republican Party as well, primaries have determined the winner of the nominations in each party. Iowa and New Hampshire—the first caucus and the first primary in the nation—have tended to sort out the candidates for us. They narrowed down the field and left the rest of the nation with two or three alternatives in each party.

These two small states have dominated the process because the contenders usually did not have the money to wage national campaigns. At the start of a campaign, they could only afford to run in these two small states. And those who had the financial resources to compete nationally (like Hillary Clinton, and Mitt Romney in 2008) were forced to battle in these two states anyway because they were the first test. Having more money didn't help that much in states so small that TV time was pretty inexpensive.

In effect, Iowa and New Hampshire have become the quarterfinals, narrowing the field to two candidates in each party who compete in the subsequent primaries. In 2000, Al Gore and Bill Bradley were the Democratic semifinalists who survived these early rounds; George Bush and John McCain were their Republican equivalents. In 2004, John Kerry and John Edwards emerged as the alternatives. In 2008, Iowa and New Hampshire winnowed down the Democratic field to Hillary Clinton versus Barack Obama and the Republican contest to John McCain versus Mike Huckabee. The other contenders—Giuliani, Romney, Edwards, Dodd, et al.—might have staggered on for a few more rounds, but their candidacies were doomed.

Now, in the Republican primaries, it will be different. The short list of contenders for the nomination will not be chosen in the early primaries. Iowa and New Hampshire will not impose their will on America. America will impose its will on Iowa and New Hampshire.

The quarterfinals will not be waged in the cornfields of Iowa or the former mill towns of New Hampshire. They will be held in the living rooms of America, among the FoxNews audience!

The share of the GOP electorate that watches FoxNews has become so dominant that the early stages of the Republican nominating process will be held on its airwaves. It is there, and not in the early-morning handshaking at factory gates in Iowa and New Hampshire, that we will meet the candidates and come to choose our favorites.

About half of those who call themselves Republicans report that they watch FoxNews every night, and two-thirds say they watch it "several times a week or more." Among Independents, 46% and even 21% of Democrats also watch FoxNews several times a week or more.[16]

FoxNews' market dominance among Republicans and Independents was not as extensive in 2008 as it is today, but its subsequent growth in market share and ratings has been phenomenal. Now its impact in Republican primaries is decisive.

In 2012, the Republicans and Independents who will choose the GOP nominee will be found watching Bill O'Reilly, Sean Hannity, Glenn Beck, Greta Van Susteren, Shep Smith, Bret Baier, Megyn Kelly, Steve Doocy, Brian Kilmeade, and Gretchen Carlson, because it is on these shows that the early narrowing process will take place.

Day after day, we will see all the candidates on FoxNews. Not just in debates, but in frequent appearances on the network's opinion and news shows. We will watch how they handle themselves, we'll learn how they answer questions, and we'll come to our decision. The Republican nominating process will resemble the TV show *American Idol*, where we watch the candidates perform and vote on who we like best.

Then, we will tell pollsters who we have come to like and those we don't like. They will record our views every few weeks and, through this process, the front-runners will emerge, candidates will surge, leaders will fall back, and the winnowing process will take place.

Normally, the early national polls don't mean much; the surveys that professionals follow are in Iowa and New Hampshire. In 2008, Rudy Giuliani and Hillary Clinton led all the early national surveys, but neither one was there on election day.

But now, surveys in Iowa and New Hampshire will show the same results as the rest of the country because all the Republicans will be watching FoxNews—the same broadcasts the rest of us are seeing. Whatever local activity is going on in Des Moines or Cedar Rapids or Manchester or Concord will be drowned out by the constant coverage Republicans will be getting on FoxNews.

And, as the polls begin to tilt to one candidate or another, campaign contributions will follow them. Those who surge ahead will attract funding and the ones who falter will find their bank accounts drying up. Mitt Romney, who will self-fund his campaign (and can count on the strong support of the Mormon community), will not face any financial scarcity, but if he falls back in the polls, his electoral appeal will fade. Money won't bring him back in 2012 any more than it did in 2008.

When the actual primaries take place, their results will tend to ratify the consensus the country has come to from watching FoxNews. Americans will impose their views on the early primaries, not the other way around.

Of course, the final decision will be made in the big state primaries that follow. There, the delegates will be selected to the nominating conventions and the winner will emerge.

So, the quarterfinals will be waged over FoxNews and ratified by the voters in the early, small state primaries.

The semifinals will take place in the big state primaries later on.

And the finals will be in November when we choose a president.

This process will favor the less well known candidates. They won't have to compete financially at first, but can rely on their FoxNews appearances to build their constituencies. Mike Huckabee, whose consistently witty, incisive, and conservative debate performances in 2008 led to victory in Iowa, will be the model for candidates to follow in 2012. Mike never had two dimes to rub together, but he defeated Romney in Iowa and outlasted him in the contest against McCain by months.

OK, but who will be the candidate?

We don't yet know. Neither of us has even met all the candidates, but here are our subjective, early impressions.

Mitt Romney

Although he led in the realclearpolitics.com average of polls from October 27 to November 21, 2010, with 19% of the Republican primary vote,[17] Romney can't get the nomination, and he shouldn't. Some object to his religion; we don't. That's not our problem with him. We object to his support of an individual mandate to buy health insurance in Massachusetts (the very provision that has been found unconstitutional by a Virginia court).

He passed and signed a bill that comes awfully close to ObamaCare in its essentials.

As Grace-Marie Turner, writing in the *Wall Street Journal*, noted, "the former Massachusetts governor enacted something very similar to the Obama health plan. It isn't working well." She said he "has been on the wrong side of the defining political battle of our time."[18]

Romney said on *Fox News Sunday* that the plan he signed into law is the "ultimate conservative plan."[19]

Really? Conservative? The *Wall Street Journal* emphasizes its similarity to Obama's program.

"Both have an individual mandate requiring most residents to have health insurance or pay a penalty. Most businesses are required to participate or pay a fine. Both rely on government-designed purchasing exchanges that also provide a platform to control private health insurance. Many of the uninsured are covered through Medicaid expansion and others receive subsidies for highly-prescriptive policies. And the apparatus requires a plethora of new government boards and agencies."[20]

Romney defends his program saying "our plan is working well."[21] But in fact, it is ruining the state's finances.

While 97% of his state has health insurance now, more than half of the 408,000 newly insured pay nothing and are entirely subsidized by the taxpayers.[22]

Like Obama, Romney promised that his program would lower health care costs, but a Harvard study said that one-third of the state residents report higher health care costs. In Massachusetts, a family of four pays almost $14,000 on health care, which is 27% higher than the national average.[23]

And, predictably, both scarcity and the inevitable de facto rationing have set in. A study by the Massachusetts Medical Society found that 56% of internal medicine physicians are no longer accepting new patients. For those who get an appointment, the average wait is seven weeks. In the words of Dr. Sandra Schneider, vice president of the American College of Emergency Physicians, in the *Journal*, "Just because you have health insurance doesn't mean there's a [primary care] physician who can see you."[24]

As the *Journal* noted, "Many patients are insured in name only: they have health coverage but can't find a doctor."[25]

Romney defends his program by pointing out that "we didn't do what

President Obama's doing, which is putting controls on our system of premiums for private insurance companies." [26]

No, indeed. But the requirement of universal coverage without any expansion in the supply of doctors and medical facilities has led insurers to request rate hikes of 8 to 32% this year. [27]

As Michael Graham wrote in the *Boston Herald*, "the disaster of Romneycare is already upon us." [28]

And so are the health care police! The *Herald* reports that the Commonwealth Health Insurance Connector "created under Romneycare [is] cracking down on more than 3,000 [Massachusetts] residents who are fighting state fines, and has even hired a private law firm to force the health insurance scofflaws to pay penalties of up to $2,000 a year." [29] Their crime? Not having health insurance!

The *Herald* summarizes the impact of the legislation: "Before Romneycare, you were on the hook for $1 billion for Medicaid and other state health care subsidies. Less than three-years later, the taxpayer bill has gone up another $750 million—a 75% increase!" [30]

Though Romney now says he will repeal or modify the heath care law, he signed a bad bill once and can't be counted on not to do so again.

After Romney, there are three front-runners for the nomination: Sarah Palin, Mike Huckabee, and Newt Gingrich.

All have three things in common:

a) They are all good, solid conservatives.
b) Each is well known and well liked by Republicans.
c) All three have massive political baggage that could drag them down to defeat.

In other years, in other elections, we might be inclined to take a chance on overcoming the baggage. But in 2012, running against the likes of Barack Obama, we don't dare do so. So the question for each of them is: can they overcome their baggage?

We will see a lot of each of them. Palin and Huckabee live on FoxNews, and Newt shows up there all the time. In the battles of 2011, we will see how they hold up and whether we sense that the American people are willing to embrace them.

Sarah Palin

Let's begin by getting one thing straight: Sarah Palin was a masterful choice for vice president. She delivered something to John McCain that no vice presidential candidate has ever given her running mate—a lead! For three weeks after the nomination, McCain led Obama in the polls. It was the only three weeks he ever did. Then McCain blew it by going back to Washington and voting for the TARP bank bailout, but that wasn't Sarah's fault.

Neither was the firestorm that greeted her nomination. Nobody has been as universally—or as unfairly—savaged by the mainstream media as Sarah Palin. Her baptism of fire stands as the greatest example of sexist bias in the history of modern so-called journalism. The media neglected her instrumental role in cleaning up Alaska's corruption, toppling a political dynasty, and working her way up on her own—without relying on a political husband or father who has been in public life to pull her up.

Instead, they focused on topics no male candidate would have had to endure: was her granddaughter really her own baby? What did she think of her daughter's out-of-wedlock pregnancy? What role would her husband play?

The interviews were ridiculous. Nobody wanted to know her opinion. These were "gotcha" traps designed to show her up. But all this damaged Sarah Palin's credibility nationally. While she is popular among Republicans and Independents, she has a 36–51 unfavorable rating among all likely voters.[31] Among Independents, though, she still has a 54–33 favorable rating.[32]

Most disturbing is the *Washington Post* poll that found that 59% of likely voters would "definitely not vote" for Palin. That's a high hurdle to overcome.[33]

The realclearpolitics.com average of all polls between October 27 and November 21, 2010, has her winning only 17% of the vote among Republican primary voters,[34] two percentage points behind Romney and one behind Mike Huckabee.

Why so low when she is so well known and, among Republicans and Independents, so well liked? Because Republican primary voters are afraid to nominate her, scared that she can't win. The price she paid for helping the GOP ticket in 2008 was egregious, and many Republicans do not want to have to spend the 2012 campaign rehabilitating the image of their candidate.

Palin did herself no favors when she abruptly resigned as governor of Alaska. She looked like a quitter. And she never adequately explained her decision. Her reasons became apparent in the subsequent months when she used her newfound freedom to write, speak out, go on FoxNews, and travel the country in support of conservatives. But she never told us why she quit . . . and still hasn't.

In fact, Sarah Palin is handling herself brilliantly these days. She is rehabilitating her image skillfully. Her reality show, her FoxNews appearances, her endorsements of real change agents across the nation, and her sponsorship of the Tea Party have all rebounded to her credit. If she continues to improve her image, Republicans may take a chance on her. They love her. They just worry that she can't win.

After all, it is quite credible to say that as governor of Alaska, suddenly plucked to run for vice president, she was not necessarily well prepared for the national stage. But now, having been there for a few years, she is becoming more and more able to handle it, more conversant with the issues, and looks more like a possible president.

We'll have to wait and see how Sarah Palin does and whether she even decides to run.

Mike Huckabee

A better, kinder, nicer man never walked the earth. His knowledge of issues is deep, his ideology heartfelt. His consistency is almost maddening. He has a great platform style, a winning debating approach, a charismatic personality, and he is viable and visible enough this time around to attract funding. He runs second in the realclearpolitics.com average of all polls between October 27 and November 21, 2010, with 18% of the vote, only one percentage point behind Romney.[35]

In contrast to Palin, he had a positive favorable rating nationally of 41–25 in the November 22, 2010, Quinnipiac Poll.[36]

But Mike's heart betrayed him when he helped to release from prison Maurice Clemmons, who subsequently killed four Washington State police officers. That could cause serious problems for Mike. He makes it clear that he didn't pardon Clemmons. He merely commuted his sentence so that he would be eligible for parole. The parole board—largely holdovers from a previous administration—voted 5–0 to release Clemmons. Huckabee's decision to commute Clemmons's sentence was based on compassion about its unusual length—a harsh sixty years for burglary and theft—and because of his age, as Clemmons was only seventeen at the time of his conviction.

After the parole board released Clemmons, following Huckabee's commutation, he was again arrested, this time for a parole violation, but prosecutors dropped the charges.

Huckabee points out that he did not free Clemmons, but just made him parole eligible. He also notes that had prosecutors pursued the parole violation, Clemmons would have gone back to prison for the remainder of his sentence.

But still, the fact remains, Clemmons later killed four police officers.

In our unforgiving politics, none of that matters. Huckabee was "blamed" for the shootings.

Why did Mike do what he did? Because he is a Christian who believes in forgiveness. When Dick handled his campaign in Arkansas, he asked Mike if he opposed parole for violent felonies. "Oh no," Huckabee replied. "The Christian concept of forgiveness demands that we always allow parole if we see evidence of change." [37]

Cory Cox, the governor's clemency advisor, explains that Huckabee believed that "everyone makes mistakes, everyone can be rehabilitated." He adds that the governor "believed racism is real, especially for people sentenced in the 1960s and 1970s." [38]

Most governors see their pardon and commutation powers as dangerous accessories to their day jobs. They don't want to have to rule on them and would rather duck the issue. Not Mike. He studied each application diligently to see if there was a basis for rehabilitation and forgiveness. He got it right a lot of the time. Many inmates genuinely changed, were released, and are living honest, honorable lives. But in the case of Clemmons, Mike got it wrong, and he might not be able to recover politically in time to win the nomination in 2012.

Huckabee also has to demonstrate that he can break out of the evangelical ghetto. In 2008, he won in Iowa largely because of the backing of the born-again Christian vote, and his primary victories came in states with huge evangelical populations—Alabama, Arkansas, Georgia, Tennessee, West Virginia, Iowa, Kansas, and Louisiana.

Ironically, Huckabee is subject to the same kind of prejudice that afflicts Sarah Palin. As a woman, she draws all kinds of special scrutiny. As a former minister, so does Mike. Never mind that he was a highly successful governor of Arkansas for a decade. Who cares that he upgraded the schools dramatically, held down taxes, and stimulated economic growth? No. The media only wants to know his position on creationism and homosexuality and what duty a wife owes to her husband. His entire record of courageous leadership is totally overlooked by the secular, anticlerical, leftist media.

But, again, we are determined, in 2012, not to swim upstream against the current. We want to win. We don't want to fight to prove a point. Sarah's negatives are unfair, as are Mike's, but we don't want to lose the election because of them. They both have to prove that they can overcome them!

Newt Gingrich

Newt is Dick's personal favorite. Eileen likes him a lot, but worries that he may be old hat for the current mood of the electorate.

The former Speaker runs fourth, at 14%, in the realclearpolitics.com average of all polls between October 27 and November 21, 2010.[39] But, as with Palin, he has very high national negatives. The November 22, 2010, Quinnipiac Poll showed him with a 30–43 negative rating nationally.[40] His unpopularity makes Republican primary voters afraid that his personal baggage will make him unelectable.

Everyone agrees that he would clean Obama's clock in a debate. He can outthink, outtalk, and outstrategize the president. He's brilliant.

But will his two failed marriages become a serious issue, especially with women?

Gingrich also emerged from his defeat in the government shutdown of 1995–96 in bad shape. Who can forget the *Daily News* front-page cartoon of Newt as a crybaby protesting that he had been seated in the back of the plane on an Air Force One trip to the Middle East for Israeli prime minister Rabin's funeral?[41] The Speaker lost the war of words with President Clinton and was beaten down in the government shutdown that followed.

Now, Newt will likely emerge as one of the key Republican spokesmen in the budget battles of 2011 and 2012. It will give him a chance to show that he can handle himself better.

More than either of the Republican Congressional leaders, he has the rhetorical ability to articulate the GOP case, and we can assume that he will be front and center in battling Obama during the fight. If the budget wars are to be Armageddon, Newt is our gladiator.

As he fights for us against Obama's socialism, voters may come to ignore or forgive his personal problems. You never know, so let's watch and find out.

On center stage again, you can bet that Newt won't blow it this time around!

Every time a party nominates a candidate to oppose an incumbent president, it does its best to choose an alternative who is the opposite in every possible respect. Clinton's detractors saw him as a draft-dodging, immature womanizer, so the Republicans named Bob Dole, an older, morally upright, combat veteran. Democrats thought Bush 41 was too old and oriented to foreign policy, so they chose Clinton, a young governor with no foreign experience.

Right now, Barack Obama is giving inexperience a bad name. He is so clearly out of his depth and doesn't seem to have a clue about how to manage the executive branch that the Republicans may see Gingrich's experience and age as a good alternative.

Will Newt even run? He didn't when there was an open seat in 2008, so why should he when he has to take on an incumbent in 2012? The answer is that Newt loves a challenge and a fight and is a true believer. He may not be able to resist entering the battle.

The Others

With one front-runner unnominatable and the three others possibly not running, the rest of the field is very important. And, with FoxNews' role in the nominating process, you don't need a whole lot of money to play. So, some of the second-tier candidates might make it into the semifinals. One of them could be the nominee. Just like Barack Obama.

So far, the potential field includes Governors Chris Christie (NJ), Bob McDonnell (VA), Haley Barbour (MS), Mitch Daniels (IN), Bobby Jindal (LA), Tim Pawlenty (MN), and Rick Perry (TX); Senators Jim DeMint (SC) and John Thune (SD); Congresswoman Michele Bachmann (MN); Congressman Mike Pence (IN); and former senator Rick Santorum (PA).

We have problems with two of them.

In our view, former Minnesota governor Tim Pawlenty has some explaining to do. In our 2009 book, *Catastrophe*, we wrote about the international effort to promote Shariah, the Islamic code of law in most Muslim countries. Shariah law is vicious. It authorizes the stoning of women, denies them funds in divorce, authorizes child brides, and encourages terrorism and jihad.

But on August 28, 2008, the Minnesota Housing Finance Agency (MHFA) board started a three-year pilot program that makes it easier for Muslims to buy homes without violating Shariah. The program authorizes the state to borrow money on their behalf and charge them monthly payments. This convoluted process is designed to circumvent their religion's prohibition against paying interest.

What business does a state have enacting a law that benefits a single religion?

Dan Bartholomay, who led the fight against the housing program, details what happened next.

"In February, 2009, the first Shariah Compliant loan was made and news of the Minnesota State–sponsored Islamic finance program hits the blogs and talk radio.

"From April to October, 2009, ACT! For America volunteers organize; various emails sent to MHFA staff; phone calls made; volunteers sit in on MHFA Board meetings; research is done.

"Nov 1, 2009–Feb 28, 2010—Twelve installments of The Bostrom Chronicles are sent to Gloria Bostrom, MHFA Board member.

"March 2010—ACT! for America volunteers, St. Paul chapter, send more than 100 letters to MHFA board members and various MN candidates for public office.

"April 15, 2010—MHFA decides to end the NMMP." [42]

Add to this tale our own condemnation of the Minnesota program in our book *Catastrophe*:

"Imagine a program for observant Orthodox Jews where the state would send in workers to turn on lights for them during the Sabbath! Or to drive them around for free so they don't have to operate a motor vehicle on Saturday. That's exactly what this Minnesota program amounts to."

"What business does a state have to jump through such hoops to help members of a specific religion to purchase homes? If anything violates the wall of separation between church and state, this is it!" [43]

Governor Pawlenty's aide, Alex Conant, sent us the following e-mail on December 13, 2010, discussing Pawlenty's role on this issue:

"This program was independently set up by the MN state housing agency and did not make any mention [of] Shariah Law on its face, but was later described by critics as accommodating it. As soon as Gov. Pawlenty became aware of the issue, he personally ordered it shut it down. Does he wish it had been shut-down sooner? Of course. Fortunately, only about three people actually used the program before it was terminated at the Governor's direction."

We're glad to hear that the program is no longer in effect. But there are several problems with the governor's reply:

- The program was in effect for more than a year and a half before it was shut down.

- During that time, activists deluged both the media and the MHFA with criticisms of the program. It is hard to understand how the governor could have remained ignorant of the program until he finally acted.

- And if, despite all this publicity and attention, Governor Pawlenty did not know about the Shariah-compliant loan program his own state housing agency had launched, what does that say about his management style?

Each of us, as Republican voters in the primary, should draw our own conclusions from these facts.

Mississippi's Governor Haley Barbour also wants to run. He's a good man and was a fine leader of the Republican National Committee, but the last thing we need is for a former lobbyist to run for president.

Here's how we break down the rest of the field of newcomers—and there are some very good ones.

New Jersey governor Chris Christie has tamed the savage beast. He took a state budget that was far out of kilter and forced a balanced budget through a Democratic legislature with no increase in taxes. It took some doing. He had to slash local school aid, which will probably cause local real estate tax hikes, but he got it done. He also killed the proposal for a new tunnel under the Hudson River connecting New York and New Jersey (there are two already). Had that project gone ahead, it would have bankrupted his state, just as the Boston Central Artery Project (the Big Dig) drained Massachusetts taxpayers for a decade. That took guts.

Virginia's governor Bob McDonnell did the same, only one better: working with a compliant Republican legislature, he was able to roll spending back to 2006 levels and avoid any tax increase. It was an amazing achievement, and that alone makes him an attractive possible nominee.

Indiana's governor Mitch Daniels has been working wonders in his state. He is promoting the first truly comprehensive version of school choice, letting parents send their children to the schools they prefer and earmarking the state's share of education spending to travel with the child to the new school. He wants to reform collective bargaining with the teachers' unions so that only wages and benefits can be discussed—not work rules or other issues. He has taken bold initiatives to reform health care by implementing a modified health savings account system for state workers (see page 101).

Bobby Jindal, governor of Louisiana, won high marks for his handling of the BP oil spill, especially after his predecessor screwed up the state response to Katrina. He is reputed to be brilliant and innovative and a real comer. Standard & Poor's raised Louisiana's bond rating and credit outlook from stable to positive in 2009 crediting the state's strong management and "commitment to streamlining its government functions."[44] A big feather in Jindal's cap!

But Jindal has hit two bumps in the road. His nationally televised Republican reply to Obama's February 24, 2009, address to Congress was panned. He talked about how poorly the government had performed during Hurricane Katrina, which Republicans said raised an issue that had hurt them politically. He also refused to veto a doubling of state legislative pay despite having opposed it while he was running. A recall petition was filed against him. He saw the light and vetoed the bill. The recall was dropped.

South Carolina senator Jim DeMint earned high marks with us when he sponsored and helped fund Republican primary challenges throughout the country, pitting Tea Party candidates and true conservatives against squishy Republican RINOs (Republican In Name Only). He didn't always win, but he deserves a lot of credit for risking his popularity by trying. In his recent book, *Saving Freedom: We Can Stop America's Slide into Socialism*, he writes eloquently about preserving American sovereignty amid the group of nations known as G-20 that is seemingly intent on making our economic decisions for us.

Indiana congressman Mike Pence, a former talk radio host, is a keen advocate of freedom and has taken the lead against Obama's efforts to squelch free speech. A solid and outspoken conservative, he may be able to summon the eloquence to match Obama and defeat him in debate. In the early going, he has earned high marks as a spokesman for the conservative cause. Many hail him as a new Reagan.

Perhaps the most intriguing of the possible candidates is Minnesota congresswoman Michele Bachmann. The leader of the Tea Party caucus in the House, she is never at a loss for words, most of them imaginative and pithy, as she responds to Democratic attacks on conservative positions. Her rejoinder to MSNBC host Chris Matthews on election night in 2010 was especially saucy. Alluding to Bachmann's ill-advised accusation two years ago that some Democrats were "un-American," Matthews asked her if she would be investigating them since she now was in the majority in the House. Bachmann refused to be baited and stuck to her talking points about how dramatic the GOP victory was. Then Chris asked: "Are you under hypnosis? Has somebody put you into a trance? Because every time I ask you about this you keep coming back with the same response."[45]

Michele shot right back that she was just expressing her feelings and asked Matthews "how's that tickly feeling up your leg tonight?" Michele was, of course, alluding to Matthews' comment during the 2008 election that hearing Obama speak sent a "tingling feeling" up his leg.[46]

Like Palin, Bachmann is often accused of saying flaky things, but her originality might make her an intriguing candidate.

Not on anybody's radar screen is non-governor, non-senator, and non-congressman Herman Cain, a charismatic orator and talk radio host. An African-American Republican conservative, Cain campaigned tirelessly for Tea Party candidates in 2010. He bought Godfather's Pizza from Pillsbury in 1988 and served as CEO and chairman for a decade. He was chairman and a member of the board of directors for the Federal Reserve Bank of Kansas City. Articulate, able, and lyrical, he could be an interesting counterpoint to Obama.

It's way too early to sort through the candidates. Enough to know that there are some very able people out there. And, undoubtedly, a bunch more will follow.

Obama has so damaged our economy that it is likely to be in the tank through much of the next two years. Republicans must focus on how the president's policies have kept us down and obliterated any prospect of recovery. And they need to use their control of the House of Representatives to undo the damage and show how low tax, free market solutions are the ones that work best.

PART TWO

HOW OBAMA HAS SCREWED UP OUR ECONOMY

The prime mission for the Republican House, of course, is to undo the vast damage the Obama administration and a rubber-stamp Democratic Congress have inflicted on the American economy.

In September 2010, the National Bureau of Economic Research, the body charged with chronicling the beginning and end of national recessions, announced—to the consternation of all—that the recession was over. According to them, it had begun in December 2007 and ended in June 2009.[1] The unemployed were irate; entrepreneurs with idle factories were puzzled; consumers who weren't spending were skeptical. The announcement became a form of grim humor in the gaunt and ravaged economic landscape left in the wake of Obama's economic policies.

But the economists had it right. The cyclical recession, part of the normal fluctuation of ups and downs of the business cycle, had indeed run its course. The usual downturn in economic activity associated with recessions was over. Things were normal again—the new normal.

And that is the most scary part! The almost 10% nominal unemployment rate and almost 20% actual rate, the negligible wage and income growth, the relative stagnation of the gross domestic product were no longer the result of a cyclical recession. They are the new permanent state of our economy!

It took a fifty-something African-American CFO of the nonprofit veterans' group AMVETS named Velma Hart to bring it all into perspective for us. Velma, who had voted for Obama, confronted the president at a town hall meeting in September 2010 that was, ironically, staged by the Democrats. Remembering the days when she and her husband had to settle for franks and beans for dinner, she challenged Obama: "My husband and I have joked for years that we thought we were well beyond the hot dogs and beans era of our lives, but quite frankly, it's starting to knock on our door and ring true that that might be where we're headed again." Then Hart asked the question on all of our minds: "Mr. President, I need you to answer this honestly, is this my new reality?"[2] she asked with a tinge of panic in her voice. It is the question we are all asking. It starts in our nightmares, then invades our quiet moments of waking anxiety, and finally, makes its way to our lips. "Is this my future?"

Why hasn't the economy recovered? Why does the malaise linger? When will confidence return? How long must the For Sale signs desecrate the lawns of our neighborhoods, tombstones marking the graves of our former prosperity, the words on the sign an epitaph to our past plenty? When can we resume our journeys up the economic ladder? Is this just the start of a new period akin to the 1930s our grandparents told us about? How long must we hold our breath and stay underwater? When can we dream again?

Beneath these urgent questions lie others, tinged with anger. What happened to the prophesies of our leaders? Where is the promised effect of the widely heralded stimulus package of new government spending? Did we accumulate all that debt and load our children with so heavy a burden for nothing? What about the change so many voted for? Why hasn't it all worked? What went wrong?

The answer is disgustingly simple. The recession that seems to follow all economic booms has, indeed, passed. Now we confront a man-made depression created by the misguided social engineering, bitter class antagonism, and animosity to prosperity of one man—President Barack Obama. In our book *Catastrophe*, we said he was waging a "war on prosperity." Now it is clear. He is winning.

Aided and abetted by a compliant Congress, he has blighted our future and is ruining our country. The fertilizer of his government spending and borrowing is rapidly overgrowing the garden of our economy with noxious weeds that are strangling the real job-creating engines. Businesses cannot borrow, capitalists can't invest, workers can't move up because government policies, taxes, borrowing, and regulation are holding them down.

The whole world entered the recession of 2007 together. But other countries did not suffer nearly the job losses that bedeviled America, and both Europe and Asia have come out of the recession much faster than we have. Why? Because we are the only country blessed with a president like Obama.

Total employment in the United States has declined by twice as much as in the G-7 countries as a whole, three times as much as in Europe, and more than seven times as much as in the United Kingdom. Since Obama took office, we have lost more than 9 million jobs.[3]

JOB LOSS IN THE RECESSION

(2007–2010)

United States	−4.6%
G-7 Nations	−2.4%
Euro Zone	−1.7%
United Kingdom	−0.6%

Source: OECD data based on all countries reporting as of September 28, 2010.[4]

Not only did the recession and its aftermath bite deeper in the U.S., it has lasted much longer than history would suggest it should. According to former senator and economics professor Phil Gramm, the average recession since World War II was short-lived and the economy regained the ground it had lost in five quarters (a year and three months). The longest was seven quarters. But, now, after eleven quarters—two years and nine months—GDP is still below what it was at the start of the recession.[5] And we are not out of the woods yet!

And the very measurement the media use—Gross Domestic Product (GDP)—is an overly optimistic one. The more accurate measure is Gross Domestic Income (GDI). Each measure the size of the economy, but they are calculated differently. Many leading economists believe that our GDP estimates are overstated and that the lower GDI estimates of growth are more likely to be correct.[6]

Writing in his calculatedriskblog.com, economist Bill McBride notes that while real GDP "is only 1.2% below the prerecession peak . . . real GDI is still 2.3% below" it.[7]

He notes that the GDI measurement "suggests the recovery has been more sluggish than the headline GDP report and better explains the weakness in the labor market. Personal income . . . was revised down for the last two quarters, and now shows essentially no growth . . . since the bottom of the recession."[8]

We are not recovering, because Obama's programs won't let us recover.

The very programs that Obama tells us are key to recovery are making it impossible. The bills that he says will stimulate job creation are, in fact, retarding it. The initiatives that he promises will speed up our economic growth are the very ones that are holding it back.

It isn't that Obama's programs aren't working. They are working, but they are moving us in the wrong direction. He is so committed to his socialist agenda that he keeps administering medicine that is destroying us as each pill moves us closer to a European socialist model.

He is like doctors of the Middle Ages, so intent on draining the sick bodies of their patients of the "evil spirits" within that they slit open their patients' veins and poured out their blood. When their patient neared death from lack of blood, they redoubled the bleedings, convinced that evil spirits still lurked. After their ministrations killed their patients, they cited the deaths as evidence of how deep-seated the evil spirits had been!

Obama's programs are paralyzing our economy because they have spawned a reign of terror, which is freezing private spending, investment, lending, or borrowing that might stimulate growth and job creation. We are scared to death of his tax, regulatory, and socialistic policies. Upon taking office as president in March 1933, Franklin Delano Roosevelt said, "The only thing we have to fear is . . . fear itself." Now our president is not soothing our fear, he is causing it.

Consumers aren't spending because they are terrified of a continuation of the recession, and specifically, about the tax increases looming in the future. Even after Obama's deal with the Republicans to extend the Bush tax cuts, he has dozens of tax increase proposals still on the table and consumers know it.

Businesses don't invest in their own company's expansion because they worry that the consumer demand won't be there.

Older entrepreneurs won't put their money back into their own businesses because they are terrified by the return of the estate tax. They know that they had better keep their assets highly liquid so that when they die, their heirs have enough liquid cash to pay a third of their estate to the government, rather than watch it all be taken away and auctioned off at fire sale prices.

The medical/health care sector, 16% of our economy,[9] can't expand or create new jobs because of the prospect of heavy federal regulation that rears its head as ObamaCare changes take effect during the next few years. Who in their right mind is going to buy a CT-scan machine and open a radiology clinic, or develop a new drug, when the feds may disallow the reimbursement next year?

The manufacturing sector, 11% of the economy,[10] is paralyzed by the threat of cap and trade legislation. How can factories expand if their output is about to be taxed at punitive levels? Owners realize that they will be forced to relocate offshore and are loath to invest in the U.S. operations. And, even if cap and trade won't pass a Republican House, they fear that limits on carbon emissions, imposed by the federal Environmental Protection Agency (EPA) under the Clean Air Act, will so crimp their businesses that they will be forced offshore just the same.

The energy sector, another 9% of our economy,[11] is likewise paralyzed, by fear of Obama's carbon tax proposals, which hit both coal and oil. There is no incentive for new investment, exploration, or drilling. Indeed, Obama's tight regulation of offshore drilling in the wake of the British Petroleum Gulf oil spill, and the prospect of new regulation on horizontal or shale drilling, make new investment highly risky. No growth there.

The financial sector, 21% of the economy,[12] is frozen in fear because of the new financial regulations passed by Congress in 2010. These rules give the Federal Deposit Insurance Corporation (FDIC) the power to take over any bank, fire its staff, replace its board, sell off its assets, and liquidate its shareholders' equity if, in its opinion, the institution has made imprudent loans, is at risk of collapse, and would impair the larger economy if it failed. With this sword of Damocles over their heads, no wonder bankers won't make loans and the financial sector won't expand or create new jobs.

The Republican House must proceed to lift these fears, one by one, and liberate these industries in order to bring our economy back to life.

We are in a man-made slump, brought on by the policies of the president. We are no longer being held down by the invisible hand of supply and demand or the cyclical oscillations of the marketplace. What man made, man can repeal.

That is the mission of the Republican House majority.

OUT-OF-CONTROL FEDERAL SPENDING

The central mission of the new Congress will be to cut federal spending. All agree that the deficit must come down. But Democrats would use the deficit as an excuse to back higher taxes while Republicans must focus only on cuts in spending.

Voters agree with the Republicans. Asked by Rasmussen Reports which they thought was more important—cutting the deficit or cutting spending—they overwhelmingly backed spending curbs.

CUTS IN SPENDING VERSUS CUTS IN DEFICIT

Which is more important:

Cutting federal spending	57%
Cutting the federal deficit	34%

Source: Rasmussen Reports [13]

Federal, state, and local government spending has risen meteorically under Obama. As noted, it now eats up 44% of our GDP. And when the health care changes are fully funded, it will go higher.

GOVERNMENT SPENDING AS PERCENTAGE OF GDP

Government 2007–2010 (in US$ billions)

Federal	2,261	3,204
State	1,178	1,431
Local	1,486	1,778
Total	4,925	6,413
GDP	14,077	14,623
Gov't/GDP	35%	44%

Source: U.S. Government [14]

In 2007, the United States ranked 16 among the nations of the world in the proportion of the economy that went to government. Now it ranks 7! [15]

In 2007, the United States had one of the smallest governments relative to its GDP, just slightly larger than that of Japan. Now the U.S. spends more of its economy on government than such socialist countries as Norway, Germany, and the United Kingdom. Even Greece, in the throes of a massive debt crisis due to overspending, only spends 43% of its economy on government, less than our 44% share. [16]

This is what Obama has done to America!

The brutal reality is that the very spending that Obama and the Democrats voted for is inhibiting our economic recovery. We cannot have a free market, free enterprise system with the government accounting for 44% of the spending. That elephant—or jackass, if you will—is too big to keep in the living room!

But if Obama raises taxes to cover his spending, he will have permanently increased government revenues to cover his insane spending and we'll never be able to bring taxes down.

We must defeat Obama's tax proposals to keep our free market, capitalist system intact.

Obama's basic solution to the recession was to embrace the ideas of British economist John Maynard Keynes and flood the economy with money. Prime the pump with government-supplied cash and the resulting increase in consumer demand and spending would jump-start the economy and restore economic growth. Like a defibrillator whose electric shock starts a dormant heart beating again, the new government money would send consumers hurrying to the store, which in turn would make businessmen run to the lending windows of their local banks to get capital with which to expand production and hire new workers to meet the new demand. Then, the new workers would spend more money, and the economic heart of the nation would start beating again. That was the theory and Obama followed it like the doctrinaire leftist that he is.

Obama poured new spending into the economy from two spigots: federal spending and the Federal Reserve Board's monetary policy.

FEDERAL SPENDING GOES WILD

In the 219 years between George Washington's taking the oath of office and Barack Obama's, the federal government borrowed a net of $10 trillion. Since Obama took office, we have borrowed $3.8 trillion more!!! [17]

INCREASE IN NATIONAL DEBT

1789	$77.2 million
2008	$9,986 billion
2010	$13,788 billion [18]

Federal spending grew exponentially, pumping out money for new programs, salaries for teachers, construction projects, tax cuts and rebates, extended unemployment, and health care benefits. The money rained down on consumers.

Obama's deluge of new spending raised federal outlays from $3 trillion to $3.7 trillion a year, an increase of almost 25%.

FEDERAL SPENDING
2008–2011

2,983 [19]	Bush's last budget
3,519 [20]	Obama
3,524 [21]	Obama
3,650 [22]	Obama

Source: U.S. Government

What did Obama spend the money on? Welfare and other domestic spending:

a.Welfare

Help to poor people. It includes unemployment compensation, food stamps, SSI (Supplemental Security Income), the earned income tax credit, the child tax credit, family support, child nutrition, welfare, and foster care. In two years, it has risen by 54%!

b.Domestic Spending

This is a catch-all that includes everything the government spends other than for entitlements and defense. It includes education, transportation, the bureaucracy, the justice system, Congress, much of agriculture, the government departments, science, NASA, government buildings and so on. Under Obama, in two years, spending in this category has soared by 41%!

Obama and the liberals like to say we need to cut Social Security and Medicare to balance the budget. Obama pushed to slice Medicare spending by $500 billion to finance his health care changes.

But they are not the culprits. The real culprits are domestic spending and welfare!

Don't believe Obama's and the liberals' myth that it is Social Security and Medicare that are bankrupting us! Nonsense. Social Security has risen by only 14% in the past two years, while Medicare has only gone up by 16%. It is domestic spending and welfare that is driving us to bankruptcy.

U.S. GOVERNMENT SPENDING BY FUNCTION

Category	2008	2010	% Increase
Welfare	$260	$400	54%
Domestic	$485	$682	41%
Medicare	$456	$528	16%
Social Security	$612	$700	14%
Defense	$612	$690	11%

Source: U.S. Government[23]

The new Republican House of Representatives must roll back this insane spending. You don't need to cut Social Security or Medicare to do so. All you need to do is to cut back the massive increases in spending that Obama and the Congress have engineered over the past two years.

Obama couldn't wait to get his massive new spending under way and demanded that Congress hike it up even before he took office. He clamored for passage of his stimulus package that, he said, would solve the problem of unemployment. First he said it would create 3 million jobs.[24] Then, he amended his prediction to say that it would create *or save* the 3 million jobs.[25] It did neither. Under Obama, our economy has lost 9,432,000 jobs.[26]

The stimulus spending was a monstrosity. Challenged to spend money, Congress acted like an alcoholic asked to taste wines. It appropriated funds for every lawmaker's pet project. The point of this kind of spending was not to do anything, but to spend money for the sake of spending money. President Obama, his cabinet, and his advisors believed that the very act of spending would inject money into the economy and would trigger growth.

With such a low threshold to justify the spending, much of the money has been wasted. It might as well have been thrown out the window for any passing pedestrian to scoop up. Consider these allocations of federal resources:[27]

- $30 million for a spring training baseball complex for the Arizona Diamondbacks and the Colorado Rockies

- $11 million for Microsoft to build a bridge connecting its two headquarters campuses in Redmond, Washington, which are separated by a highway

- $219,000 for Syracuse University to study the sex lives of freshman women

- $3.4 million for a thirteen-foot tunnel for turtles and other wildlife attempting to cross US 27 in Lake Jackson, Florida

- $2.3 million for the U.S. Forest Service to rear large numbers of arthropods, including the Asian long-horned beetle, the nun moth, and the woolly adelgid

- $2.5 million in stimulus checks sent to dead people

- $380,000 to spay and neuter pets in Wichita, Kansas

- $148,438 for Washington State University to analyze the use of marijuana in conjunction with medications like morphine

- $3.1 million to transform a canal barge into a floating museum that will travel the Erie Canal in New York State

- $6 million for a snowmaking facility in Duluth, Minnesota

But it's one thing to appropriate the money and another to actually spend it. Obama found that he could spend only a small portion of the stimulus money right away. The only thing Washington could do well was to pass out money. Fully 85% of the tax rebates went out the door in the first year, as did 73% of the new entitlement spending.[28]

But the heralded construction projects that were supposed to jump-start the economy took a long time to get going. By the end of 2010, in fact, only half of the stimulus money allocated to contracts, construction, grants, and loans had actually been spent. It took time to select projects, design buildings, let contracts, and start the money flowing.

It turned out that Obama's urgency to get his hands on the stimulus money was not motivated by any immediate need to spend it to get the economy moving, it was to expand the size of government and use the recession as an excuse to jam his big-spending agenda through quickly in the first hours of his presidency.

While this orgy of spending was going on, the Federal Reserve Board fulfilled its part of the Keynesian design by a dramatic lowering of interest rates and massive creation of new money.

THE FEDERAL RESERVE'S MONETARY MAYHEM

The Federal Reserve Board matched Obama's massive spending by slashing interest rates, functionally, to zero and almost tripling the money supply. The theory was that these measures would keep business well lubricated with credit, stop bankruptcies, cut layoffs, and give companies the resources they needed to grow and expand.

When the recession first hit, the Fed rapidly lowered interest rates as far as it could—to one-quarter of 1%. The steep fall in interest rates demonstrated the panic that had seized Washington's economic and political establishment. In the space of a few months, short-term rates tumbled to almost zero and ten-year bond interest was cut in half.

THE FED SLASHES INTEREST RATES

Date	Interest Rate	
	One Month	Ten Year
July 23, 2007	4.88	4.97
March 17, 2008	1.16	3.34
Sept 15, 2008	0.36	3.47
Dec 10, 2008	0.00	2.64
Oct 26, 2010	0.14	2.67

Source: U.S. Treasury[29]

The idea, of course, was that if interest rates are kept very, very low, businesses will borrow money and use the cash to expand and create jobs. The demand side of the economy was being watered by massive government spending, while the supply side was fueled by low interest rates to encourage business growth.

But it didn't work. Even with interest rates rivaling Elton John's famous song "Too Low for Zero," businesses didn't borrow, didn't invest, and didn't expand.

So the Fed resorted to a novel strategy for flooding the economy with money—"quantitative easing," a euphemism for printing money.

Of course the Fed didn't literally operate a printing press. It would have taken too long to churn out enough hundred-dollar bills. Rather, the Fed went to America's banks and inquired gently if they were interested in selling their mortgage-backed securities.

Were they ever! These bankers had been glumly contemplating their piles of mortgage-backed securities, purchased from Fannie Mae and Freddie Mac at the height of the real estate boom. Once coveted investments, now they were worth nothing. Most were underwater (the debt was more than the land and buildings were worth) and no payments were coming in. Who wouldn't want to sell these worthless pieces of paper, this confetti?

When the Fed offered to buy them at 100 cents on the dollar, it was as if Santa Claus had just walked in the door.

Banks flocked to the Fed, eager to unload their mortgage-backed securities and the Fed obliged, buying $1.065 trillion of them, pumping huge amounts of cash into America's banks. In addition, the Fed bought up $832 billion of U.S. Treasury notes and $151 billion of debt issued by other federal agencies. In all, the Fed's shopping spree injected about $2 trillion into the economy.[30]

The money supply more than doubled from $853 billion in October 2008 to $2 trillion in October 2010.[31]

GROWTH IN MONEY SUPPLY*

(in US$ billions)

07/01/07	$853
08/01/08	$872
10/01/08	$1,136
10/21/10	$1,969

*Adjusted Monetary Base (Cash and Excess Reserves)
Source: Federal Reserve Board

The Fed eased up on its purchase of bonds and securities in March 2010, but it is back at it again. Fearful that the economy is in a permanent state of torpor, the Fed is now ratcheting up its purchase of bonds and notes to pump more money into the economy—to do more of what has not worked to date.

Now we are saddled with a vastly expanded money supply, which is growing every day. At the moment, the money is in hiding, awaiting a better economic climate. Consumers, businesses, and banks are all sitting on it and waiting for times to improve.

But one day they will improve and all that money will come out of hiding. All at once. Too much money will be chasing too few goods and services and the result will be awful, untamable, runaway inflation. The classical formulation of the Fed's role is to dampen the economy once it is moving up. In the words of William McChesney Martin, "to take away the punch bowl just as the party gets going." [32]

But now taking away the punch bowl won't do anything. Everybody has their own private flask of liquid stimulant in their pocket! We all have paid down our credit cards and other debt, businesses are awash in cash, and banks have huge reserves.

The Fed speaks bravely about soaking up the extra money before it can be spent, but has no real plan for doing so.

And why did we accumulate all that debt? What was the big spending for? Why did we print so much money? None of it worked.

BUT IT DIDN'T WORK

So the Keynesian model was fully implemented, beyond anyone's wildest dreams. And it didn't work. Nada. Zero. Nothing.

The Keynesian defibrillator sent forth its charge, but the nation's economic heart didn't respond. Maybe a beat or two, not much more. The cash for clunkers program triggered a few car purchases. The home buyer tax credit led to some sales. But as soon as the stimulus stopped, so did the buying.

Consumers wouldn't spend. Businesses wouldn't expand. Banks wouldn't lend. The Keynesian stimulus did no good.

Why didn't it work? Because you can lead a horse to water, but you can't make it drink!

Obama can pump all the money he wants into the economy, but he can't make us spend it. And we didn't.

Look at the data. People didn't buy cars or appliances or other consumer products. They just pocketed the money.

According to the U.S. Department of Labor, consumers decreased their average spending from 2007 to 2009 by 1.15% per year.[33] Almost all categories of products and services suffered cuts in consumer spending.

CUTS IN CONSUMER SPENDING, 2007–09

(average annual reduction)

Food at home	−8.3%
Food away from home	−1.8%
Housing	−0.2%
Alcoholic beverages	−4.8%
Apparel and services	−8.3%
Entertainment	−0.2%

Source: U.S. Department of Labor[34]

The only increases in consumer spending were in health insurance (up 15.5% per year) and education (up 13% per year).[35] Of course, health insurance spending is largely involuntary—and stoked by the prospect of the new insurance regulations under ObamaCare—and education spending is vital for workers looking to move out of unemployment.

Instead of using the money to buy goods and services, we used it to pay down credit card debts, reduce our student loans, pay off car loans, and put money in the bank. Meanwhile, we didn't spend it on anything that would stimulate the economy or create new jobs. The savings rate rose from 3.2% in 2007 to 8% in 2010.[36] People sat on their wallets. Sales were flat even as the stimulus money flowed out of the Treasury.

Since the middle of 2008, Americans have cut their total debt by almost $200 billion—an average of $2,700 for a family of four. In August 2010 alone, Americans reduced their credit card debt by $5 billion and their car loans by almost $2 billion.[37] Good for them, but not much use for the economy.

Companies didn't spend their money either. At the end of March 2010, the *Wall Street Journal* reported that "nonfinancial companies" had socked away $1.84 trillion in cash and other liquid assets as of the end of March, up 26% from a year earlier and the largest-ever increase in records going back to 1952. Cash made up about 7% of all company assets, including factories and financial investments, the highest level since 1963.[38]

So American companies are sitting on almost $2 trillion of cash—money that could be invested in new factories, a larger sales force, technological improvements, new product lines, or services for consumers. Instead, the companies would rather just sit on the cash and not invest it. No jobs created there.

And the companies, of course, pay a steep price for keeping their cash liquid. They have to be content with the small earnings an almost 0% interest rate can provide. Or they can play the stock market. Or visit Vegas.

Why didn't consumers spend? Why did business sit on its money? Why didn't the horse drink the water? Why didn't Keynesian economics work?

Because consumers and the people who run businesses are not automatons and aren't crazy. They knew that the checks that flowed from Washington were not going to last forever. They realized that good times were still a long way away.

People are not stupid. They can tell the difference between standing under a shower and standing in the rain. In both cases, you feel water pouring on your head, but one will end as soon as you—or the government—turns off the water, and the other will go on for a while.

The *Wall Street Journal* phrased it more elegantly: "Consumers are unsettled by the dismal job market and the need to repair household balance sheets badly damaged by the housing bust and the recession."[39]

And if consumers aren't spending, business won't either. Deutsche Bank economist Torsten Slok noted that "the problem . . . is that even though they [American companies] have the wherewithal to bring on new workers, they are holding off until they see more willingness of consumers to spend." Slok calls it "a vicious cycle of everyone sitting around doing nothing."[40]

It should not have come as a surprise that everybody sat on their money. We warned in our book *Catastrophe* that this is exactly what would happen:

"If taxpayers get refunds and workers get paychecks, why won't they spend the money? Because people have brains. They're not animals who respond automatically to stimulation; they know what's going on. They know the tax refund checks they get are one-shot gifts that won't come around again. Their anxiety over the future paralyzes their ability to respond to the economic stimulus of the moment the way the economists had hoped."[41]

Massive stimulus spending didn't work in Japan in the 1990s. The ratio of government debt to GDP rose by 217% as politicians spent $1 trillion (double it to find the U.S. equivalent) in a fruitless effort to stimulate the economy. Economic growth averaged 0.6% a year during this period.[42]

It didn't work when President George W. Bush sent out rebates to every American household in 2008. He sent out $100 billion in checks, a pittance compared to Obama, but only 10–20% of the money was actually spent on goods and services.[43] They saved the rest or used them to pay down bills and loans.

And why didn't the banks lend out the money the Federal Reserve Board was sending their way? The banks sat on the money because of their worries about the economy, but also because they had something much better to do with their newfound wealth: lend it back to the government!

Why should banks take risks on new mortgages, car loans, business development, commercial real estate, manufacturing expansion, or entrepreneurial initiatives when the government is ready to borrow all the money they can lend?

Remember that banks got their capital, essentially, for free by selling the Fed their worthless mortgage-backed securities or by borrowing from the Fed at interest rates close to zero. Banks incurred no cost in acquiring their capital. These bankers instead lent their new cash back to the federal government from whence it had come at an interest rate averaging 3.5%. This spread between the cost of acquiring capital and the earnings it generates is enough for any banker. No stockholder could expect more.

And, of course, the government loans are risk-free. By definition, they are guaranteed by the full faith and credit of the United States government. You can't get any safer than that. No matter how overextended our exchequer becomes, the power to tax the largest economy—by far—in the world lies behind the debt, securing its repayment.

So why should bankers fool with lending money to a pair of young geniuses who are nursing the next big idea in their garage? So what if it might sprout into the next Microsoft or Dell if they could get capital? Better to be content with an adequate return on your loans with a government guarantee. Nothing is safer or more certain to make you money. After all, getting capital for free and lending it out at 3.5% makes it impossible *not* to make money and bankers know it.

So banks wouldn't lend to the private sector, consumers didn't buy new goods or services, and companies refused to part with their cash or make investments in expansion.

Obama's principal strategy for solving the recession didn't work. When he took office, unemployment was 7.7%. By November 2010, it was 9.8%, with not much prospect of going down.[44] And even these stats understated the problem. When you add the underemployed who work part-time for economic reasons and "marginally discouraged workers" (folks interested in working who have looked for a job in the past year, but are not now actively searching for jobs) the rate grows to 17.1%.[45]

The rest of the world has been recovering. But not the United States. We are getting over the recession much more slowly than any other industrialized country.

U.S. GROWTH RATE COMPARED

(Second quarter, 2010)

Country	Average Annual Growth
U.S.	1.7%
Euro Zone	4.0%
United Kingdom	4.8%[46]

What's the difference? We have Barack Obama as our president and they don't!

OBAMA'S REAL AGENDA

Why was Obama so wrong? Why did he bet so heavily on an economic theory that had been so discredited? Was he stupid? Crazy?

He was crazy like a fox! Barack Obama is not stupid. He could not really have imagined that his massive stimulus borrowing and spending would grow the economy.

The truth is that he didn't care. His goal was not recovery. Not improving America. Not making things better. Not stimulating private sector growth.

He wanted to use the recession to expand the public sector. As Rahm Emanuel, his first chief of staff, famously said early in Obama's presidency, "You never want a serious crisis to go to waste."[47]

The new spending was not a means to the end of recovery. The additional outlays were themselves the goal. Barack Obama wanted to expand the public sector to make us into a government-centric economy. He wanted to diminish the private sector and expand the role of government. In short, he wanted to raise the level of public spending in the United States to more nearly approximate that of Western Europe with its socialist democracies.

The goal of increasing public sector spending has long been deeply embedded in liberal ideology. John Kenneth Galbraith, the leading economist of the left, pled constantly in his books during the 1960s and '70s for an expansion in government spending and investment in the public sector.

American liberals looked with jealousy at the vast public sectors of Western Europe and were determined to pick up the pace of U.S. government outlays.

Obama simply took an eight-year wish list of spending projects and passed it all in one week. His hope was not that the spending would encourage the private sector. He wished the exact opposite—he wanted government spending to replace the private sector.

Obama, of course, realized that a higher deficit would make the pressure for higher taxes inevitable. And *that* was also his goal. He wants a tax policy that takes from the rich and gives to the poor—a Robin Hood increase.

Obama's campaign promise that he would not raise taxes on the middle class does not give us much comfort. We don't believe him in the first place. And even if we did, we have all come to realize that a tax hike on some of us impacts us all.

The recession has changed American opinions about tax policy. In 2008, voters did not mind taxes rising on the rich as long as they were not personally affected. But the recession has shown us all that any tax on anyone depresses the economy and saps economic growth.

We are finding out that while class warfare makes great politics, it is lousy economics. According to new research from Moody's Analytics, the top 5% of Americans by income account for 37% of all consumer outlays. Outlays include consumer spending, interest payments on installment debt, and transfer payments.[48] And consumer spending generates 70% of our Gross Domestic Product.[49]

A Rasmussen Reports poll on September 13, 2010, found that, by 51–44%, U.S. voters wanted to extend the Bush tax cuts—including those for rich people. (This poll was conducted before Obama conceded the point.) Offered a choice between extending the tax cuts for all Americans and extending them for everyone but the wealthy, 48% opted to extend them for everybody, and just 41% wanted them for all but the rich.[50] A majority of our countrymen now realize that even if they don't personally pay more in taxes, they will end up paying by losing their jobs.

Obama has abandoned, for now, his efforts to repeal the Bush tax cuts on those making more than $250,000 a year. But don't be fooled. He will return to his demands after the extension has expired two years hence, if he is re-elected. Only by defeating him can we defeat this tax increase in the future.

By threatening to raise taxes on the big spenders, Obama is once again placing his social priorities in the way of our economic needs. He is so anxious to soak the wealthy and redistribute income that he is willing to kill the goose that lays the golden egg.

His goal is to spend and tax us into his vision of a reengineered society. That's his idea of "social justice."

But Americans are realizing that the big spending programs he is passing are stopping us from recovering from the recession.

AMERICA BECOMES A DEBT SLAVE

Each new stimulus bill, every additional dollar of deficit and debt, each new federal regulation or tax or fee drains our economic corpus of the very blood it needs to survive and prosper. But Obama keeps draining away the blood, oblivious to its effect on us as he focuses, like Captain Ahab, on his ideological objective of income redistribution.

But Obama's spending did a lot more than just fail to lead to recovery. It has transformed the United States into a debt slave, perhaps permanently, because every dollar the government spent, it borrowed.

His new spending caused the federal deficit to explode beyond all reason. After decades of deficits that hovered around 3 or 4% of our economy, we now have one that has reached almost 10% of our GDP.[51]

Obama's defenders say that the Bush administration racked up a deficit of $1.3 trillion and that the 2009 shortfall of $1.6 trillion is only slightly greater. But this argument is a sleight of hand. The final Bush deficit, in his 2008–09 budget, was supposed to be $458 billion.[52] But, because of the recession, it had risen to about $713 billion by the time he left office.[53]

In September 2008, the banking system collapsed and the administration rushed in with loans to shore it up. The TARP (Troubled Asset Recovery Program) lent out $700 billion to financial institutions to stop them from going under. Because the federal budget makes no distinction between spending and lending, all $700 billion went on the balance sheet, driving the deficit for FY2009, up to $1.4 trillion—of which half was the TARP loans (the $713 billion of real deficit plus the $700 billion of TARP loans.)

Most of the $700 billion in TARP loans was never spent. Banks just held on to the money (or asked the Fed to hold on to it for them) so that nobody would have cause to doubt their financial solvency. There would be no runs on banks as there were in 1933. After a few months, banks repaid the money. Among private companies, only AIG, the most seriously impaired one, couldn't repay its loans. And, of course, the two federal government agencies that borrowed TARP funds—Fannie Mae and Freddie Mac—were awash in insolvent debt so that they, too, could not repay it.

In all, about $500 billion of the $700 billion Bush had lent out was paid back. But no sooner did the money come back to the Treasury than Obama sent it back out again in new federal spending. This time, however, the money went out never to return. It was spent, not lent. The budget deficit, which should have dropped to about $900 billion once the $500 billion in TARP money was paid back, went up to $1.6 trillion instead—or 10.6% of GDP.[54] But this time, the deficit was permanent—the money wasn't coming back.

Obama's massive spending and borrowing did nothing to stimulate the economy, but just added to the deficit and the debt. Families and businesses pocketed the extra cash, reducing their debts. All Obama really managed to do was to transform private family and business debt into government debt.

This level of government debt has made recovery impossible. Every dime he borrowed cut the money that could flow to businesses and consumers in private sector lending. The spending and the borrowing it triggers are like a tapeworm embedded in the innards of our economy. Whatever capital we generate, savings we accumulate, or resources we aggregate go first to keep our government afloat. After the government's appetite for borrowing—which now runs to $150 billion per month[55]—is satiated, there is nothing left over for the rest of the economy.

The interest on the debt will cripple our government and force high taxes and spending for years—or decades—to come.

We have yet to feel the full impact of Obama's insane borrowing because, as fast as the debt has increased, interest rates have declined. In fact, the total the government has to spend servicing the debt has risen from $237 billion in FY2008 to $251 billion in FY2011.

But this statistic is illusory. It only works while interest rates are low. Once the rates rise, our debt payment obligations will soar.

With the Fed pouring money into banks buying up securitized mortgages, interest rates are extremely low. Insecurity about the euro in the wake of the financial difficulties of Greece, Portugal, Spain, Italy, and Ireland has generated a flight to the dollar by cautious investors. Holding dollars instead of euros, they buy U.S. government bonds with their money, holding down interest rates.

Sooner or later, however, rates are going to rise because the world is simply running out of money. Every country is running a deficit and has to turn to the bond market to borrow enough to pay its bills. Eventually, the Fed has to stop printing money or massive inflation is inevitable. When it begins to taper off its purchase of securities and bonds from banks, a global shortage of capital will undoubtedly set in.

The world produces $60 trillion of goods and services[56] each year (global GDP) and, by the broadest indication of its money supply, has $58.9 trillion of capital.[57]

But global debts far outstrip these resources. The governments of the world, combined, owe $40 trillion.[58] Private companies, banks, and individuals owe an additional $120 trillion.[59]

So a world worth $60 trillion owes itself $160 trillion. As soon as the current euro-panic subsides and the Federal Reserve stops printing money, interest rates will have to rise to attract the kind of capital needed to repay or even to service that kind of debt.

HOW MUCH DEBT IS THERE?

Government Debt	$40 trillion
Private Debt	$120 trillion
Total Debt	**$160 trillion**

Source: The Economist

So who will lend us the money for Obama's deficits? Not the Chinese or Japanese. They are divesting themselves of U.S. government debt as fast as they can. The key lender will be none other than the Federal Reserve Board itself. The Fed will lend money to the federal government. Where will it get the money? It will create it. It will print it. At some point, this Ponzi scheme has to catch up with us and the credibility of the dollar has to come crashing down.

As these pressures are beginning to come to a head, interest rates on federal debt are bound to increase. No longer will the government be able to borrow money at its current rate of about 3.5% interest.

And, when this happens, the drain on the United States budget will become especially severe. As deficits continue, each year adding to the debt, and interest rates rise, the debt service obligations will absorb more and more of the federal budget.

The United States will become like a family inveigled into taking out a subprime mortgage by initially low teaser rates. Then the rates go up, and they find that their monthly mortgage bill is too high and they can't pay their debt. Though the U.S. will pay its debt, it will do so with an ever greater sacrifice in other important public spending. Or, worse, it will pay the debt by printing money, debasing the currency and setting the stage for inflation like that which gripped Germany in the 1920s.

The chart below tells us how much we would have to pay in debt service from our federal budget if the deficits that we expect do materialize (no cut in spending) and interest rates rise:

HOW MUCH WE WOULD HAVE TO PAY IN INTEREST ON OUR DEBT IF RATES RISE

	Debt Levels (In US $ billions)	Annual Debt Service at Varying Average Interest Rates (In US $ billions)			
Fiscal Year	Total Debt	3%	4%	5%	6%
2010	13,562	406.86	542.48	678.10	813.72
2011	14,904	447.12	596.16	745.20	894.24
2012	15,818	474.54	632.72	790.90	949.08
2013	16,565	496.95	662.60	828.25	993.90
2014	17,289	518.67	691.56	864.45	1,037.34
2015	18,082	542.46	723.28	904.10	1,084.92
2016	18,976	569.28	759.04	948.80	1,138.56

Annual debt levels as projected by the CBO.
Total Debt for Fiscal Year 2010 is actual as reported by the U.S. Treasury.[60]

Our debt service obligations could take over our entire federal budget. If rates went to 5%—a likely scenario—we would soon be paying more than $1 trillion in interest on the debt. That is about equal to our current Medicare and Social Security spending combined!

This huge and growing debt service obligation will force Congress and the president to cut the deficit and reduce the rate of growth in the national debt. The question is: how?

Our task is to make sure that it is not through tax increases!

OBAMA'S PENDING TAX HIKES PARALYZE THE ECONOMY

During the spending phase of Obama's presidency, the government proffered an open hand filled with cash. But everybody knows that just over the horizon loom huge tax increases, particularly on those most prone to spend their cash. Like hogs in a stockyard, we look skeptically at each day's feeding trough, knowing that the day of slaughter is coming. We have all come to realize that we are being fattened up for higher levels of taxation and we are hoarding our cash in anticipation.

The consumer anxiety that is bottling up spending and causing cash to stay in checking accounts, CDs, or credit card balance sheets is not just a general angst about the economy. It is a very specific and very well-deserved fear of looming tax increases.

Some have assumed that once Obama agreed to extend the Bush tax cuts, he wouldn't raise taxes. That is a fool's assumption. Not only will he raise rates on those making more than $250,000 a year, but he has a long list of new taxes he wants to impose in the meantime.

We must stop him!

Already, he has succeeded in reimposing the inheritance tax as part of his deal to extend the Bush tax cuts. Starting in 2011, and for the next two years, the tax will be 35% on estates of more than $5 million.

The problem with the inheritance tax (or death tax, as the GOP calls it) is not the relatively small number of rich people whose heirs will have to pay more from their estates. They can fend for themselves. The problem is that no tax is more certain to kill economic growth than a levy on estates.

Consider the case of the aged millionaire contemplating his mortality with increasing concern. If he reinvests his profits in his business, creating more jobs, he'd better not die anytime soon. If he does, his heirs will have to pay 35% of his estate (minus an exemption of $5 million) to the federal government. If all his money is tied up in the business (or in farmland or housing), the only way to pay the estate tax would be to sell off assets—a forced quick sale that will not fetch the best price. To assure that his heirs don't have to do that, the wise elderly entrepreneur will hoard cash and not invest his profits in his business. When he dies, his heirs will just cash out some CDs and pay the taxman. But, before his death, his wealth does us all no good, because he is keeping it liquid.

And Obama is determined to reduce what little relief from taxes the current system of deductions affords us. Americans have come to depend on the deductions they take for home mortgage interest payments, state and local taxes, and charitable deductions to decrease their tax exposure. The home construction industry and charities of all shape and size depend on these deductions to provide incentives to build or donate. And politicians in state and local governments earnestly hope that their tax hikes will be better received by irate constituents if they can deduct them on their federal income tax forms.

But Obama wants to cap the deductions for mortgages, taxes, and charitable donations at the 28% bracket. This would reduce the value of your deductions by between a quarter and a third depending on your income.

If you are in the top tax bracket of 35%, Obama wants to let you deduct only 28% of your tax, mortgage, or charitable payment. So you will lose 7%, or one-fifth, of your current deduction. Those in the 33% bracket would lose 5%—or one-sixth—of their current deduction.

The National Commission on Fiscal Responsibility and Reform, appointed by Obama and the Democratic majority as a fig leaf for their tax proposals, went even further and recommended replacing the mortgage interest and charitable donations deduction entirely with a 12% tax credit for the actual amount of the mortgage payment or the charitable gift. This would cut the amount the deductions for charitable and mortgage interest save taxpayers even more drastically.

For a family that is in the 25% tax bracket with a monthly mortgage bill of $1,000, this would cut the amount they save in taxes in half. Under the Obama Commission proposal, they would lose a deduction that saves

$3,000 in taxes and replace it with a credit that would save only $1,440—half as much.

Currently, the deduction is available to all mortgages of under $1 million. The Commission would only make the new tax credit apply to loans of under $500,000.[61]

And Obama would also limit deductions for state and local taxes to 28%. Taxpayers are able to survive high federal and state tax rates because their state taxes are deductible on their federal tax return. But now Obama would deny this relief.

Unwilling to violate his campaign commitment not to raise taxes on the middle class, Obama has decided to reduce their deductions instead! If you fail to see any difference between these approaches, join the club.

So this president, who pledged not to raise *federal* taxes on the middle class is, in effect, forcing a state tax increase by limiting the amount of the state and local income tax deduction.

The most important impact of the Obama tax deduction changes would fall on the 67% of Americans who own their own homes.[62] Home owners facing foreclosure or falling behind on their mortgages will suddenly find that the limitations on the deductibility of their mortgages will add thousands to their real debt burden.

A full quarter of all tax filers—and about half of those who actually pay federal income taxes—take a mortgage interest deduction. In 2010, it saved them $104 billion in taxes and, by 2013, it will save them $135 billion—if Obama and the Democrats let it live![63]

The president's proposals will not only soak the taxpayer, they will snuff out whatever growth there still may be in the home construction industry.

While the Federal Reserve Board is busy printing money to try to keep mortgage interest rates low and stimulate home buying and construction, Obama will be raising taxes on mortgage interest and making most mortgages one-quarter or one-third more expensive. With mortgage interest rates now running at 4.6% for a thirty-year fixed mortgage,[64] that is the equivalent of adding 1.2 to 1.6 points of extra interest! On a $100,000 mortgage, that adds between $100 and $133 to the payments each month! Some incentive to buy or build homes!

Home ownership has fallen to a ten-year low with the high rate of foreclosures and tighter lending restrictions, according to the National Association of Realtors.[65] Could Obama pick a worse time to cut back on the mortgage interest deduction?

Chairman of the Mortgage Bankers Association Michael D. Berman said, sensibly, "A rollback of the mortgage interest deduction as proposed by the commission would have a devastating impact on both present and future homeowners in this country. It would immediately stop in its tracks any stabilization we are seeing in the housing market and would effectively increase the cost of homeownership for millions upon millions of people."[66]

Reducing this deduction would also cost us a huge number of jobs. The construction of 100 homes generates 305 jobs, $14.5 million in wages, and $8.9 million in tax revenue.[67]

The National Association of Realtors estimates that cutting the mortgage interest deduction so drastically "could critically erode home prices and the value of homes by as much as 15%, according to our research."[68]

Carlos Bonilla wrote for the American Action Forum, a center-right policy group, that it would be reasonable to expect that "housing prices will fall" by an amount equal to the decreased value of the deduction. "Homebuyers don't get the tax deduction for nothing—they've actually paid for it in the cost of the house they purchased. It has simply been capitalized over the years they will be paying their mortgage."[69]

"This would result in an enormous blow to the 60% of Americans who presently own their homes," Bonilla goes on to say. "We've already experienced double-digit home value declines in the past few years; do we really want to see them drop another 10–15% instantly because of a change in tax policy?"[70]

And Obama has also taken aim at charitable giving. Most cynically, this president, who trumpets concern for the poor, will undermine charities across the nation by limiting the deductibility of their donations. With national charitable giving at about $304 billion a year,[71] his proposal would increase taxes on those who give by $35 billion a year.[72]

As with curtailing the mortgage interest deduction, the Obama-appointed National Commission on Fiscal Responsibility and Reform goes even further in cutting the charitable donation deduction. The Commission would give taxpayers a credit worth 12% of their donations—but only if they contributed 2% or more of their adjusted gross income to charity.[73]

The proposal would confine the benefit to the wealthier donors who give that high a proportion of their income to charity. The average church-goer who earns $50,000 a year would be hard pressed to equal the $1,000 threshold that would trigger the deduction.

And it would, of course, slash the deduction for wealthier taxpayers. A $1,000 donation to the Red Cross by an upper-income taxpayer (assuming he is above the 2% threshold) would lead to a tax savings of $350 under current law. But if the Commission's proposal passes, it would save only $120 in taxes, a cut of more than two-thirds.

USA Today reports that "wealthy givers are more sensitive to the impact of tax policy on their contributions than they've been in the past, according to a new survey by the Center on Philanthropy at Indiana University and Bank of America." [74]

"People give because they care about a cause or for other reasons, but certainly, tax conditions affect the timing of the gift, the level of the gift and the manner in which they give," says Una Osili, director of research at the Center on Philanthropy." [75]

When you combine Obama's proposed increases in the federal tax brackets (i.e., letting the Bush tax cuts expire) with his plans to limit deductibility, the effect is horrific—about a 25% increase in federal tax payments!

Consider a home owner in Nancy Pelosi's San Francisco:

Option One—Household Income: $75,000

If the family makes *$75,000* a year
And has a mortgage of **$120,692.67**
And has property tax payments of **$1,404.86**
And has to pay *$4,983.90* in state income tax
And gives **4%** of their income to charity
Then, they will find their federal income taxes rising by *27.9%*, or **$1,459.81**, under Obama's proposals.

Option Two—Household Income: $150,000

If the family makes *$150,000* a year
And has a mortgage of **$166,780.22**

And has property tax payments of **$1,941.32**

And has to pay **$12,483.90** in state income tax

And gives **4%** of their income to charity

Then, they will find their federal income taxes rising by *3.7%*, or *$661.61*, under Obama's proposals.

Option Three—Household Income $250,000

If the family makes *$250,000* a year

And has a mortgage of **$352,229.68**

And has property tax payments of **$4,099.95**

And has to pay **$22,483.90** in state income tax

And gives **4%** of their income to charity

Then, they will find their federal income taxes rising by *15.4%*, or *$5,147.65*, under Obama's proposals.

Option Four—Household Income: $400,000

If the family makes *$400,000* a year

And has a mortgage of **$536,324.26**

And has property tax payments of **$6,242.81**

And has to pay *$37,483.90* in state income tax

And gives **4%** of their income to charity

Then, they will find their federal income taxes rising by *29.9%*, or *$19,618.54*, under Obama's proposals.

These scenarios assume the following tax changes recommended by Obama or by his Deficit Reduction Commission:

1. An increase in the top rates to 39.6% and 36%
2. An increase in the FICA ceiling to $150,000
3. Replacement of the mortgage interest and charitable deductions by a 12% tax credit
4. Capping the state and local tax deduction at 28%
5. Cutting the payroll tax by 2% as adopted as part of the deal extending the Bush tax cuts
6. Eliminating the Child Tax Credit

And there's more: Obama's Commission also recommended eliminating or curtailing the Child Tax Credit, which gives low- and moderate-income parents a $1,000 credit on their income taxes for each child.[76] A "refundable" credit, it really amounts to a welfare payment for those who either pay no taxes or pay less in taxes than the credit allows.

It also called for reduction or elimination of the Earned Income Tax Credit (EITC), a program that assures that anyone who goes to work, full-time, and finds that their paycheck does not lift their family out of poverty, will get the difference as a refundable tax credit. Alone among the social welfare programs, this one makes great sense. It guarantees that work pays, and it is key in the success welfare reform has had in cutting poverty even as it slices the welfare rolls.

But Obama is not stopping there. While he promised during the campaign that he would not raise taxes on the middle class, his Deficit Reduction Commission has recommended a steep hike in Social Security taxes for families making more than $106,800, but less than $150,000 per year—middle class by anybody's definition.

Right now, employers, employees, and the self-employed only pay FICA taxes on the first $106,800[77] of income (a sum indexed to inflation). Now, Obama's Deficit Reduction Commission has proposed raising the ceiling to $150,000 per year. That means that any family whose joint income exceeds $106,800 will now have to pay Social Security taxes on their entire income up to $150,000. Eighteen million American households will see their taxes rise.[78] Now Obama is defining the "middle class" as having incomes below $100,000 per household!

That blessed day—usually in the fall—when our paychecks go up because they are no longer taking out Social Security taxes will not happen for most Americans.

For families making $150,000, this amounts to an almost 50% increase in their Social Security taxes. And Obama will have a hard time describing families whose joint income is between $106,800 and $150,000 as wealthy.

All these tax increases are on the table and very possible in an Obama-dominated world.

The recommendations of the Obama commission on the deficit were endorsed by most of the Democrats on the body. That's no surprise. What is shocking is that Republican senators Mike Crapo (ID), Tom Coburn

(OK), and retiring senator Judd Gregg of New Hampshire all voted to back the tax increases recommended by the Commission. There must be something in the water supply in Washington that turns good men like these into taxers and spenders. Hopefully, the conservative Republicans of Idaho and Oklahoma will learn of their apostasy and will press them to recover their sense of fiscal conservatism on the Senate floor.

And there are still more tax hikes coming! The administration has floated all sorts of new ideas for torturing our taxpayers.

Copying the European socialist model, Obama's people have trumpeted a value-added tax (VAT) as a possible solution. This tax, hidden from view, is imposed at each stage of a commercial transaction. When the raw material suppliers sell to the manufacturer, they pay a VAT. When the manufacturer sells his products to a wholesaler, he pays a VAT. And when the wholesaler sells to a retailer, he too pays a VAT. By the time the product reaches the consumer, each layer of taxation is already built into the price of the product or service. The customer has no idea how much tax he is paying, the product just seems to cost a lot.

"Fair tax" advocates like talk show host Neal Boortz have urged a VAT for America, but *only* as a replacement for the federal income tax. Obama doesn't want to replace any tax. He just wants to add on. Since the Sixteenth Amendment to the Constitution isn't likely to be repealed anytime soon, a fair tax could be dangerous. Politicians could just sneak back and keep the income tax *in addition to* the VAT levy.

. . . And Obama's not through yet. The House passed an income tax surcharge for families with incomes of $250,000 or more in its early version of the ObamaCare legislation. Though the provision died in the Senate, it will likely be revived when the time comes to pass around the hat to pay off the deficit.

. . . No, not finished yet! Obama also wants to cut "spending" on what budget types call "tax expenditures" (i.e., deductions or tax credits). He wants to sweep through the tax code and slash or eliminate tax breaks that businesses and individuals get.

The Obama liberals flagged their intentions when President Clinton's former chief of staff, John Podesta, proposed cutting tax deductions and credits in a memo from his think tank, Center for American Progress. (Progress toward bankruptcy!)

Podesta's group proposed:

- Ending deductions for business meals and entertainment. Currently we can deduct half the cost of the meal. No more.

- Taxing life insurance benefits for the dead. Right now, the earnings your life insurance premiums gather are not taxable. Obama would tax them at the time of your death. This is in addition to reimposing the inheritance tax. Don't die under Obama!

- Eliminating tax breaks for farmers.

- Increasing taxes on credit unions.

- Increasing taxes on Blue Cross and Blue Shield. At the same time health insurance premiums are soaring due to ObamaCare!

- Taxing timber companies more heavily.

- Raising taxes for nonprofit life insurance companies.

- Eliminating the real estate investment tax shelter. This will cripple efforts to provide good housing in the inner city.

- Taxing the interest on state and local bonds for privately owned infrastructure projects. At the same time he is spending like mad on infrastructure, he would cripple states and cities trying to build sewage treatment plants, hospitals, airports, energy plants, etc.

- Eliminating all tax deductions for state and local bonds and replacing them with a flat subsidy. With the municipal bond market on the verge of collapse because of concerns over the solvency of many states, this proposal will just make things a lot worse.

- Ending tax breaks for businesses that locate in inner-city areas. Great for a president pledged to help our cities!

These "tax expenditures" will be billed as closing loopholes or ending "welfare for the rich," but they will be tax increases just the same, each draining money from our economy—dragging it down—and transferring wealth to the government.

To stop these tax increases, Republicans will have to hold the line against any increase in levies and propose deep spending cuts to reduce the federal budget deficit.

TAX HIKES WON'T CUT THE DEFICIT

Obama's tax proposals will not cut the deficit, but will lead to an ever steeper downward spiral in the economy that will swell the deficit by adding to entitlement payments and will necessitate greater and greater tax increases.

The increases in taxation will dampen economic growth. Each new tax increase will generate less and less of the expected new revenue as it soaks up money that should have fueled consumer demand and business expansion. With each new rung up the tax ladder, economic activity will decline and revenue growth will fall shorter and shorter of anticipated levels.

And, as the economy staggers under the impact of higher taxes, entitlement spending will rise. More people will need welfare, food stamps, unemployment compensation, and Medicaid. While Obama may initially propose higher taxes as part of a combination of spending cuts and tax increases, the inability of the tax hikes to generate enough revenue and the growth of entitlement spending will ensure his failure to close the deficit. That will trigger a pattern of higher and higher taxes and less and less economic growth.

That was exactly what happened in 1982, when President Ronald Reagan agreed with the Democratic Congress to go along with higher taxes. The deal was that for each dollar in tax hikes, they would cut $3 in government spending. Sounded like a good deal. But although the taxes went up, the spending never came down. In fact, it rose. From 1983 to 1988, federal outlays increased from $808 billion to $1.1 trillion[79]

And, when Bush 41 caved in to Congressional Democrats in 1990 and broke his "read my lips" pledge of "no new taxes," he agreed to a 2:1 ratio of spending cuts to tax hikes. Once again, taxes rose on schedule, but the spending cuts did not materialize. In fact, spending rose from $1.25 trillion in 1990 to $1.53 trillion in 1995.[80]

If Obama has his way and gets a mix of spending cuts and tax increases, we will wind up with the same result we had after Reagan and Bush 41 made similar concessions—higher taxes and higher spending.

On the other hand, tax cuts can balance the budget because they stimulate the economy, which grows tax revenues and decreases entitlement spending.

Again the historical record makes the case clear:

When President Ronald Reagan cut the capital gains tax rate from 39% to 28%, the economy grew by 4.4%—about 1.3% higher than the historic average.[81]

And when Reagan cut the top rate of the income tax from 70% to 50% and cut the capital gains rate form 28% to 20%, economic growth averaged 5.3% over the ensuing three years—2.3% above historic norms.[82]

And when Clinton cut the capital gains rate from 28% to 20% (it had risen back in 1986), growth averaged 4.6% over the next three years—1.6% higher.[83]

The history of tax cuts stimulating the economy is clear.

The Americans for Tax Reform note that the Congressional Budget Office "projects that every tenth of one percent increase in economic growth over the next decade will increase federal tax revenues by $247 billion." If we can adopt policies that grow the economy 1% faster (including strategic tax cuts), we can trigger $2.5 trillion of new revenues over the next ten years without higher taxes.[84]

In 1995, President Clinton suggested that the Federal Reserve Board was being unduly conservative in its growth policies. He noted that draconian budget cuts and tax hikes could be avoided by a policy that allowed the economy to grow its way out of the deficit. The president wanted to deliver a speech to underscore this point, but he was hooted down by his economic advisors who were wary of offending the Fed. Apparently, Clinton and then Fed chairman Alan Greenspan had reached a nonaggression pact in which each agreed to refrain from criticizing the other. But Clinton's point was absolutely right, and the performance of the economy after he cut the capital gains tax proves it. We had growth with no inflation.

The fact remains that the only tax that stimulates the economy is a tax cut! And the record proves it over and over again.

PART THREE

HOW THE REPUBLICAN HOUSE CAN UNDO THE DAMAGE OBAMA HAS DONE

In one of the greatest electoral upheavals in American history, the Republican Party regained control of the House of Representatives in the midterm elections of 2010 and cut the Democratic margin in the Senate to a narrow 53–47. There are now fewer Democrats in the House of Representatives than at any time since 1938! The tremors of the massive Republican earthquake have toppled Democratic dynasties in many of the fifty states.

Having abused the American people by using their mandate for "change" to socialize health care, grow government to monumental proportions, and take over broad swaths of America's private sector, Obama's Democrats were repudiated—soundly—by outraged American voters.

But this massive victory simply begs the question: what should the GOP do with its newfound political power? How can it turn America around, reinvigorate the economy, and at the same time expose the Obama presidency and economic program for the fraud that it is?

The Republican Party has the power to save our nation and end our drift into a decade-long depression. But how should it proceed?

Some have wondered if a Democratic Senate can make a Republican House impotent. Hardly. If the issues that faced us were primarily those of policy, the breach between the two Houses might indeed sap Republican momentum. But they're not. The issues we face are largely financial: how do we lower the budget deficit by slashing federal government spending and returning it to pre-Obama levels?

Even when issues of policy are involved, as with Republican efforts to roll back Obama's changes in health care law, they become fiscal very quickly. While Republicans cannot repeal ObamaCare—they lack the votes to override a presidential veto of such a bill—they can focus on defunding it. So even health care becomes a financial issue, not just a policy question.

On financial issues, a majority in the House of Representatives goes a long, long way.

First, of course, the federal Constitution requires that money bills originate in the House. So it is there that the nitty-gritty of structuring the federal budget begins.

Moreover, it takes two houses of Congress and a presidential signature to pass a budget, raise the debt limit, or to OK appropriations bills. If the House of Representatives says no, the spending doesn't happen.

Alex Castellanos, a Republican political consultant, said it best on election night of 2010 on CNN. "America decided to put a brake pedal on Barack Obama's car tonight, stop spending, stop the health care, the expansion of government, but you only need one brake pedal."[1] You don't need two.

With Republican control of the House, a huge confrontation with the president over cuts in spending versus increases in taxes is sure to dominate the landscape of the coming political cycle.

And the Democratic control of the Senate might prove more apparent than real, as was their control of the House in the wake of the Reagan victory of 1980. In that Republican landslide, the GOP only captured the Senate, but left the House in the skilled hands of Democratic Speaker Tip O'Neill (the exact reverse of the 2010 outcome). Many worried that the Reagan revolution would die in the House committees and on the floor. But it didn't.

O'Neill and the Democrats were so intimidated by the Reagan sweep of 1980, and so determined to avoid a fate similar to their defeated Democratic Senate colleagues, that they passed the Reagan agenda with few demurrals.

We saw an early indication of the weakness of the Democratic Senate majority during the lame duck session in December 2010 after the Republican victory. Even though the Democrats still had their old 2009–10 majority meeting for one last time, they couldn't roll back the Bush tax cuts on the wealthy. Indeed, four moderate Democrats—Senators Jim Webb (D-VA), Joe Manchin (D-WV), Ben Nelson (D-NE), and Joe Lieberman (I-CT)—voted with the Republicans. All but Lieberman are up for reelection in 2012. They read the handwriting on the wall and voted with the Republicans to support the tax cuts.

The Democratic majority cannot afford to lose four votes in the future because it holds the Senate by the tenuous margin of 53–47. With other endangered Democratic senators up for reelection in 2012, more defectors might join the four in abandoning Obama's program. They are likely to ask themselves, Why should I stick my neck out and vote with Obama and incur the wrath of my home state voters, when, even if I vote the way the Republicans want, Obama will veto the bill and it cannot be overridden?

So the House is likely just to push the Senate aside, taking advantage of its cowardly Democratic moderates (call them opportunists), and face the president one-on-one.

Will President Obama move to the center?

He can't. Obama has dragged our politics so far to the left that what he might now call the center is what used to be the left. When Obama took office, the federal, state, and local governments ate up 35% of our nation's economy (GDP). Now they consume 44%. We need to roll it all back to 35% so that our private sector can have room to breathe and grow.

On this fundamental question, there is no middle ground. If Obama moves to what he might define as the center and proposes to cut spending back to, say, 40%, it would be unacceptable. It would freeze in place and make permanent a massive expansion of government.

In the *New York Times* of December 1, 2010, Matt Bai's article "Debt-Busting Issue May Force Obama Off Fence" illustrates how the liberals will try to portray what used to be the left as the new center. How they will try to pretend Obama is moving toward compromise, when all he is really doing is protecting far-left positions and huge spending increases.[2]

Bai writes that "Mr. Obama has almost invariably sought to position himself halfway between traditionalism and reform." He goes on to "take the example of Mr. Obama's first initiative, the roughly $800 billion stimulus, which independent and conservative voters revile as a huge government handout, while liberals deride it as too small and too timid." For a second example, Bai cites "the health care law, which struck independents as liberal overreach and yet bitterly disappointed the left because it didn't include a government-run plan."[3]

Only in the *Times*/liberal fantasy world could an $800 billion spending bill that nearly tripled the federal deficit and a health care law that radically overhauled our entire system be called middle choices between the left and the right. Yet Obama will constantly be featuring such "compromises" in an attempt to sell the notion that he is moving to the center.

For example, he tried to dress up his surrender to the Republicans in agreeing to extend the Bush tax cuts as a "compromise." It was no compromise. The concession Obama made in extending the Bush tax cuts was a surrender and a rout! There is a big difference between moving to the center as an act of strategy and policy and fleeing to it because you don't have a choice.

We cannot be fooled!

If the Republicans manage their power well and seek important and specific confrontations with the administration, they can sweep the national elections again in 2012, replacing Obama and adding to their gains in Congress.

The key is to take Obama on, but be smart about how we do it. We need to engage the liberals from well-prepared positions, countering their socialist spending with proposals that enjoy the support of the American people. The GOP will not succeed if it avoids confrontation. Nor will it do well if it confronts the president without a careful eye on public opinion. But well-managed and staged battles, with good strategy and tactics, can stop the economic skid, while at the same time leading to Obama's defeat in 2012.

HOW TO REDUCE THE DEFICIT WITHOUT RAISING TAXES

Republicans have skated through the 2010 elections with vague promises to rein in spending, but largely have not had to spell out exactly how they plan to do it. Now they will have to walk the walk, having spent the election talking the talk.

Democrats always love to portray budgeting as a zero-sum game where you have to subtract over here in order to add over there. But the reality is totally different. The fact is that subtraction—tax cuts—usually leads to addition, i.e., increased federal revenues.

But any credible plan to reduce and eventually eliminate the deficit must rely on spending cuts as well as economic growth. This is true not just because we want to lower the deficit, but, more important, because we don't want to ratify the huge federal spending that Obama has enacted whether or not growth makes it possible to afford it. The growth of government under Obama is dangerous for the economy and will lead to a European-like economic strangulation. We must reel it in!

But we also need to reconsider one of the great fictions promulgated by liberals and Democrats: that cuts in government spending hurt the poor. It is true, of course, that when you spend less on social services, you are giving the poor less or reaching fewer of them. But if these cuts reduce the deficit, stimulate economic growth, and let the job market flourish, they will more than make up in employment opportunity and the chances for advancement what they take away in public services. Especially when one considers the heavy component of administrative cost in federal outlays, cutting spending and therefore reducing the deficit do not need to hurt poor people. And even cutting taxes on the rich helps the poor, since the rich account for one-third of all consumer spending in the country. That consumer spending means jobs for poor people!

As President John F. Kennedy said, "A rising tide lifts all boats."[4] And, as Ronald Reagan said, "The best social program is a job."[5]

Because of decades of reckless and wasteful government spending, it will be surprisingly easy to cut government down to size. Fortunately, the Americans for Tax Reform, a group led by Grover Norquist and committed to economic growth and no new taxes, has pioneered the work in this field.

Let's start by understanding the size of the federal deficit now that we have extended the Bush tax cuts permanently and stopped the AMT from eating us alive. (The AMT is the Alternative Minimum Tax, originally passed to make sure rich people pay some taxes despite their shelters and deductions. But, not indexed for inflation, it has reached more and more middle-income taxpayers. The Obama-Republican budget deal on extending the Bush tax cuts stopped the AMT's growth.)

THE PROJECTED FEDERAL DEFICIT

(in billions)

Year	Deficit
2010	$1,342
2011	$1,265
2012	$ 960
2013	$ 885
2014	$ 840
2015	$ 960
2016	$1,091
2017	$1,142
2018	$1,183
2019	$1,318
2020	$1,438

Source: Congressional Budget Office

We will need sharp cuts in spending and pro-growth tax policies to bring the deficit down.

HOW TO CUT FEDERAL SPENDING

The law requires that Congress pass budgets for the ensuing ten years. While this provision seems to enable long-term planning, it really results in theoretical fights over fanciful numbers in the out years that never really materialize.

When Clinton agreed with the Republicans on a plan to balance the budget in 1997, their goal was to eliminate the deficit by 2005. Instead, economic growth, largely kindled by tax cuts, brought the budget into balance by 1998. So much for forecasts!

Let's focus on the next three years, when we can reasonably anticipate what economic conditions are likely to be.

As you can see from the tables on the previous page, the deficits for these years are now predicted by the Congressional Budget Office to be:

2012	$960 billion
2013	$885 billion
2014	$840 billion

So how can we cut these deficits?

In fact, it won't be that hard. Democrats and liberals like to sell us a bill of goods telling us that to cut the deficit through spending reductions alone will require huge cuts in Medicare and Social Security. They speak of how hard the sacrifice would be for the average American and for the elderly in particular.

Nonsense. The budget deficit was not primarily caused by increases in Social Security or Medicare and it need not be solved by cuts in those programs. It was caused by increases in welfare, Medicaid, and domestic spending and can be solved by cutting welfare, Medicaid, and domestic spending. You don't need taxes. You don't need to cut Social Security. You don't need to cut Medicare! At least not in the short term.

First, let's understand what makes up the federal budget. It is divided into two broad categories: mandatory and discretionary.

- **Mandatory programs** includes interest on the federal debt or entitlement programs like Social Security, Medicare, Medicaid, and various forms of welfare like food stamps. Congress does not limit spending on these programs. The budgets it passes each year are really just predictions of how much they will cost, not limitations. In effect, Congress just signs a blank check and authorizes the administrators to pay out benefits to all who qualify.

- **Discretionary programs** are those for which funds are appropriated each year. Spending is limited to the amounts specified by Congress.

Budgeteers divide discretionary spending into two categories: defense and nondefense. The nondefense part includes outlays for things like education, transportation, homeland security, public safety, etc.

In FY2009, the budget broke down like this:

Total Budget:	$3,526 billion
* Mandatory	$2,289 billion
* Discretionary	$1,237 billion
* Defense & Intl.	$699 billion
* Nondefense	$538 billion

We propose the following steps to cut federal spending and the deficit:

HOW TO CUT SPENDING

1. Roll back discretionary, nondefense spending to 2008 levels and then freeze it there for three years (through 2014).
2. Roll back Medicaid to 2008 levels, adding a retroactive 3% annual increase. Then let it rise by only up to 3% each year in the future. Block grant the aid to the states and let them run the programs.
3. Reduce our troop levels in Iraq and Afghanistan to 60,000 combined by 2015.

Together, these simple steps will cut the deficit to manageable proportions by 2014.

No cuts will be required in Social Security or Medicare and no tax increases will be necessary . . . or tolerated!

Now let's go into the details:

The first thing to do is to roll back the huge increase in discretionary nondefense spending with which Obama has saddled our country. Drop it back down to pre-Obama levels.

If we did so, we would save $126 billion in FY2012. In FY2013, we would save an additional $118 billion. In FY2014, we'd save $117 billion.

SAVINGS FROM FREEZING NONDEFENSE DISCRETIONARY SPENDING AT '08 LEVELS

Fiscal Year Savings from Freeze

2012	$126 billion
2013	$118 billion
2014	$117 billion

But we need to go further.

We should transform Medicaid from an entitlement to a block grant to the states, setting an annual amount for each state keyed to the 2008 spending levels plus a factor of 3% for inflation.

States should get the flexibility to administer Medicaid funds as they wish, adjusting benefits and eligibility as needed to make the numbers work.

Unless we impose caps on Medicaid, it will double in nine years. More than any other, this is the entitlement we must rein in.

Such a cap would save $62 billion by 2014.

BLOCK GRANTING MEDICAID

(allowing 3% annual increase)

Year	Currently Budgeted	Proposed	Savings
2008	$201 billion (baseline)		
2012	$270	$226	$44
2013	$283	$233	$50
2014	$302	$240	$62

And we propose ratcheting back our troop levels in Iraq and Afghanistan to a total of 60,000 by 2015. If we did that, we would save $72 billion by 2014:

IMPACT OF CAPPING IRAQ/AFGHAN AT 60,000 TROOPS BY 2015

	Savings
2011	$1 billion
2012	$6
2013	$34
2014	$72

So . . . by 2014, if we . . .

a. Freeze nondefense discretionary spending at 2008 levels for three years
b. Block grant Medicaid and limit its increase to 3% a year
c. Cut troop levels in Iraq/Afghanistan to 60,000

. . . we would cut the deficit by $251 billion by 2014, bringing it down to $589 billion, or 3.4% of GDP.

Economists feel that a 3% deficit is desirable. They call deficits at that level "primary balance." It is the standard set by the European Union for its members—even though it is hardly ever met—and it is a good yardstick for us. A deficit of 3.4% would bring us back to the levels of the Reagan years. In his eight years as president, the deficit averaged 3.9% of our GDP.

BUDGET DEFICITS UNDER REAGAN

Year	% of GDP
1981	2.5%
1982	3.9%
1983	5.9%
1984	4.7%

1985	5.0%
1986	3.2%
1987	3.0%
1988	2.8%

Source: U.S. Government[6]

And this could be done without cutting the defense budget, Social Security, or Medicare and while extending the Bush tax cuts!

What programs would be cut? Here's a partial list. As you can see, nothing proposed here will bring down the republic!

- *Highways* Three-quarters of the money we spend on highways is for new roads. Only one-quarter is for maintenance and enhanced safety on existing roads. We could do without any new roads for the next three years.
  Three-year savings: $90 billion.[7]

- *Climate Research and Energy* We spend $2 billion a year on climate research and another $2 billion annually on "innovative technology" loan guarantees and renewable energy supply programs.[8] Eliminate them.
  Three-year savings: $12 billion.

- *Federal Aviation Administration* We could save $3.6 billion a year (about 20% of the FAA budget) by making passengers and airlines pay for improvements to local airports, rather than burden the taxpayers with the cost.
  Three-year savings: $10.8 billion.[9]

- *National Institutes of Health* Cut their grants by 10% and save $2.4 billion a year. This would eliminate about 5,000 grants a year. Let the bureaucrats do some prioritizing!
  Three-year savings: $7.2 billion.[10]

- *Federal Land* We should sell off a lot of the land Washington owns, but, until we do, we should make grazing fees equal the cost of operating the bureau, saving taxpayers $1.1 billion a year.
  Three-year savings: $3.3 billion.[11]

- *Congress* Roll back the cost of Congress to 2008 levels and save $500 million a year. They don't deserve a raise.
  Three-year savings: $1.5 billion.[12]

- *Forests and Fish* Cut spending for the Forest Service, Fish and Wildlife Service, and so forth, in half. Save $4.3 billion a year.
  Three-year savings: $12.9 billion.[13]

- *Army Corps of Engineers* 15% cut in Army Corps of Engineers civil projects would save $700 million a year.
  Three-year savings: $2.1 billion.[14]

- *Diplomacy* 20% cut in our diplomatic missions and foreign service staff. Save $2.5 billion a year.
  Three-year savings: $7.5 billion.[15]

- *Pork* The National Infrastructure Innovation and Finance Fund is an Obama pork creation. Eliminate that and save $4 billion a year.[16] Build America Bonds is another Obama brainchild that needs to be repealed. Up to now, all state and local bonds were guaranteed by their governments, which paid back the interest and principal out of local revenues. Obama is now picking up the tab to the tune of $11.5 billion a year. Eliminate the program entirely.
  Three-year savings: $46.5 billion.[17]

- *Agriculture* We now spend about $15 billion a year on agricultural subsidies. According to the Cato Institute, the largest 10% of America's farms get almost three-quarters of the money. We also spend about $4 billion annually on agricultural research. Cut this spending in half.
  Three-year savings: $28.5 billion.[18]

- *Pensions* Federal pensions are all indexed for cost of living adjustments based on the rate of wage inflation. Changing it to price inflation would save $3.5 billion.
  Three-year savings: $10.5 billion.[19]

- *Scholarships* Obama wants to make Pell Grants into entitlements. Right now they are discretionary. That means that anyone who qualifies can get one and Congress will have no control over how much it costs. Bad idea. What we don't need now is a new federal entitlement. We should keep it discretionary. We should cut the spending level Obama proposes by 9% in 2015, saving $3.7 billion a year.
  Three-year savings: $11.1 billion.[20]

- *State Aid* Grants to states for rehabilitative services and disability research are another Obama giveaway to help bail them out of their fiscal problems. Cut it out and save $3.3 billion a year.
  Three-year savings: $9.9 billion.[21]

- *Education Research* Cut it by $1.2 billion.
  Three-year savings: $3.6 billion.[22]

- *Corporation for Public Broadcasting* Eliminate this left-wing media subsidy. Save $500 million.
  Three-year savings: $1.5 billion.[23]

- *National Endowments for Arts and Humanities.* Eliminate them. Let the private sector and charities pick up the slack. If we kill Obama's proposal to cut back deductions for charitable contributions, it will help. Save $500 million a year.
  Three-year savings: $1.5 billion.[24]

- *Department of Education* Cut out Obama's proposed increases and save $7 billion a year.
  Three-year savings: $21 billion.[25]

- *Environmental Protection Agency* A 10% cut would save $1 billion annually.
  Three-year savings: $3 billion.[26]

- *Special Aid to District of Columbia* Why not eliminate it and just give them the aid we give to all the states? Save $700 million a year.
  Three-year savings: $2.1 billion.[27]

- *Corporation for National and Community Service* A Clinton-era campaign promise we can't afford. Eliminating it would save $2.3 billion annually.
  Three-year savings: $6.9 billion.[28]

- *Housing Assistance* Obama plans to spend $47 billion on housing aid, the bulk of it—$41 billion—on Section 8 rent subsidies. We should make no new Section 8 commitments, saving $5 billion annually.
  Three-year savings: $15 billion.[29]

- *Federal Pay* Obama finally got the voters' hint and announced, in December 2010—two years too late—that he would freeze federal salaries. We have got to adjust federal pay to bring it into line with the private sector. The American Enterprise Institute and the Heritage Foundation have estimated that federal employees earn $14,000 a year more in pay and benefits than their private sector counterparts—a disparity of 30–40%.

  The new government in the United Kingdom, headed by Conservative David Cameron, has frozen the salaries of the top 72% of government employees. We should follow that example until private sector incomes catch up.

  Ryan Ellis, tax policy director for the Americans for Tax Reform, writes that "according to the Bureau of Economic Analysis, federal pay and benefits per employee is about $120,000 per year. There are 2.4 million civilian federal employees, so that comes out to $288 billion this year." Ellis estimates that their pay and benefits grow by 7% a year. A freeze would save about $20 billion annually.
  Three-year savings: $60 billion.[30]

Americans for Tax Reform's Grover Norquist identifies several other areas where we can cut back federal spending without inflicting great harm on our society. They include:

- *Repeal the Davis-Bacon Act* This law requires that federal construction contractors pay the "prevailing wage" to their workers. As Americans for Tax Reform notes, "there is a high frequency of errors" in computing the wage rates, which drives them up by 22%, pushing up federal construction costs by $9 billion a year. We should repeal Davis-Bacon.[31]

- *Sell off government assets* The feds own 650 million acres of land, about one-third of the area of the United States! The Bureau of Land Management says that 3.3 million acres are suitable for sale to the private sector. But we haven't sold them. The Heritage Foundation estimates that we spend $25 billion a year maintaining unused or vacant federal properties. Sell them off![32]

But none of these cuts will mean much if the members of the Congress just put the money back in the budget through earmarks.

Here's what earmarks are: when a federal agency gets its budget from Congress, it can spend it pretty much as it wants. But members of Congress often pass special interest amendments to the budget directing that certain sums be spent on certain projects. These projects eat up a large portion of these agencies' budgets.

If we are going to freeze discretionary nondefense spending at 2008 levels, we at least have to give the agencies flexibility in how to spend the money. After all, earmarks are, by definition, projects that the agencies themselves felt weren't worth funding.

For example, the National Institutes of Health (NIH) get about $25 billion a year, partially to fund cancer research around the nation. We want those funds to go where they will do the most good—to those programs that offer a real insight into licking this horrible disease. The administrator of the Institutes scrutinizes all the research programs and decides which merit funding.

But then Senator Big Bucks, up for reelection this cycle, comes in and demands that his program at Small Town U get research money, even though it is not doing anything particularly useful to cure the disease. The NIH administrator will say no. Then Senator Big Bucks appeals to Congress and gets an earmark for Small Town U in the budget, and the money the NIH gets is diverted to this useless program.

Useless? For curing cancer maybe, but not for the senator's reelection campaign. Because Small Town U hired the ABC lobbying firm to get it an earmark. And the lobbyists at ABC are so grateful to Senator Big Bucks for getting the earmark funded that they contribute tens or hundreds of thousands to his campaign. See our chapter on The Democrats We Must Defeat—Part IV of this book—to find out who gets what in the earmarks-for-donations racket.

House and Senate Republicans voted to oppose earmarks in the 2012 budget. We need to put a ban on earmarks into the budget and fight for it. We need to kill all the Democratic earmarks, from the Senate, to maintain fiscal discipline.

The cuts we have suggested are, of course, just rough examples of what can be done. None of these reductions is particularly onerous and none would cause enormous amounts of pain. They can all be done with little risk of political blowback.

None of these cuts will endanger our welfare or safety. We can roll back discretionary spending to 2008 levels without damaging our country.

While we are at it, let's cut unnecessary defense spending as well.

HOLD DOWN DEFENSE SPENDING

Under Obama—the liberal—defense spending has actually risen more rapidly than it did under Bush—the conservative.

As Mattie Corrao, writing in the *Daily Caller*, notes, "President Bush, who created a new federal department charged with domestic security, waged two new offenses in the Middle East and initiated the War on Terror, kept [defense] spending an entire percentage point lower than the current average."[33]

Even though Obama is fighting a war—and Bush was too—this kind of increase is unjustified. We need a strong defense, but we need a robust economy, too. We cannot allow defense spending to weaken our basic economic power and drive us into unsustainable deficits.

As we withdraw from Iraq and wind down our surge in Afghanistan, we must accept limits on our defense spending.

Congress must do its part too to hold down defense increases. Earmarks have long saddled the defense budget with programs, armaments, airplanes, and bases that the Pentagon neither wants nor needs, but that congressmen and senators insist upon to bolster their local economies— and, as noted, their campaign kitties. The defense budget is not an economic stimulant. It is for the safety of our country in an unsafe world. A curb on earmarks will do a lot to hold down defense increases.

Paul Kennedy warns in his *Rise and Fall of the Great Powers* of imperial overreach, the tendency of great military powers to spend beyond their means and bankrupt themselves in the process. We need look no further than the old Soviet Union to find the consequences of letting defense spending rise to unsupportable levels.

Mindful of this excessive spending, Defense Secretary Robert Gates has identified $30 billion of spending cuts he says can be achieved by greater efficiency. But he plans on "redirecting those [savings] to other areas within the DOD [Department of Defense]. The federal government would save around $25 billion if most of those savings were simply applied to deficit reduction instead,"[34] according to the Center for American Progress (admittedly, a liberal group).

And then there are savings we can achieve by curtailing and canceling weapons we just don't need.

WEAPONS WE DON'T NEED

- V-22 Osprey. Save $2 billion.

- DDG-51 Arleigh Burke class destroyers. Buy one instead of two and save $1.9 billion.

- CBN-80 aircraft carrier. Buy two instead of three and save $1.5 billion.

- Littoral combat ships. Buy two per year instead of four. Save $1.3 billion.

- Marine Corps' expeditionary fighting vehicle. Defense Secretary Gates wants to cancel this program and save $600 million.

- F-35 Joint Strike Fighter. Cut the procurement in half—to 35 for the Air Force and 10 for the Navy—saving $4.8 billion.

- Virginia class submarines. Maintain the current policy of buying one a year rather than increasing it to two as now planned. Save $2.8 billion.

Total Savings: $14.9 billion[35]

Defense Department Civilian personnel A 10% cut in Defense Department civilian personnel would save $8 billion a year.[36]

Combined, these defense cuts would reduce the Pentagon budget by close to $50 billion.

BLOCK GRANT MEDICAID

It is not only discretionary spending that is driving federal deficits ever higher, it is also entitlements. We don't want to cut Social Security or Medicare. They didn't cause this deficit and cutting them is not the way to solve it. But we do need to cut the growth of the other entitlement programs like Medicaid. As noted, during Obama's tenure, welfare programs have increased by 54%.[37]

We should limit spending on these entitlements (other than unemployment benefits, Social Security, and Medicare) to an annual increase of about 3%. Such a limit would not cut any program, but would simply limit its future growth. States would get the money in block grants from Washington and could allocate the funds as they see fit.

Some states might want to cut back on who is eligible for Medicaid. Others might want to limit the services covered, perhaps restricting dental or psychiatric care or reducing the scope of benefits.

States may also want—and Washington should permit them—to experiment with changes in how Medicaid works.

The best option would be a voluntary program in which people could either keep their current coverage or opt for a Health Savings Account (HSA).

An HSA would pay people a flat amount every year for their health care (typically about $2,500 per person). They would pay for their premiums and medical costs out of that check and could keep whatever they did not spend at the end of the year, tax free. If their medical expenses exceeded the HSA payment, the government would pick up a rising percentage of the extra cost. Once it passed a certain threshold, say $6,000 in a year, the gov-·ernment would pay the entire tab. The HSA approach gives the health care consumer himself an incentive to hold down spending and help save money.

An HSA plan could let the states absorb the reductions in the rate of increase of Medicaid without reducing the quality of care.

Indiana governor—and possible presidential candidate—Mitch Daniels implemented just such a policy for state workers. Seventy percent of them chose to sign up. The state gives them $2,750 for health care each year, but 94% of them don't use it all and keep what they do not use. So far, the unused amount comes to about $2,000 per employee. The program has saved the state $20 million or 11% of its usual employee health care budget.[38]

Governor Daniels notes, "In 2009 . . . state workers with the HSA visited emergency rooms and physicians 67% less frequently than co-workers with traditional health care. They were much more likely to use generic drugs than those enrolled in the conventional plan, resulting in an average lower cost per prescription of $18. They were admitted to hospitals less than half as frequently as their colleagues."[39]

Obama's health care program provides for a massive expansion of Medicaid over the next decade. His bill requires that states expand their programs to cover people with incomes of up to one-third above the poverty level (133% of poverty). In most parts of the country, this mandate requires free health care for all earning up to about $30,000 a year.

Some states have already reached or exceeded that level. New York, for example, covers up to 150% of the poverty level for adults and Massachusetts tops out at 133%. California covers up to only 106%, but other states are very low. Florida covers up to 53% and Arkansas, Mississippi, and Texas are even lower. All these states will be required to raise their Medicaid spending to at least the 133% mandated in Obama's law.[40]

For the first year (the law takes effect in 2014), the Feds will pick up all of the cost. For subsequent years, the states will have to pay 5%.

The impact of this Medicaid expansion on the federal budget will be crushing. Right now, the Feds pay only between half and two-thirds of a state's Medicaid bill, depending on how poor the state is. But, under Obama's bill, the federal share of the cost of the program expansion will zoom to 95%.

Federal Medicaid spending has already risen from $118 billion in 2000 to $251 billion in 2009. Since Obama took office, it has gone up by $50 billion. Under Obama's program, it will cost $3.9 trillion between 2011 and 2020. We must repeal the section of ObamaCare that mandates new Medicaid coverage. Together, these ideas will bring the budget deficit down dramatically, likely to less than 3% of our GDP by 2014.

We keep saying not to cut Medicare and Social Security. But something must be done, in the longer term, to keep these two entitlements secure by reining in the rate of increase in their spending. Here's how we might do that:

WARNING: HANDS OFF SOCIAL SECURITY AND MEDICARE!!!

Conventional wisdom says that we can never cut the deficit without reining in Social Security and Medicare. But Clinton did just that and we can do it again now. Cuts in discretionary spending, curbs on other entitlements, block grants to the states, and the other measures recommended by Americans for Tax Reform can get us a large part of the way there.

Eventually, we will need to make Social Security viable and keep Medicare costs in line, as much to balance the budget as to protect both systems.

But we don't have to do it in 2011 and 2012!

We can't afford it politically and we don't need to do it financially. Social Security and Medicare have risen by 14% and 16% respectively on Obama's watch. Domestic spending is up by 41% and welfare is up by 54%. That's where the cuts should fall.

Having gotten elected over fighting the $500 billion Democratic cut in Medicare, Republicans would get their heads handed to them if they went with cuts of their own in the program.

And let's not have a reprise of 2005 when Bush squandered his political capital after his reelection victory by proposing the voluntary diversion of a portion of each person's Social Security tax payment into alternate investment vehicles. Democrats pounced on the idea, saying that it endangered

Social Security by diverting its revenues. They were wrong about that. But the proposal didn't live long enough to prove it.

Republicans would be giving away the 2012 election—reelecting Obama—if they chose to slay either of these sacred cows before the next election. And they don't need to in order to reduce the deficit significantly.

When Dick briefed President Clinton on the poll he conducted right after the Republican victory in 1994, he asked him if he wanted to hear the four-hour briefing or the one-word summary. The one-word version was: Medicare. When the Republicans cut the rate of growth in the Medicare program, they destroyed their chances of winning the budget fight and of recapturing the White House in 1996. Vice President Gore and others expanded the message to include Medicare, Medicaid, education, and the environment. But the core message was: don't cut Medicare.

Three political movements have met their death over proposing cuts in Medicare:

- Clinton lost control of Congress in 1994 largely because of Hillary's plan for government-run health care.

- Gingrich's revolution ground to a halt and Clinton was reelected over the Speaker's plans to cut Medicare.

- Obama's revolution was stopped dead in its tracks in the elections of 2010 mainly because of his health care changes and their Medicare cuts.

The Republican resurgence of 2010 must not be the next casualty!

Why did the Republicans propose to rein in Medicare in 1995–96? It wasn't to balance the budget. The budget got balanced without making any cuts in either program, just as Clinton said it would. (It actually came into balance more because the economy improved and because we cut capital gains taxes than because of any budget cuts.)

The Republicans proposed those Medicare cuts primarily because they wanted to shrink the size of government. Good idea. But let's focus now on what we need to do to bring the deficit down without new taxes. Then, when we win the White House, let's go on to deal with entitlements.

But what *is* the real answer? How do we save Social Security and Medicare?

According to Wisconsin's Congressman Paul Ryan—probably the single most brilliant member of the House (not to damn him with faint praise)—it won't be that hard. After crunching the numbers with the best actuaries available, Ryan, in his famous "Roadmap" for America, concludes that two steps would suffice to assure the long-term solvency of the system.

HOW TO SAVE SOCIAL SECURITY

1. *Raise the retirement age* by one month every two years. By 2100, it would be 70 years of age. This is hardly an onerous proposal. When Social Security was started, in 1937, life expectancy was 65 for women and 60 for men. A lot of folks would never make it to 65. Now, it's 76 for men and 81 for women. Most of us will last well past 65. Why should we pay for ever longer retirements as people get healthier and stay younger longer? Raising the retirement age as Ryan proposes would keep pace with increased life expectancy, assuring the same length of retirement, on average, that we guarantee today.

2. *Adjust cost-of-living increases.* There are two ways to compute the annual cost-of-living adjustment for Social Security. You can base the measurement on either price inflation or wage inflation. (Price inflation is usually about 1% more.) Now the Social Security system uses price inflation. Ryan proposes continuing that for anyone on Social Security who makes $75,000 a year or less, but urges using wage inflation for those making more. And he would phase in this change so it would not affect anyone now on Social Security or now over the age of 55. It makes sense. Why should we use wage inflation to calculate a cost-of-living raise for retired people? They don't get wages. They pay prices. Use the rise in prices as a yardstick for raising their pensions.

These two minor changes are enough to guarantee the solvency of the Social Security system for the next 100 years. So don't sweat it.

Ryan's other proposal, which also makes sense, is a variant of the one Bush made that was shot down in 2005. He says that we should permit people now under 55 to pay part of their Social Security taxes into a separate fund, which they could invest in funds approved by the government that might bring a higher return. Their downside would be protected in that they would get back their tax payments in pensions even if those went up in smoke in the stock market.

His idea is a good one. But if we propose any of these changes now, before the 2012 election, the Democrats will accuse us of cutting or privatizing Social Security. We cannot give them that club to beat our candidates over the head with!

Saving Medicare may be a bit harder. The key is to replace the current system with a health savings account approach, as Governor Daniels has done for public employees in Indiana. Just give the elderly a flat amount at the start of the year and let them keep whatever they don't spend. As noted above, if their medical costs exceeded that flat amount, the government would pay a progressively larger share. But this also gives the elderly a reason to cut back on their use of medical facilities.

No healthy man ever visited more doctors than my father did before his death, in 2010, at ninety-nine years, nine months, and ten days. He would visit the dentist, the eye doctor, his GI doctor, his GP, his hearing doctor, his heart specialist regularly, and other doctors occasionally. It was, as he aged, his principal reason to leave his home. And why not? Medicare picked up the tab. But give him a flat payment to cover his costs so that he had to weigh whether or not to spend the money on each visit, and his cost of Medicare would have dropped substantially.

HOW TO DEFEAT OBAMA'S TAX-AND-SPEND BUDGETS

Obama will open the budget battle by saying he is moving to the center. He has convened a National Commission on Fiscal Responsibility and Reform, co-chaired by the superannuated former Wyoming Republican senator Alan Simpson and Clinton's former chief of staff Erskine Bowles. Bowles is an ardent advocate of deficit reduction, but never shies away from using tax increases to try to do it.

The Bowles-Simpson Commission recommended a 2:1 ratio between spending cuts and tax increases, just as previous commissions have done. But history is clear. As noted, the tax increases take effect on schedule, but the cuts somehow never materialize. Even if the reductions in discretionary spending are voted by Congress, the tax hikes slow the economy and, as noted, this drives up entitlement spending, which eats up the planned reduction in discretionary outlays.

Any "compromise" that includes spending cuts and tax increases is really just a tax increase. Period.

To avert the spiral of tax hikes—slowed economic growth—and higher entitlement spending, we need to stop Obama from raising taxes. They would put us on a downward path to economic stagnation. We must say no.

Hell no!

But we need to be clear on our objectives. As noted earlier, we propose a nine-part program for which we must fight throughout the year. Whenever Obama needs a specific piece of legislation—a new budget, spending appropriations bills, or an increase in the debt limit, Republicans must be there with their agenda demanding concessions as we tick off the nine items:

1. Stopping tax increases
2. Rolling back government spending
3. Bringing the deficit down to 3% of the economy
4. Defunding ObamaCare
5. Blocking the EPA from imposing a carbon tax
6. Stopping the NLRB from killing the secret ballot
7. Freeing small banks to make loans again
8. Blocking the FCC from undermining free speech
9. Eliminating earmarks from the budget

The FY2011–12 budget debate will really begin in the spring of 2011 when the federal government's huge deficits catch up with it and it needs to raise its statutory debt ceiling. The debt ceiling is a fiction voted by Congress and regularly and routinely raised whenever the debt rises up that high. Congress always just rubber-stamps the debt increase the president wants.

Not this year!

The newly elected Republican senator from Illinois Mark Kirk has proposed that the GOP resist raising the debt limit unless we wring specific spending reductions and other concessions from Obama. And then we need to keep coming back for more. Senator Kirk proposes that we raise the debt limit for only three months at a time. When the federal government needs more money they will have to come back to Congress asking for an increase in the debt limit. And each time they do we need to be there with our list of demands in hand asking for additional concessions.

Then the debate over the actual budget for FY2012 will begin in the spring and summer of 2011. Republicans, who will control the House of Representatives, will have the constitutional responsibility to initiate spending bills. They will have the primary task of making the spending cuts necessary to cut the deficit. Their work will position the Republican Party for the battle ahead.

They must provide a credible deficit reduction and a path to further cuts without opening the can of worms of Social Security and Medicare.

The Democrats will howl about the severity of the spending cuts and will portray Republicans as heartless.

In 1995–96, these pleas fell on deaf ears and did not move the American people to oppose the cuts until two developments changed the equation: (a) Clinton took dead aim at the Medicare cuts; and (b) Clinton proposed a path to a balanced budget that did not cut Medicare or raise taxes.

Obama won't have the option of attacking Republicans for proposing Medicare cuts if the Republicans don't propose any, and he sure won't articulate a path to a balanced budget that doesn't involve tax increases.

But if Republicans stay away from Social Security and Medicare, these attacks won't diminish popular support for their program. A Rasmussen Reports Poll taken in November 2010 showed that by 52–25%, voters believe that "decreases in government spending will help the economy." On the other hand, by 18–58%, they feel that tax increases "will hurt the economy."[41]

With the support of the American people, the Republicans will carry the day.

Some worry that the Republicans need to propose a way to bring the budget into actual balance. A zero deficit is attractive, but, ultimately, the only way to achieve it is to stimulate economic growth as we did in the 1990s. If we can cut the deficit appreciably, bringing it into "primary balance" (i.e., 3% of GDP) without new taxes, the Republican Party will have taken the first step. Then, after the election of 2012, we need to take the next step by adopting tax cuts and reforms in Social Security and Medicare. But let's get step one done this year!

It won't be easy.

Obama will doubtless veto any increase in the debt ceiling that contains budget cuts and he will also veto any Republican budget that cuts his big-government programs. The GOP will lack the votes to override. A game of chicken will begin. The government will have no ability to borrow money and no budget. The Republicans will agree to an interim budget or debt limit increase that includes their spending cuts, as they did in 1995, but Obama will veto it, as Clinton did. The government may shut down, as happened in the 1990s. Or the Congress may pass temporary resolutions to keep it open without giving in on its budget proposal.

Armageddon will ensue—a public war between the legislative and the executive. At stake will be the central issue of whether to cut spending or raise taxes.

The Republicans need to hold firm and fast to their guns and not retreat a step. They need to use all the tools of modern communication to convince people that they are right and that Obama is wrong.

If the deadlock persists until well into 2012, so be it. If the question of spending cuts versus tax increases becomes the central issue in the presidential race, so much the better. Republicans can fight on that issue and win!

When Dick was orchestrating Clinton's side of the government shutdown in 1995–96, he got the Democratic National Committee to purchase about $1.5 million in ads every week to back up the president's position. The Republicans did not follow suit (or apparently even realize that Clinton was advertising). In 2011–12, Republicans and their allies, such as Americans for Prosperity, Karl Rove's American Crossroads, League of American Voters, Superpac USA, and 60 Plus, need to plaster the airwaves with their message.

But the real battle will not be on television. It will be in the streets. Here, the Tea Party movement will prove our salvation.

These dedicated activists—some old, some young—thronged to rallies across America to protest Obama's health care changes and to battle for the GOP victories of 2010. Now they must rise up again and dominate the landscape of American politics.

In Greece, London, and Paris, demonstrators ask that government do more for them. In the United States, the Tea Party's central demand is that it do less.

Many have criticized the Tea Party for challenging Republican establishment candidates in the primaries of 2010. In Nevada, Alaska, South Carolina, New York, Kentucky, Delaware, Utah, and other states, Tea Party leaders vanquished the regular Republican candidates in primaries. Unfortunately, in three cases—the Senate races in Delaware, Colorado, and Nevada—they snatched defeat from the jaws of victory. The Tea Party–backed Senate candidates went down to defeat in November where the establishment candidates would likely have won. (Even had they all won, Republicans would still have fallen short of a Senate majority.)

But the tradeoff will have been worthwhile if the primary defeats strike fear into the hearts of Republican politicians from coast to coast and induce them to hold the line against taxes and for cuts in spending.

If Mike Castle, an eighteen-year Republican congressman at large from Delaware, could lose a Republican primary after serving as a popular lieutenant governor and governor, any Republican is vulnerable anywhere. The shock waves from Christine O'Donnell's upset primary victory are still reverberating in the souls of GOP pols. She was, in a way, to Republicans the same kind of warning signal that the victory of GOP candidate Scott Brown in Massachusetts was for the Senate Democrats in early 2010. Democrats ran right through the warning and voted for ObamaCare anyway. But they paid the price in November 2010. Republicans must heed the warning and stand strong for spending cuts and no tax hikes.

It is up to the Tea Party to police the ranks of Republicans to hold them in line behind a no-tax position. Those who might go squishy need to see a hail of protests in their home states and face the prospect of primary fights down the road if they stray. Those whom the Tea Party elected, the Tea Party can defeat, and the GOP establishment knows it full well.

The cacophony in the streets must be deafening to sustain Republicans in their no-tax position.

The pressures on the other side will be enormous. Investors will condemn the Republican position as irresponsible. The International Monetary Fund (IMF) will warn of dire consequences if tax increases do not pass or the debt limit is not raised. The Federal Reserve Board will go all-out to sell the tax hikes and debt limit hike and to convince Americans that the GOP is demagoguing the issue. China and Japan will weigh in and raise doubts about buying more American bonds. The whole world will join in, demanding higher taxes on the American people.

Except, the American people will hold firm. They will stand up to the pressure from the establishment media because they know full well that our system of free enterprise is more important to them than it is to the established elites, particularly those that come from communist nations like China or the socialist countries in Europe or government-dominated economies like Japan's. They will stand up for American independence and against tax increases and will win the day.

And, just as the elections of 1996 were structured by Clinton's victory in the government shutdown of 1995, so the results of the 2012 election will be dominated by the outcome of the budget fights of 2011–12.

Americans will hold fast to no new taxes because they will realize that their country is on the line.

THREATS TO REPUBLICAN UNITY—KEEP AN EYE ON 'EM

But there are other issues that will be wrapped into the great budget and debt limit debates, particularly the need to defund the ObamaCare program. The Republican budget must zero-fund the key provisions of this law, and Obama will undoubtedly stand stubbornly against defunding. As the overall debate swirls about taxes versus spending, a debate within the debate will heat up about the future of ObamaCare.

DEFUNDING OBAMACARE

The threat of new taxes and the looming federal budget deficit are raising our fears of a continued economic recession. But entire sectors of our economy are being paralyzed by the looming threat of federal regulation. No industry is more affected than the health care sector, a full 16% of our economy. Who can expand? Who can hire new people? Who can grow with federal regulations just around the corner?

Arrogantly, the Democratic Congress passed Obama's health care legislation, even as polls showed that the vast majority of Americans opposed it.

Never has such a major piece of legislation been passed by a simple party-line vote without any crossovers to help it pass. On Election Day 2010, Americans loudly registered their opposition to the health care law changes. As the *New York Post* wrote: "Democrats who supported the health care bill lost in droves. Eight Democrats in the House . . . switched from opposing the bill on early votes to supporting it for final passage. Six sought reelection; five . . . lost. Arizona and Oklahoma passed ballot measures opposing the law's individual mandate [to buy insurance] . . . Missouri voters had already done so earlier this year . . . A Rasmussen telephone poll found 59% of voters in favor of repeal." [42]

Now, in the wake of the Republican victory in the House, the question is: how do patriots mitigate the damage to our medical system?

Obviously, repeal is impossible. Even if the Republicans were able to muster enough votes in the Senate to pass a repeal bill, Obama would veto the bill and we would lack the votes to override it.

The best option is to defund the bill; to strip it of its enforcement provisions and make it impotent. Then, if Republicans succeed it dethroning Obama in 2012, they can pass a repeal bill and be rid of the nightmare entirely.

ObamaCare would bring huge changes to our health care system: [43]

- By enrolling tens of millions of people in private health insurance plans, whether they like it or not.

- By forcing millions of families to pay absurdly high percentages of their income for health insurance before any federal subsidy kicks in.

- By vastly expanding Medicaid, covering 16 million new people.

- By establishing standards for private insurance, requiring what must be covered and enforcing compliance.

- To promote health care rationing (proponents call it efficiency), it will mandate cost comparative metrics and limit the options a doctor has to provide care.

- By creating a new commission to cut Medicare by $500 billion.

- Through field experiments and demonstration programs on what it calls controlling spending, but that we know is rationing of health care.

Meanwhile, the bill does not appropriate enough money to do any of these things. It only authorizes the spending. Federal bureaucrats use authorization bills to wrap up fish! It is the appropriations that count! And these require approval of the newly elected Republican House of Representatives.

According to the *New England Journal of Medicine*, the legislation contains 64 specific authorizations to spend up to $105.6 billion and 51 general authorizations to spend "such sums as are necessary"[44] between 2010 and 2019.

The Congressional Budget Office (CBO) estimates that there is "at least $50 billion in specified and estimated authorizations of discretionary spending that might be involved in implementing [ObamaCare] legislation."[45]

The only actual appropriation in the bill was for $1 billion to the Department of Health and Human Services (HHS) to implement the bill, only between one-fifth and one-tenth of the amount the Congressional Budget Office says will be needed.[46]

And it doesn't appropriate a dime for the Internal Revenue Service (IRS) to make sure everybody signs up for health insurance. It authorizes grants to the states to help create the "health insurance exchanges" from which people will buy policies, but doesn't actually appropriate anything. It also fails to appropriate, or even authorize, funding for the administrative costs states will incur in expanding their Medicaid programs.

As the *New England Journal of Medicine* noted, "without large additional appropriations, implementation [of ObamaCare] will be crippled."[47]

And that is precisely our intention! *The New England Journal* spells out how defunding might work:

> If [ObamaCare] opponents gain a majority in either house of Congress, they could not only withhold needed appropriations but also bar the use of whatever funds are appropriated for . . . implementation, including the implementation of the provisions requiring individual people to buy insurance or businesses to offer it. They could bar the use of staff time for designing rules for implementation or for paying subsidies to support the purchase of insurance. They could even bar HHS from writing or issuing regulations or engaging in any other federal activity related to the creation of health insurance exchanges.[48]

The *New York Times* notes that "the number and variety of restrictions Congress can impose in spending bills is almost unlimited." The newspaper cites the example of a rider attached to an energy bill in 2009, which provided that "no funds appropriated in this act may be used for the transportation of students or teachers in order to overcome racial imbalance in any school,"[49] hardly a germane amendment, but binding anyway. "House Republicans could easily pass similar provisos stating that no federal money could be used to carry out specific sections of the new health care law," the *Times* noted.[50]

And that is just what the House Republican leadership must do. "They'll get not one dime from us," incoming Republican House Speaker John A. Boehner said recently. "Not a dime. There is no fixing this [program]."[51]

The incoming House Majority Leader Eric Cantor (R-VA) underscores the Republican plans: "If all of ObamaCare cannot be immediately repealed, then it is my intention to begin repealing it piece by piece, blocking funding for its implementation and blocking the issuance of the regulations necessary to implement it."[52]

As attractive as the Boehner-Cantor position is to those of us who oppose this legislation, it may be wiser to concentrate on defunding key provisions that are highly unpopular. Such a strategy will force Obama to fight on unfriendly turf.

Here's how divided government works: if a president proposes a program to Congress, his opponents there usually concentrate on the aspects of the proposal they—and the public—dislike the most. That way, the whole debate focuses on that one part of the overall proposal.

For example, in 1994, President Clinton proposed an omnibus anti-crime package to the Republican Congress. It had three major provisions:

- One, which was very popular, stiffened penalties for crimes, authorized funding for more prisons, limited plea bargaining, and established a federal death penalty. Both Republicans and Democrats supported it and it passed without controversy. It was hardly ever mentioned in the national debate (so the voters forgot it was ever passed).

- A second provision instituted strict gun controls on assault weapons and required a waiting period and background checks for handgun purchases. Republicans hated this provision, but the public, as a whole, supported it. Republicans voted against it, but—because they knew the public wasn't on their side—wisely did not make it their key objection to the overall bill.

- The third part, which drew all the public debate, set up public works projects to improve life in the inner city. It famously authorized "midnight basketball" courts on which young people could expend their energies. The public, rightly, saw it as a boondoggle and the Republicans made the entire debate about this one provision.

The bill barely passed and so drained the president's popularity that it contributed to his loss of Congress a few months later.

The point is that when you make a proposal in Washington, the opposition decides what to focus on and that becomes the major issue. Your bill or your plan is only as strong as its weakest link.

The weakest links in the health care debate are:

- Obama's expansion of the IRS as an enforcement vehicle to make sure everybody has an insurance plan that the government finds acceptable and that employers cover all their workers

- His $500 billion cut in Medicare spending and the health care rationing it will trigger

- His expansion of Medicaid to cover 16 million new people (including those earning up to $30,000 a year)

- The state insurance exchanges, which the law requires, the cornerstone of the entire program

Let's concentrate our defunding efforts on these four fronts.

DEFUNDING THE IRS

The requirement that individuals buy health insurance (the individual mandate) and that businesses either provide coverage or pay a fine for failing to do so (the employer mandate) is the key to the whole bill. Destroy this and you cripple the entire program. And the bill happens to assign to the most hated and feared agency in the government—the IRS—the happy duty of enforcing these provisions. (After Congressional reforms in the 1990s, the IRS has done a lot to clean up its act and to be more professional and fair, but the public still regards it with a large load of apprehension.)

Obama proposes to vastly expand the IRS to enforce his legislation. The IRS says it will need to hire as many as 13,500 additional agents to administer and enforce the individual mandate.[53] Congressman Dave Kamp (R-MI), the ranking Republican member of the House Ways and Means Committee, puts the number even higher, saying that the "IRS could have to hire 16,000 agents, auditors, and other workers" to enforce these provisions.[54] This expansion would add 15% to the current IRS staff of 106,000 employees.[55]

The Ways and Means Committee estimates that the IRS will have to spend about $10 billion enforcing the individual mandate provision of the ObamaCare bill.[56]

Republicans should take aim at defunding the IRS expansion. If they do this, they will have an enormously popular position from which to fight.

The ObamaCare legislation authorizes the IRS to fine individual taxpayers 2.5% of their total incomes if they don't have insurance. The minimum fine is to be $695 and the maximum will be $2,085 for anyone caught without having "minimum essential coverage."[57] This enforcement provision is the Achilles' heel of the law. The fine is heavy enough to be a real threat to the average taxpayer.

After all, an American with a net taxable income after deductions and credits of $50,000 a year has to pay about $9,000 in federal taxes. To add an additional $1,250 onto it (2.5% of his income) for failing to have health insurance will be a steep penalty, which comes to a tax increase of more than 14%.[58]

But the alternative will be even more expensive. ObamaCare requires a family making $50,000 a year to pay about 7% of its income for health insurance—about $3,500—before any subsidy kicks in. So they will be between a rock and a hard place: pay a $1,250 fine and get no health coverage or pay $3,500 and get covered. Either way, that's a hefty chunk gone from family budgets already stretched pretty thin.

A family making $80,000 would have to pay a fine of $2,000 or buy a health insurance policy that costs 9.5% of its income, or $7,600.

REQUIRED PREMIUM PAYMENTS UNDER OBAMACARE BEFORE SUBSIDY KICKS IN

Income	What You Must Pay
Up to $29,000	$ 580
$29,000–$33,000	$ 870–$1,320
$33,000–$44,000	$1,320–$2,772
$44,000–$55,000	$2,773–$4,427
$55,000–$88,000	$4,427–$8,360

Source: Kaiser Foundation[59]

Neither choice will be popular with the average family. By defunding the enforcement provision, Republicans will be echoing the resentment of most American families at having to bear such a burden in the midst of a recession. While the individual mandate will not kick in until the start of 2014 (so as to move it conveniently after Obama stands for reelection), the IRS will have to start gearing up to enforce it now.

ObamaCare also would force employers whose businesses have fifty or more workers and do not offer insurance coverage to pay a fine of $2,000 per employee. This provision will also be enforced by the IRS.

The Republican House should defund the IRS enforcement of both provisions, not only by cutting the funding, but also by passing explicit language in the legislation itself banning the use of any appropriated funds for enforcement of the ObamaCare law. Any federal employee who violates the law should be subject to specific criminal penalties.

Without such a provision, the IRS will be free to shift resources from other parts of the agency to cover the costs of the enforcement of the individual mandate to buy insurance.

Republicans will doubtless pass the defunding legislation soon after they take power in the House of Representatives. Then it will either die in the Senate or pass. (Much legislation like this will attract the votes of so-called moderate Senate Democrats anxious to cover themselves to avoid defeat in 2012.) But even if it passes the Senate, Obama will, of course, veto it.

So the Republicans should fold the defunding of ObamaCare into any legislation raising the debt limit and, failing that, into their 2012 budget appropriations. Then the battle over funding ObamaCare will become a central part of the test of wills between the parties that will dominate the 2011–12 period and play itself out before a national audience. The addition of the IRS enforcement ban to the national debate can only help the Republicans win the battle.

In December 2010, the United States District Court for Virginia declared the individual mandate provision of the ObamaCare law unconstitutional. As we predicted in our previous book, *2010: Take Back America—A Battle Plan*, the interstate commerce clause of the Constitution, on which the administration relied in justifying the bill, cannot cover ObamaCare's mandate. It is neither interstate nor is it commerce.

It isn't interstate because insurance companies are specifically barred from selling their policies across state lines. And it isn't commerce because a failure to buy health insurance cannot be called an act of commerce.

ObamaCare faces a long and tedious journey through the federal courts. It will win some and lose some, and then the U.S. Supreme Court will likely decide the issue. But, until then, we must focus on defunding the enforcement of this mandate through Congressional action.

DEFUNDING MEDICARE CUTS

America's elderly registered their sharp opposition to the cuts to Medicare that finance half of ObamaCare. They were so outraged by this $500 billion cut that they turned out in huge numbers to fight Obama in the 2010 election.

According to pollster John Zogby, senior citizens (over 65) cast 23% of the vote in the midterm elections, although they are only 18% of the adult population. And they voted more heavily Republican (57–38) than any other age group.[60]

Blocking these cuts by cutting off administrative funding must be a key priority for the House Republicans.

The Medicare cuts are to be administered by a new Independent Payment Advisory Board that will oversee the program. The Commission will be charged with deciding how to cut Medicare by $500 billion over ten years. These cuts will go into effect automatically unless stopped by specific legislation. With Medicare slated to cost $7 trillion over the next decade, the cut would amount to a 7% slash—no easy task to achieve.

We need to zero-fund this Payment Advisory Board. No money. No staff. No overhead. No offices. Zero. And we must prohibit the diversion of any other monies from other budgets to pay for their evil work. And should the Board actually make any cuts, we must override them in amendments to the debt limit and budget appropriations bills. If Obama vetoes these bills, then let the government shut down before we allow cuts in Medicare.

By contesting the Medicare cuts in the budget and appropriations bills, wrapping them into the overall debate, Republicans can turn the tables on the Democrats. During the Clinton years, Democrats beat back Republican attempts to cut Medicare, and their success dominated the outcome of the government shutdown crisis and the subsequent elections of 1996. Now it would be the Republicans who are trying to stave off cuts in Medicare. The issue would work for us, not for the Democrats, and give Republicans a key edge in the ensuing struggle.

A closely allied provision of ObamaCare requires the Department of Health and Human Services (HHS) to set up a Patient-Centered Outcomes Research Institute to compare costs and results of various treatments for illness to analyze which work the best and the cheapest. This analysis will provide the basis for care rationing decisions about what medicines and treatments doctors may offer their patients under the program. The ObamaCare legislation authorizes—but does not appropriate—$500 million a year to carry out the research.[61]

Note that these metrics are all based on one common and false assumption, that one size fits all. HHS is charged with deciding what the treatment should be for everybody afflicted with a vaguely similar illness. Of course, one size does not fit all, and the art of medicine involves assessing often subtle variations in each patient's condition and need for care. But HHS will handcuff doctors and stop them from using their judgment in deciding what course is right for each particular patient.

It will also probably go well beyond assessing the viability of treatments or medications and start looking at the viability of patients themselves. Who can get a heart transplant? What age? Smokers? Diabetics? People with chronically high blood pressure? If the data says they aren't likely to live a lot longer with a new heart, the omnipotent Research Institute may issue guidelines denying them treatment. Rationing. Literally, death panels.

During the debate over ObamaCare, the public outrage over the potential of the bill to encourage premature euthanasia became so intense that the administration dropped a provision authorizing Medicare payments to reimburse doctors for talking to their patients about their desired end-of-life treatment as part of an annual checkup. Critics like Sarah Palin called this provision, coupled with the rationing ObamaCare would force, the equivalent of death panels.

Now the Obama administration is planning to implement by executive order that which it had to withdraw from its legislation. The *New York Times* reported—on Christmas Day of 2010—that Obama had decided to impose a new rule saying that "Medicare will cover 'voluntary advance care planning,' to discuss end-of-life treatment, as part of the annual visit."[62]

"Under the rule, doctors can provide information to patients on how to prepare an 'advance directive,' stating how aggressively they wish to be treated if they are so sick that they cannot make health care decisions for themselves."[63]

We must defund all three forays into government-sponsored euthanasia and health care rationing. The Republicans must delete funds from the Independent Payment Advisory Board, the Patient-Centered Outcomes Research Institute, and the new authorization for Medicare reimbursement for end-of-life counseling. Without funds to administer either the 7% cut in Medicare or the research to accumulate metrics to decide on which care to allow and which to disallow or to support end-of-life counseling, neither effort can proceed. Are these folks willing to work without pay or benefits? Case closed.

DEFUNDING MEDICAID EXPANSION

The Republican House must also focus on the vast expansion of Medicaid. President Obama's legislation expands coverage to 16 million people not now eligible and will likely compel tens of millions more who are now eligible to register.

ObamaCare requires states to cover everybody earning up to 133% of the poverty level (up to about $30,000 income per year). Its costs will not only wreck the federal budget, but will also force states to impose new, high taxes to finance their share of the costs.

Beyond the general tactics of refusing to vote funds for the expansion of Medicaid and prohibiting the use of other appropriated monies from being used for this purpose, Republicans may be able to use a special tactic to defeat the Medicaid growth. Because of the high costs the expansion imposes on each state, even many Democrats are eager to exempt their states from the provision. The *New York Post* reported that "Democratic Senator Ron Wyden of Oregon . . . asked for his state to be exempted from many of the law's provisions."[64]

Republicans might form a coalition with Democrats who are worried about being responsible for triggering tax hikes in their states to exempt state after state from the Medicaid expansion. In classic log-rolling, legislators could condition any one state getting an exemption on all of the states that want them winning it. Such tactics might even produce enough votes to override the veto of an increasingly unpopular president.

DEFUNDING HEALTH INSURANCE EXCHANGES

A final key point of attack is defunding the "health insurance exchanges" for small businesses and individuals. These state-level exchanges are designed to force insurers to offer plans that provide a minimum level of benefits and are competitive in price. Writing for BNET, the CBS Interactive Business Network, Ken Terry explains how defunding the exchanges might work:

> Should Congress block funding for these exchanges, it could cripple a centerpiece of reform and trigger a cascade of unintended consequences. Here's how that could happen. First, some states might bail on their plans to set up exchanges, citing their unaffordability in the absence of federal support. Second, the feds would have no money to set up its own exchanges in states that fail to do so . . . Any failure to create exchanges . . . by 2014 would in turn block federal insurance subsidies to individuals and tax credits to small firms in those states. So individuals would still be required to buy insurance . . . on their own without government help. The natural result: a consumer revolt in which many people would simply refuse to buy coverage, preferring to pay the government fines instead.[65]

And, Terry notes, "if a large number of people remained uninsured, but insurers were required to accept everyone who applied for coverage, health plans would naturally jack up rates to handle the increased risk of covering the population. That would set off a health insurance death spiral, with more businesses dropping employee coverage, boosting the ranks of the uninsured and inevitably making insurance too expensive for most anyone to afford."[66]

These fights will not be easy. The defunding effort will only succeed if there is a mobilization of concerned citizens and activists akin to that which opposed the passage of ObamaCare in the first place and which animated the massive Republican wins of 2010. Everybody must donate, take to the streets, rally, demonstrate, and demand defunding. The rally cry must shake the nation!

Our health care system's fate is in our own hands. If we fight for it, we can preserve it, even now, from the ravages of President Obama and his socialist cronies. But it will take a massive effort from all of us. All hands on deck!

REPEALING THE DEATH TAX

The budget deal reached between Republicans and President Obama called for reinstitution of the inheritance tax for the next two years at a 35% rate with an exemption for estates of $5 million or more. The fact that a lame duck Congress—filled with Democrats in control of both houses—agreed to this extension does not take the issue off the table.

The conservatives now in control of the House must press for its elimination as part of their budget position.

The reimposition of the inheritance tax (or death tax) looms large over American investors and entrepreneurs. It freezes their efforts to expand their businesses or invest their capital in creating new jobs. The chance that they might die and saddle their heirs with a large tax liability forces them to keep their capital liquid, readily available to pay the taxman if they should pass away.

A study by no less than Obama's former economics advisor Larry Summers and economist Laurence Kotlikoff found that "intergenerational transfers" account for a very large portion of all capital in the United States. Summers and Kotlikoff found that "between 41% and 66% of capital stock was transferred by bequests at death or through trusts and lifetime gifts." The study concluded that "patterns of savings don't validate" the idea that rich people spend down their savings. Instead, they pass them along to their heirs. "A major motivation for saving and building businesses," Summers and Kotlikoff noted, "is to pass assets on so children and grandchildren have a better life." [67]

If rich and elderly businessmen and investors knew that their heirs did not have to ante up 35% of the value of their estate in taxes, they would feel much freer to reinvest their profits in business expansion and new job creation rather than keep it under the mattress (or in CDs, T-bills, or stocks) to pay the estate tax.

While the number of properties involved is small—and Obama likes to dwell on how few people pay the tax—the economic impact is huge. A 2009 study by Douglas Holtz-Eakin and Cameron Smith found that repealing the inheritance tax would create 1.5 million new jobs.[68]

The report said that repeal would increase small business capital by more than $1.6 trillion, increase payrolls by 2.6%, and expand investment by 3%.[69]

The death tax falls especially hard on farmers and others whose estates are illiquid. The Heritage Foundation notes that "families often must sell such assets that do not regularly trade in active markets to raise money to pay the death tax. Due to the lack of an active market, these families must often accept prices for these assets that are lower than they would have received if they had more time to sell the property."[70]

And all this tax burden is totally unnecessary! The death tax is totally useless, a tax that produces no additional revenue! All the property covered by the tax is also subject to the capital gains tax (except for cash). Where an estate is not subject to the inheritance tax, the heirs must pay a tax on their capital gains anyway. The only difference is that the inheritance tax is fully payable when the parent dies and the capital gains tax is charged when the heir sells the property.

The Heritage Foundation explains that "currently, the heirs 'carry over' the basis of the original owner's assets when they acquire the possession in question. The capital gains tax is calculated on the difference between the sale price the heir receives when he sells the item and the price the deceased paid when he acquired it."[71]

It is so much fairer, better, and more economically productive to wait to charge the tax until the possession is sold. That's when the heir has the liquid capital to pay the levy; he makes it back in the sales price. Having to pay the tax at the time he inherits the property means he has to scramble around, sell off assets for a fraction of their price, and take a huge loss in order to pay the Fed. But at the time of sale, the capital is right there and it is easy to decrease the profit from the sale by the amount of the capital gains tax.

Repealing the death tax would have only a minimal impact on the U.S.

budget. In 2008, it yielded only $24 billion, just 1% of all federal tax collections,[72] and, were it repealed, capital gains tax revenues would increasingly offset the loss from death tax collections.

The only folks who gain from the tax are estate planners, insurance companies, and big businesses.

Estate tax lawyers and planners reap large fees helping families avoid the inheritance tax. They have an obvious interest in continuing it.

Life insurance companies are no less interested in its extension. Families who cannot afford estate lawyers and planners to help them avoid the inheritance tax usually purchase life insurance policies that will pay their heirs enough to cover the tax liability triggered by the inheritance tax. Of course, the fees of estate planners and/or life insurance premiums siphon money away from small business owners who might otherwise invest it in creating jobs.

Publicly owned big businesses also gain a competitive advantage over smaller, family-owned firms because most of their capital passes on to the next generation in the form of readily tradable stocks and bonds. The size of the total portfolio of the company's stocks and bonds is so big that even a large stockholder selling off his holdings would usually not impact the price much, while a small family-owned business takes an enormous hit to satisfy its death tax obligation.

And big businesses often are able to scoop up smaller businesses—whose heirs are forced to sell to raise money to pay the death tax—at bargain basement prices.

But repealing any tax will take a great deal of work. Explaining to Americans why they should care about a tax most of them will never have to pay is a challenge. But it is no harder than explaining to those who earn less than $250,000 a year why they should care about tax increases that affect only their wealthier compatriots. A tax on anyone hurts us all. The money may not be paid by each of us in checks to the U.S. Treasury, but it is paid just the same in stymied economic growth, unemployment, and recession.

We need to work to spread the information about how the death tax hurts us all!

ENDING THE BANKING REIGN OF TERROR

Banks are not lending. Those four words summarize, more than any other, the key reason why our economy has not recovered. The crisis of 2008–09 triggered "reform" legislation in 2010, which has, in turn, frozen bank lending. Commerce has not ground to a halt only because of market conditions or economic sluggishness. It has evaporated also because banks are terrified by the new regulations Congress has passed.

Banking is based on lending. And lending always entails risk. That's why we pay interest on our loans—to give the lender an incentive to take the risk. But bankers are no longer willing to take the risks they once did. Particularly small banks are fearful that if their loans go bad, the Federal Deposit Insurance Corporation (FDIC) will use the new regulatory powers it got under the Dodd-Frank Wall Street Reform and Consumer Protection Act to close them down, fire their boards, dismiss the management, and wipe out shareholder equity.

The banks keep their stone facades, their pediments and columns. They may still look like ancient Greek temples, but they are no longer banks. They are mausoleums. The commerce that once thrived inside is dead, killed by the fear of federal regulation.

Bryan Real, president of United Food Group in Elgin, Illinois, put it best: "Banks don't want to lend. The last three years have been the worst for small business lending I've ever seen." Mr. Real sought financing to develop a coffee and condiment dispenser but got turndowns from four banks.[73] He had 6,000 orders for the new equipment, but couldn't get the loan to pay for the start-up.

He's not alone. The National Small Business Association reported in July 2010 that 41% of small business owners could not obtain the financing they wanted.[74]

The Federal Deposit Insurance Corporation reports that, nationally, banks' small business loan portfolios dropped from $711 billion in the second quarter of 2009 to $652 billion in the second quarter of 2010.[75] And when banks don't lend, small businesses can't grow. According to the Federal Reserve, small businesses get more than 90% of their financing from banks.[76]

Ben Bernanke, chairman of the Federal Reserve, noted that "it seems clear that some creditworthy businesses have had difficulty obtaining the credit that they need to expand and, in some cases, even to continue operating."[77]

Some small businesses have given up and are not even applying for loans anymore. The National Federation of Independent Businesses survey found that while only 27% of small business owners reported that their credit needs had been met, 52% so despaired of the marketplace that they didn't want to borrow money.[78] Barlow Research Associates reported that only 17% of small businesses had even applied for additional credit in the past year, about half of the proportion that normally do.[79]

It isn't just small, community banks that are closing their loan windows to small businesses. Chase made $2.1 billion in small business loans in 2010, down 40% from the $3.5 billion it made in the first half of 2008.[80]

A cycle seems to have set in where banks won't lend, small businesses don't expand, jobs are not created, sales dry up, and small businesses don't want to borrow.

The loser, of course is the American economy. The Census Bureau reports that small businesses create 72% of the new jobs in the United States while medium-size companies generate only 16% and large firms only 12% of the new jobs.[81]

Small banks, which make the bulk of small business loans, are particularly unwilling to lend in the new financial and regulatory climate. And it is these banks that provide two-thirds of all loans to small businesses throughout the nation,[82] even though they have only 12% of all bank assets. Big banks—those with $100 billion or more in assets—make only 22% of small business loans.[83]

Why aren't small banks lending to small businesses?

It's not that they don't have the money. In the third quarter of 2010, banks with assets of less than $5 billion hoarded their cash, lending out just 82% of their deposits, compared with 91% at bigger banks.[84]

The regulatory reign of terror that has stopped lending to small businesses has been induced by the Dodd-Frank Wall Street "Reform" and Consumer "Protection" Act of 2010. The Act vastly expands the power of the FDIC to close down financial institutions, even those that do not avail themselves of its deposit insurance.

It confers new powers on the FDIC that would make Fidel Castro or

Hugo Chavez envious. It lets the agency "seize, break-up and wind down a failing financial company whose failure threatens financial stability in the United States." This power covers bank holding companies, nonbank financial companies supervised by the Federal Reserve, a company that is "predominantly engaged in activities that the Federal Reserve has determined are financial in nature or incidental thereto, and subsidiaries of these companies."[85]

The FDIC can move in if two-thirds of the Federal Reserve Board and a similar proportion of its own board find that the financial company "is in default or danger of default" and that its failure would have "serious adverse effects on financial stability in the United States." The FDIC also has to get an order from the U.S. District Court for Washington, D.C., or the consent of the financial company's board of directors.[86]

Once the FDIC moves in, its powers are almost unlimited. It can

- Take over and manage the assets of the bank

- Merge the bank with another company

- Transfer its assets or liabilities without getting anyone's consent

- Remove the managers and employees who are "responsible for the failed condition" of the bank[87]

- Ensure that "shareholders . . . do not receive payment until all other claims . . . are fully paid."[88]

When Dodd-Frank was going through Congress, the administration justified the expanded FDIC powers to the public saying that they were necessary to police financial institutions that were too big to fail—i.e., that their collapse would engender the same kind of national panic that hit when Lehman Brothers went bankrupt in the fall of 2008. But the FDIC is using its new powers to close down small community banks and financial institutions whose failure would barely cause a blip on Wall Street radar screens. The main consequence of these takeovers is to obliterate entire towns, robbing them of the cornerstone of their economy: the local bank.

It has the same impact that closing the train station used to have—it wipes out communities.

Granted, the economic crisis has been hard on small banks. In 2010, 143 of them have failed, in addition to 140 that went under in 2009.[89] But the FDIC's regulatory hit list goes much further. It fingers 829 small banks— one in eight—that it says are at risk of failure.[90]

Or at least at risk of FDIC takeover.

The spread of the FDIC's oversight powers has terrified small-town bankers. One West Virginia small bank owner commented that "we see federal regulators looking over our shoulders and [we] just won't make loans that they might consider risky. We don't want to lose our bank."[91]

One Tennessee banker noted that beyond the danger of losing his bank, he felt hobbled by the need to hire layers of professionals, accountants, lawyers, and other staff to comply with the new federal regulations. The costs that can easily be absorbed by a big bank can make the difference between a profit and a loss at a smaller one.

Time magazine tells the story of Community Bank & Trust (CBT) of Cornelia, Georgia. The FDIC took over CBT on January 29, 2010. It claimed that the bank was on the brink of insolvency. Thirty-five homes and 189 businesses underwritten by CBT had already been foreclosed and another 1,500 were listed as in serious trouble.[92]

The effect of the FDIC seizure on Cornelia was traumatic. *Time* notes that "CBT's $1.2 billion in assets represented 75 times the county's $16 million annual budget."[93] Ed Brown, president of the Habersham County Historical Society, said, "A lot of people put a lot of stock in the bank, and when it failed, it shook the whole town."[94]

The FDIC decimated CBT after the takeover. It forced a sale to an out-of-town bank, South Carolina Bank and Trust, which, in turn, fired 100 of CBT's 400 employees, closed ten branches, and moved more than 200 loans toward foreclosure.[95]

CBT lay at the very core of Cornelia. As *Time* noted, before the town "got a sewer system, Cornelia got a bank."[96] The bank was the town's economic lifeline. By 2005, it held nearly half of the residents' bank deposits.[97] CBT had an honored place in the community. A famous story in town was that when the bank president's eldest son, who worked at the bank, said that he and his wife were going to live elsewhere, his father said "not and work in this company, you're not." He promptly fired his son.[98]

Now, under the new management of the South Carolina Bank and Trust, it's a new day. Cornelia city manager Donald Anderson says that the South Carolina bank "is really killing the town, and I blame the FDIC." He and other Cornelians worry that South Carolina Bank and Trust "is sucking the assets out of Cornelia to help build business in the larger city of Gainesville, 24 miles to the southwest, a fear fueled by the fact that CBT's new market president, Jeff Fulp, has chosen to live in Gainesville rather than Cornelia. 'It's like Invasion of the Body Snatchers,' says Don Bagwell, a [Cornelia] city commissioner."[99]

Should the FDIC have taken over CBT and forced a shotgun marriage to the South Carolina Bank and Trust? Some Cornelia residents wonder if the Feds were way too quick to pull the trigger. After all, the new South Carolina owners have foreclosed on just 2.14% of the business loans and only 1.75% of the residential mortgages. Were things so dire that the bank would have failed had the Feds not stepped in?

We'll never know. What we do know is that one-eighth of the small banks in the U.S. are in danger of an FDIC takeover, a chilling prospect for these companies and for the small businesses that depend on them for credit.

Another example of the FDIC's overreach comes from the heart of Obama country—the Chicago suburb of Oak Park, where Park National Bank, a small, community financial institution, was closed prematurely by federal regulators out for scalps with which to festoon their walls.

Park National was owned by Michael Kelly, who put together a group of nine privately held community banks under his holding company FBOP. The banks had $19 billion in assets combined.[100]

A philanthropist, Kelly devoted all the profits of his banks—27% over two years—to charity work aimed at helping the poor. Rather than pay himself dividends, he gave to schools, parks, affordable housing, social services, and community organizations. His banks refused to make subprime loans and offered banking services, according to inthesetimes.com, to "predominately black Chicago neighborhoods otherwise served only by predatory payday lenders and currency exchanges."[101]

FBOP got into trouble when quasigovernment mortgage guarantors

Fannie Mae and Freddie Mac went under in 2008–09, costing Kelly's banks $756 million of their capital, about half their total holdings. The Treasury Department came to the rescue, and announced that $545 million in TARP funds would go to FBOP as part of a package of small bank loans.[102]

But then TARP changed its mind and refused to process the loan. Kelly, who had previously secured $600 million in private capital commitments, found that the stigma of having been turned down by TARP led his alternative capital sources of dry up. "It was the kiss of death," Kelly says.[103]

Despite the losses, Park National remained profitable, but two other banks owned by FBOP were critically undercapitalized. Inthesetimes.com recounts that the "FDIC invoked an optional rule—used only six times over two decades—that made the two stronger banks liable for the losses of all the other banks in the group. The FDIC notified FBOP that it had the standard 90 days after its warning to meet capital requirements."[104]

"As the . . . deadline drew close, FBOP presented a plan for private investment but asked for a week's extension, a common courtesy in such cases, to finalize the details. The bank knew—as did the FDIC—that the following week Obama planned to sign new legislation allowing corporations to carry losses forward for more years in the future to write off against taxes. That would have effectively given FBOP up to $200 million, making it possible to raise the capital it needed from just one investor."[105]

But the FDIC wouldn't wait. It had already cut a deal to sell all FBOP banks to U.S. Bancorp (America's sixth largest bank) with a $2.5 billion taxpayer subsidy to pay for loan losses, terms that would easily have saved FBOP, had they been offered.

Irony of ironies, on the morning of October 30, 2009, Treasury Secretary Tim Geithner went to Chicago to hold a press conference honoring the Park National Bank for its service and presenting it with $50 million in tax credits for expansion of its community development work. At 5 p.m. that same day, the FDIC seized the bank and turned it over to U.S. Bancorp!

They wouldn't wait the week.

The other end of the takeover equation is that large banks are feasting on the corpses of their smaller competitors, often with a generous subsidy in hand from taxpayer funds.

For example, after BankUnited was taken over by the FDIC, it was bought by a group of private investors with a taxpayer subsidy. According to Reuters news service, "the FDIC lost $4.9 billion when it sold BankUnited." Part of the reason for the loss is that the federal agency is "guaranteeing more than 80% of the bank's assets and the future income stream from the FDIC to the bank is worth a whopping $800 million." [106]

Reuters summarizes the lucrative FDIC-banker connection this way: "It certainly looks as though the FDIC is selling dimes for a nickel to its highly exclusive group of qualified buyers, and that purchases from the FDIC have invariably turned out to be fabulous deals. That's not the boring banking that the US wants to see: instead, it's the kind of high-stakes deal making which makes Wall Street so resented in the heartland, and which, clearly, is never going to die." [107]

Anxious to appear to address the shortfall in lending to small businesses, President Obama is responding not by alleviating its cause and reining in the regulators, but by throwing money at the problem. He induced his Democratic rubber-stamp Congress to pass a $30 billion program to infuse small banks with capital.

But capital is not the problem. As Reuters reports, "community banks don't need the money . . . the industry is relatively flush. In the third quarter [of 2010], banks with assets of less than $5 billion on average had tangible common equity equal to 9.62% of tangible assets. That's a stronger capital position than big banks, whose equivalent ratio stood at just 7.97% on average, according to SNL Financial." [108]

With small banks in such relatively solid financial condition, the question looms: is the FDIC right to be so aggressive in taking over these institutions? Or has it gotten a bit high from its new sweeping regulatory powers?

One thing is clear: until someone reins in the FDIC and ends its reign of terror over small banks, small business lending will not resume anytime soon.

Patriots must demand that Congress recognize that it was big banks and Wall Street whose irresponsible behavior caused the financial meltdown, not small banks and their lending practices. The crisis of 2008–09 was not akin to the savings and loan debacle of the 1980s. Then, small banks and their clubby ties to small-town cronies fueled the collapse.

The modern problems were caused by federal policies that induced mortgage lenders to take big risks and got quasigovernment entities Fannie Mae and Freddie Mac to guarantee their loans. Then, big bankers sliced and diced the resulting mortgages and spread the risk onto the balance sheets of banks around the world. When the underlying mortgages collapsed, so did the global banking system.

The small, community banks now in the FDIC's regulatory sights played little role in the process. Most of the subprime mortgages that underlay the crisis were issued in the first place by either larger banks or by nonbank financial companies like Countrywide Financial, New Century, Ameriquest Mortgage Company, HSBC, and Fremont.[109]

It was not the small, community bank that let us down, so why should these banks be under the gun?

Washington Monthly, commenting on the relatively good fiscal condition of smaller banks, noted that "one reason community banks are doing so well right now is simply that they never became too clever for their own good. When other lenders, including under-regulated giants like Ameriquest and Countrywide, started peddling ugly subprime mortgages, community banks stayed away. Banking regulations prevented them from taking on the kind of debt ratios assumed by their competitors, and ties to their customers and community ensured that predatory loans were out of the question." [110]

So what is the justification for the FDIC coming down so hard on them?

Patriots may suspect that President Obama's expansion of federal regulatory power and the increasingly broad swath of takeovers of small, community banks is not a response to the crisis, but part of his overall goal of taking over the American economy. Socialism is about ownership—and what better way to take over the economy than to take over its banks? Large Wall Street banks are usually willing to act as directed by Washington. Look at how they cooperated in the auto industry takeovers, much to the pain of their own depositors whose assets were obliterated. But small banks are subject to less discipline and tend to march to the beat of their local communities. Obama is determined to change all that and to increase federal control.

We must stop him. The Dodd-Frank bill does not do enough to regulate large banks and does too much to put small banks under the Fed's regulatory thumb. The Republican House must act decisively to free local banks from undue federal regulation and, through legislation and Congressional hearings, rein in the FDIC, restraining its takeover rampage. When the chill of terror is lifted, local banks will once again start lending to small businesses now that each loan no longer has the chance to lead to the loss of their bank.

STOPPING THE EPA FROM KILLING U.S. MANUFACTURING

Election? What election? The massive repudiation of the Obama administration's environmental policies and its proposal for cap and trade to cut carbon emissions appears not to have registered with the Oval Office or the federal Environmental Protection Agency (EPA).

While all concede that it is now politically impossible to persuade the people's elected representatives in Congress to pass this legislation, the EPA announced on Christmas Eve of 2010 that it is planning an end run around Congress and will impose the very same regulations on greenhouse gases by bureaucratic rule that the democratically elected Congress rejected.[111]

Obama's proposed cap and trade legislation passed the House in June 2009. The Waxman-Markey bill squeaked through by 219–212, but never made it through the Senate. Even when Obama had a 60-vote majority, the opposition of Democratic senators from coal states such as West Virginia (Jay Rockefeller and Robert Byrd) blocked its passage.

But the very threat of its enactment did its damage nonetheless. Manufacturing businesses from coast to coast—and especially in America's heartland—were paralyzed by fear of its passage. They didn't expand. They didn't launch new product lines. They didn't create jobs, because they worried that the energy tax that was the centerpiece of the legislation would lead to their ruin. Faced with the likelihood that cap and trade would make them move offshore—perhaps to China or India, which had no such tax—they dared not put more money into the facilities in the U.S.

Once again, the Obama reign of terror stopped business growth in its tracks.

But, apparently, losing the election of 2010 has not dulled the ardor of the EPA bureaucrats. Now that it is clear that Obama can't get cap and trade through Congress, the federal EPA is planning to declare carbon dioxide a toxin and enact administrative regulations that will have the same effect as cap and trade.

Wisconsin Republican Rep. Jim Sensenbrenner warns that EPA is planning "to regulate greenhouse gas emissions by fiat." [112] It is using the old Clean Air Act, passed in 1970, to justify the new regulations. When this legislation was passed, of course, nobody considered the issue of global climate change. It was aimed at curbing pollution that caused disease. One of the most successful laws in recent history, it is now being used for an entirely different and alien purpose.

FoxNews.com reports that "the tactic of shoehorning global warming regulations into the 1970s Clean Air Act seemed far-fetched until the Supreme Court opened the door for it with their decision in *Massachusetts v. EPA* in 2007. That 5–4 decision instructed the EPA to decide whether or not to pursue global warming regulation based on the language of the statute.

"A reasonable EPA would have reacted to the Court by citing the enormous administrative burden and absurd results of trying to stop global warming using a 40 year-old law designed for very different problems and deferred to Congress on the issue." [113] But not the Obama EPA, led by Lisa Jackson, which is charging straight ahead to do by administrative rule what the Congress refused to pass.

The new EPA regulations would fine businesses for their emissions and deny permits to any that want to locate in already "polluted" areas.

After Congress rejected cap and trade, it seemed to be dead. But Myron Ebell, director of the Center for Energy and the Environment with the Competitive Energy Institute, says, "I would like to have a party and say we won, but the truth is we are still in the middle of it. The problem is now that the administration changed strategy and is using existing laws and regulations, like the Clean Air Act, the Endangered Species Act and EPA regulations to implement its agenda. And unlike the cap and trade effort, it is much harder to get the public excited about rule changes." [114]

Nick Loris of the Heritage Foundation echoes Ebell's concern: "Obama will try a piecemeal approach. And they have a much better chance of becoming law than cap and trade ever did." [115]

The EPA has set a goal of reducing permissible greenhouse gases from 75 million parts per billion to 60 million. It has asked each state to evaluate its power plants, industries, and other pollution emitters to determine what is the "best available technology" to reach this goal.[116] States will have no voice in determining the standard, but will have to pick the means of achieving it. It's like being asked if you prefer lethal injection or the electric chair.

But here's the thing: instead of using a national standard of 60 million parts per billion, the EPA will apply this standard to every community in the country. It will ask any community seeking to attract business: can you meet the greenhouse gas standard? If an area can't—if the industries in that community already emit too much in greenhouse gases—no business will go there, since it would not be able to get a pollution permit from EPA if it did.

The *Washington Examiner* reports that "University of Mississippi professor William Shughart II . . . notes that many jurisdictions across the country can't meet the present greenhouse gas standard, much less reach the lower threshold anytime soon. 'If a county or city is not in compliance, its economy won't be able to grow, so the EPA's proposal would spell economic stagnation for many communities,' Shughart contends." The *Examiner* warns that "without the proper pollution permits, existing facilities and new construction projects across the country either will grind to a halt or never get started."[117]

If the EPA bases its regulation of carbon dioxide emissions on community-wide or statewide data, it dooms certain communities or even entire states to economic stagnation.

What is the rationale for approaching these standards geographically?

Why do we punish oil-producing states like Texas and Louisiana because, in supplying America's energy needs, they emit a lot of greenhouse gas already? Why should they be unable to attract new industry because their existing plants emit a lot of CO_2?

Were these regulations really about pollution, this geographic approach would be understandable. If the lungs of those Texans who live near their energy plants were already filled with pollutants, the EPA would be justified in limiting their further exposure.

But we are not talking about pollution here! We are talking about greenhouse gases—carbon dioxide—the same stuff we breathe in and out every moment of every day! Carbon dioxide doesn't make you sick. The reason for regulation is not the health of those who are exposed, but the supposed need of the planet Earth to limit its emission of such gases to retard global climate change. Whether this goal is worthy or not, what difference does it make that the carbon dioxide comes from Texas, whose industrial mix includes a lot of CO_2 emissions already, or New York, which may not?

The only rationale for geographic quotas on emissions is political. The energy-producing states are in the South and prone to vote Republican. Could this be the motivation?

The EPA regulation will hurt the entire nation, reducing the GDP by $1.7 trillion and costing us 7.3 million jobs by 2020, the Manufacturers Alliance estimates. But it will hit certain states the hardest. Texas will lose 2.7 million jobs, Louisiana 938,000, California 846,000, Illinois 396,000, and Pennsylvania 351,000.[118]

The EPA regulations really are a declaration of war against coal. But most American electricity comes from coal—the deadliest of sins in the environmentalist world—and it's the industry that would bear the brunt of cap and trade taxes.

The United States is making enormous strides in getting away from carbon-based electric power generation without punitive taxes or crushing regulation. The proportion of power that comes from coal has dropped from 52% in 1996 to 49% in 2007 to 45% in 2009. Meanwhile, natural gas sourced power and renewable sources have doubled in the proportion of our electricity they generate since 1996.

CHANGE IN AMERICAN ENERGY SOURCES

Source	1996	2009
Coal	52%	45%
Natural Gas	13%	23%
Nuclear	20%	20%
Renewable	2%	4%

Source: U.S. Energy Information Administration [119]

While the socialists would like to use America's dependence on coal-fired power to overhaul our free enterprise system and impose government controls, auctions for permits, and energy taxes, our capitalist system is doing quite nicely on its own! Natural gas production and renewable source based power is soaring and coal use is dropping. And, as environmental information spreads, the drop in coal dependency has accelerated. EPA regulation is just not needed to cut coal emissions. They are coming down on their own!

It looks increasingly like we can keep our manufacturing base, retain our energy independence in electric power generation, and still satisfy the demands of those who are focused on the human contribution to climate change. But Obama's socialists don't care. They want the regulatory power anyway.

EPA also wants to tax emissions from oil refineries, raising the cost per barrel by 20 to 50% by 2015 and doubling or tripling the cost by 2030,[120] a cost increase that will soon make its way to the gas pump.

The Heritage Foundation details the horrific impact of such regulation, whether by Congressionally enacted cap and trade legislation or an EPA-imposed regulatory alternative.[121]

- Cumulative GDP losses of between $1.7 trillion and $4.8 trillion by 2030 (in inflation-adjusted 2006 dollars). Each year, at least $155 billion in national production of goods and services would be destroyed.

- Half a million to one million jobs would be lost each year until 2030.

- The annual cost of emission permits to energy users would be at least $100 billion by 2020 and could exceed $300 billion by 2030.

- The average household will pay $467 more each year for its natural gas and electricity (again in 2006 dollars).

- Gasoline prices will rise by 64 cents per gallon.[122]

American manufacturing has faced and largely met the challenge of low-wage competition throughout the world. As more and more products are made in Asia, the United States has preserved its share of the global manufacturing market at 25%. Despite the competition, the U.S. still leads the world in manufacturing as it has done every year since World War II. Why? Because we automated. But taxing energy taxes the machines that replace workers and makes manufacturing industries uncompetitive.

WHO MAKES IT?
MANUFACTURING BY COUNTRY

Country	$ Total Manufacturing Output, 2007
United States	$1,831 billion
China	$1,106
Japan	$ 926
Germany	$ 670
Russia	$ 362
Italy	$ 345
United Kingdom	$ 342
France	$ 296
South Korea	$ 241
Canada	$ 218

Source: http://www.wisegeek.com/what-are-the-top-manufacturing-countries.htm.[123]

How have U.S. manufacturers been able to keep their market lead, with foreign workers earning only about a tenth of what our people do? Essentially, we have replaced people with power. The U.S. has lost 5 million manufacturing jobs over the past three decades, but production has continued to expand to keep pace with global demand,[124] with machines doing the work men and women once did.

Chicago Fed economist William Strauss points out that the increasing productivity of the U.S. manufacturing sector is extraordinary. He explains that "inflation averaged 3.7% between 1980 and 2009, while at the same time the rise in prices for new vehicles averaged 1.7%. U.S. manufacturers are making stuff better and cheaper and faster than ever before. Those who imagine 'we don't make anything anymore,' as Donald Trump claims, don't grasp the magnitude of America's industrial productivity gains." [125]

But machines need energy, and lots of it. By taxing energy, as the EPA proposes to do, we tax the key equalizer that has let the United States keep its manufacturing sector vibrant and productive. We eliminate the edge we have over low-wage countries. (This policy from a president who campaigned on opposing outsourcing of U.S. production!)

Dr. Tim Nerenz, executive vice president of the Oldenberg Group, a large manufacturing firm based in Wisconsin, prophesizes that he will have to move his businesses offshore if a carbon tax is imposed. He explains that "automation in my factories is not a lights out process. We still need people, but fewer of them. Machines make it possible for one person to do the work several once had to do. But the machines consume large amounts of energy. Cap and trade would force me to close factories and move." [126]

Dr. Nerenz points out that the proposal would also force him to operate his trucks only four days each week, cutting his ability to service his customers. "It would be a disaster," he says. [127]

The threat of cap and trade legislation or EPA regulation is already costing us jobs. Brent Vassey, writing for townhall.com, points out that "manufacturers are making decisions about their future capital investments today. Whether or not [cap and trade] . . . is embraced by the U.S. . . . is a critical decision, because America will lose opportunities to compete and create jobs in the future as long as the threat of an economy-crushing tax scheme like 'cap & trade' exists in the public debate." [128]

Meanwhile, American coal companies, increasingly barred from burning their product here, are busily exporting it to China, which has no compunctions about carbon emissions. Coal exports to China have been soaring!

U.S. COAL EXPORTS TO CHINA

Year	Tons of Coal Exported to China
2009	2,714 tons
2010 (first six months)	2,900,000 tons

Source: *International Herald Tribune*[129]

No, this is not a typo. The exports of U.S. coal to China have actually increased one thousandfold between all of 2009 and the first six months of 2010!

No student of global warming could maintain that there is any difference to the globe's climate if the coal is burned here or in China. It's the same planet and the same atmosphere. So Obama's EPA regulations are having a wonderful effect—sending our coal to China to burn!!!

Some states are suing the EPA to block the new regulations. Specifically, Texas, the most heavily affected state, has advised the agency that it will not cooperate or comply with the new regulations until a court orders it to do so.

EPA assistant administrator Gina McCarthy "rejected claims that the first-ever nationwide U.S. limits on carbon pollution will hurt business. 'The Clean Air Act for 40 years has found a way to issue permits in a way that allows the economy to grow,' she said. 'We aren't going to stop that with the greenhouse-gas' best-available process.'"[130]

But forty years ago (when the Clean Air Act was passed), the U.S. did not have to compete in a global economy like we do today. It did not matter that much if China or India limited pollution or let their people breathe poison and die young. Whereas, with today's porous international borders and prolific foreign trade, it would be economic suicide to force American business to meet standards their competitors don't.

And remember that the Clean Air Act was passed amid a clear national consensus that it was more important to preserve health than to allow polluting industries to operate in populated communities. But there is no such unanimity on the need to control carbon dioxide emissions, which have no health consequence other than their supposed contribution to global climate change.

Finally, Ms. McCarthy ignores the fact that the Clean Air Act was phased in over decades. First it applied to particulates, sulfur, and lead. Then it was expanded to nitrous oxides. Each new regulation affected specific industries, but none had the potential to cripple our whole economy. But curtailing carbon dioxide emissions can do just that. It is a federal regulation that impacts all industries, all manufacturers, all producers, all energy generators. All at once. To impose regulations over this ubiquitous gas will cause massive disruption.

Patriots must work to make sure that the Republican House passes a law to stop all regulation of greenhouse gases, using existing legal authority. If the EPA wants to expand its regulatory umbrella to include carbon dioxide, let them convince the people's elected representatives in Congress.

It is very possible that we will be able to pass such legislation in the Senate, and there is an outside chance that we will win by such a margin as to be able to override a presidential veto. Some liberal Democratic senators from coal-producing states—such as Jay Rockefeller (D-WV)—have already backed such legislation.

In an e-mail, the senator said, "Such an unstable regulatory environment prevents companies from making long range investment decisions."[131]

If we cannot pass a delay or a ban on EPA regulation as a regular bill, the issue of carbon dioxide regulation will have to be wrapped up in the debt limit expansion debate or the battle over the FY2012 budget. In either case, it will become a key point of contention in the deadlock between the White House and the House of Representatives.

Welcome to the budget battle! If the same fight that pits big taxes versus big spending cuts also pits ObamaCare versus defunding and EPA regulation versus lower electric bills and manufacturing jobs, so much the better! It makes the fight a lot easier to win.

KEEPING THE SECRET BALLOT IN UNION ELECTIONS

The key goal of big labor—and a major fear of most American private sector businesses—is the end of the secret ballot in union elections. It is the secret ballot that stops union thugs from intimidating their fellow workers into supporting unions they would otherwise oppose. Unions are determined to end secret balloting so they can coerce workers into approving unions.

Card check legislation, which would eliminate the secret ballot, was the key legislative priority of the AFL-CIO when the Democrats took sixty seats in the Senate and full control of the House. President Obama pushed for the new law. But it still didn't pass.

No worries! The National Labor Relations Board (NLRB), like the EPA, is planning to do by fiat what the Congress has rejected doing democratically.

To get a union now, a majority of workers must check off on cards indicating that they want one at their workplace. When 50% plus one have checked the cards, the NLRB orders an election—with a secret ballot—to determine if the workers really want the union. In many cases, a majority of workers sign and check cards saying they want a union, only to have a majority of the same workforce vote it down when the ballot is private, proving that the secret ballot is the only way to stop the coercion of workers to back unionization.

That's why Congress refused to pass card check legislation. After it passed the House, it died in the Senate.

But that hasn't deterred the Obama administration. That which it has sought and failed to get passed in Congress, it is now seeking to do by administrative rule.

To pave the way for this end run around Congress, Obama appointed Craig Becker, the top lawyer for the SEIU (Service Employees International Union) as head of the NLRB. It was like inviting the fox to watch the chicken coop. SEIU is the most radical of unions and has been instrumental in Obama's political machine.

Given his record, the Senate refused to confirm Becker, even with an overwhelming Democratic majority, so Obama gave him a recess appointment in March 2010 that did not require Senate approval.

Then Becker, who was appointed without Congressional approval, began to attempt to eliminate the secret ballot requirement, again bypassing Congress.

The requirement of a secret ballot stems from the NLRB decision in the

2007 *Dana Corp.* case (351 NLRB No. 28), which, as the *Wall Street Journal* reported, ruled that "card check was an inferior substitute to secret ballots." The NLRB held "that when a company recognized a union via card check, workers had the right to force an immediate secret vote on whether they really wanted to join that union." [132]

Now Craig Becker is trying to reverse the *Dana* decision. At the end of August 2010, the NLRB, by a 3–2 party-line vote, decided to "revisit" *Dana*. It requested briefs from all parties by November 1, 2010, and will, likely, shortly reverse it. If so, it will invite massive coercive unionization to proceed.

In our minds, for Becker there is a clear appearance of a conflict of interest on the question. The *Journal* points out that "the labor lawyer has already refused to recuse himself from cases involving the SEIU, his former employer." The newspaper adds that "now it turns out that he had filed a brief for the AFL-CIO in the original *Dana* case arguing that there is no essential difference between card check and secret ballots." [133]

The voters in Arizona, South Carolina, South Dakota, and Utah quite clearly saw a big difference between card checks and secret ballots. In the 2010 election, all four approved ballot measures to require secret ballots in union elections. In Arizona and Utah, the measures passed with 60% of the vote. In South Dakota, it got 79%, and in South Carolina, 86%.[134] Citizens' groups in four other states—California, Florida, Mississippi, and Florida—are planning to seek similar votes in the 2012 elections.

These states are, of course, trying to blunt the possible impact within their borders of an NLRB decision reversing the *Dana* ruling. At stake is more than justice for their workers. Their ability to create jobs is on the line.

Why do these states worry that private sector unionization will cost jobs? They need look no further than the auto industry. For decades, the United Auto Workers (UAW) played industrial hardball, routinely striking unless their demands were met. By the time the U.S. auto industry collapsed under the strain, wages and benefits had risen to $70 per hour. Health benefits for retirees and workers added $1,200 to the cost of each vehicle General Motors made in 2007. The UAW ended up destroying itself. Membership crashed as employment cratered. After peaking in 1979 at 1.5 million members, the union's ranks dropped to 355,000 in 2009.[135]

The impact of unionization on job loss is most evident in the manufacturing sector. While unionized manufacturing jobs decreased by 75% between 1977 and 2008, nonunion manufacturing jobs actually rose by 6% over the same time period. While unions tend to raise wages—most studies show they are about 15% higher in unionized companies—they definitely cost jobs, too.[136]

Good deal: higher wages but no job!

Part of the reason unions so adversely affect job retention and creation is that they slow investment. The Heritage Foundation reports that "one study found that unions directly reduce capital investment by 6% and indirectly reduce capital investment through lower profits by another 7%. The same study also found that unions reduce R&D activity by 15 to 20%."[137]

In the construction industry as well, unionization has cost jobs. Since the late 1970s, unionized construction jobs fell by 17%, while nonunion employment in the industry rose by 159%. The union percentage in the construction industry fell from 38% to 16% of all building jobs since 1977.[138]

A consulting firm modeled what would happen if union membership expanded as a result of the repeal of the secret ballot. It found that for each 1% increase in the proportion of the labor force in unions, there would be a 1.5 million increase in unemployment![139]

Whether by legislative action or administrative fiat, the repeal of the secret ballot in union elections represents a threat to the norms of democracy, the rights of workers, and our economy's ability to create jobs. But President Obama is deeply beholden to labor unions for their political support, manpower, and funding. His failure to pass card check when Democrats held overwhelming power sharply disappointed his union allies. Now, through the autocratic proceedings of the NLRB, he hopes to make things right with his labor friends.

The Republican House must push for legislation barring the NLRB from abolishing the secret ballot in union elections. Such legislation would have a good chance of passing even in the Democratic Senate. Becker's confirmation as NLRB director got only 52 votes in the Senate (falling short of the 60 needed for cloture), and some of those voting yes have been replaced by Republicans who would vote against abolishing secret ballots.

Obama would veto the bill, of course, and there is no reasonable chance that we could override his veto.

So card check must also go into the debt ceiling and budget battles of 2011. Patriots must demand that the appropriations bill for the NLRB ban the use of any funds to reverse the *Dana* decision and to ratify any union election in which a secret ballot was not offered to the workers.

Adding this provision—along with that defunding ObamaCare and blocking the EPA from regulating carbon dioxide—will make the battle over the budget even more important for the preservation of our liberty.

So all three of the trifecta of highly controversial Obama policy proposals—health care, cap and trade, and card check—will end up in the debt limit and budget debates. Republican efforts to rein them in will stand or fall based on the game of chicken that will ensue as the GOP refuses to raise the debt limit or to pass a federal budget without these key defunding provisions.

That's great! The more important legislation is crammed into this debate, the better able we will be to mobilize patriots to battle against Obama's budget and program.

KILLING EARMARKS

The House and Senate Republicans have voted to eschew earmarking in this Congress. A few Republicans, like Senator James Inhofe (R-OK), have said they will continue earmarking anyway, but most senators and congressmen have foresworn the practice.

In the House, of course, with a majority, the Republicans will be able to stop any earmarks from reaching the budget. But in the Senate, they will be outvoted by the Democrats, and the odd stray Republican, and earmarks will find their way into the budget.

It is very important that the Republican House demand that the budget be totally free of earmarks and that it defeat all the Senate earmarks, whether Democrat or Republican. By holding the line, the Republican House can end this terrible practice.

Earmarks cost us $15.9 billion in 2010.[140] If we freeze discretionary nondefense spending at 2008 levels, as noted, we will save $126 billion. Stopping earmarks will put us one-eighth of the way toward our goal.

Earmarks are bad because they invite corruption. The practice of trading earmarks for campaign donations has become so widespread that it is corrupting our entire political process.

Incumbent senators and congressmen are raising large portions of their campaign war chests from lobbyists who give money in return for seeing their clients' earmarks inserted into the budget. See Part IV of this book, where we discuss the individual Democratic senators who are up for reelection in 2012, to see how pervasive the practice has become.

We must stop it here and now!

PROTECTING FREE SPEECH

It is customary for a party that has lost an election decisively to scapegoat its leaders and campaign strategists. But the Democrats, in the aftermath of their drubbing in 2010, chose to attack the free speech rights of their opponents.

As soon as the results came in, one of Obama's appointees to the Federal Communications Commission (FCC), Michael J. Copps, proposed that a "public value test" should replace the current licensing system for television and radio stations.[141]

Speaking at the Columbia School of Journalism thirty days after the election of 2010, he said that he wanted to require "a renewed commitment to serious news and journalism."[142] His kind of news.

He wraps his desire to squelch conservative radio in the language of "localism." The goal, he says "is more localism in our program diet, more local news and information, and a lot less streamed-in homogenization and monotonous nationalized music at the expense of local and regional talent." The *New York Times* reports that he "suggested that 25% of prime-time programming should be locally or independently produced."[143]

Of course, by "local" he means not national. Not Rush Limbaugh. Not Sean Hannity. Not Neal Boortz. Not Michael Savage. Not Dennis Prager. Not Mike Gallaher. Not Laura Ingraham. Not Mancow. And certainly not Glenn Beck.

Using localism, he wants to drive stations off the air if they do not comply. The *Times* reported that "Mr. Copps said the public value test should occur every four years. Currently, stations have to renew their licenses every eight years. If a station were to fail the public value test and did not improve a year later, he added, the agency should 'give the license to someone who will use it to serve the public interest.'"[144]

Every four years. Hmm. What happens every four years in the United States? Could there be a connection here?

Not content with controlling content, he also wants to restrict political advertising and called on the FCC to "determine the extent of its current authority" to compel stations to disclose the interest groups behind political ads.[145]

Copps masks his desire to interfere with free speech by complaining, "It's a pretty serious situation that we're in. We are not producing the body of news and information that democracy needs to conduct its civic dialogue, we're not producing as much news as we did five, ten, fifteen years ago and we have to reverse that trend or I think we are going to be pretty close to denying our citizens the essential news and information that they need to have in order to make intelligent decisions about the full direction of their country."[146]

Is he kidding? We now have three full-time, 24-hours-a-day cable news networks and hundreds of talk radio shows where once we had only sitcoms and top forty music! Our air waves are choked with news and information. And what about the Internet? Can Copps seriously argue that we have less access to news today when we have every piece of national or local news available with the click of a mouse?

Congressman Joe Barton (R-TX) immediately took Copps to task. "I hope," he wrote in a letter to the FCC commissioner, "that you do not mean to suggest that it is the job of the federal government, through the Federal Communications Commission, to determine the content that is available for Americans to consume.[147]

"Although your concern for providing American citizens information they need to 'make intelligent decisions about the full direction of their country' may stem from the very best of intentions, increasing the federal government's role in the composition of the information Americans have at their disposal—in an information marketplace that is bigger and more easily accessible than ever before—is unwise policy and raises serious questions of constitutionality," Barton wrote.[148]

Of course, that's just what Copps and the liberals who now rule the

FCC have in mind. In our book *Fleeced* (written in 2008), we warned that "liberals are planning a far more insidious and destructive attack on conservative talk radio—one that would go much further than the Fairness Doctrine, not just regulating the content of talk radio programming but also forcing basic changes in [station] management and ownership."[149]

Arguing that we need to increase local control, community input, and minority ownership, the FCC is planning to try to eliminate talk radio as we know it.

They also want to use the argument that we need "net neutrality" to pave the way for federal regulation of the Internet.

The *Washington Times* explains that the controversy stems from the complaints of consumer groups and Internet-based businesses like Netflix that the "big telecommunications firms have slowed or blocked access for heavy users from competitive sites to give their own movie and entertainment sites a competitive advantage."[150]

The *Times* notes that "big telecommunications firms counter that they cannot justify huge investments in Internet infrastructure if they must offer access to all comers on basically the same terms."[151]

But the debate is about more than just the terms of Internet use. It is about whether the government can control the Internet.

The *Washington Times* writes that "critics see the net neutrality push . . . as a government power grab and a threat to the major telecommunications companies such as Comcast and Verizon who are building the nation's fast-growing broadband and smart-phone networks."[152]

Incoming House Majority Leader Eric Cantor (R-VA) says that "imposing net neutrality requirements would significantly harm a key industry by shackling it with unnecessary and anti-competitive regulations at a time when we can least afford it."[153]

Congresswoman Marsha Blackburn (R-TN) wants to give Congress the sole oversight of the Internet, taking the power away from the FCC.

The House must include explicit language prohibiting the FCC from interfering in the content, management, ownership, or coverage of radio stations and in taking away its power over the Internet in the debt limit expansion and the FY2012 budget.

So that's the fight. It's not just over the budget. It's over the entire direction of our nation.

To repeat the list we gave earlier, it is about

1. Stopping tax increases
2. Rolling back government spending
3. Bringing the deficit down to 3% of the economy
4. Defunding ObamaCare
5. Blocking the EPA from imposing a carbon tax
6. Stopping the NLRB from killing the secret ballot
7. Freeing small banks to make loans again
8. Blocking the FCC from undermining free speech
9. Eliminating earmarks from the budget

If we do those nine things, we will have done a lot! We will have saved this country.

As Theodore Roosevelt said as he launched his Bull Moose Party in 1912: "We stand at Armageddon and we battle for the Lord!"[154]

Patriots, take note!

The budget battle will begin in May and June as the House begins to shape its spending plan and will really heat up as the federal fiscal year comes to a close on October 1.

But the first major clash of the 2011 legislative season will focus on the looming bankruptcies of state and local governments, and this battle will set the stage for the great confrontations later in the year.

THE COMING STATE BANKRUPTCIES

California, New York, Illinois, and New Jersey are the new Greece, Portugal, Spain, and Ireland. Their finances are so out of whack that they only stave off bankruptcy by depending on the repeated infusion of federal funds. Other states, like Michigan and Connecticut, are not far behind.

In the opening months of the legislative session, these profligate states will line up to get their annual federal subsidy. Like addicts at a methadone clinic, they will ask Washington to renew their fix—the grants they got in the stimulus package—so that they can balance their budgets, albeit precariously, on the backs of the taxpayers in other states.

These states are on the verge of bankruptcy. Their revenues are falling so far short of their spending that they are meeting their state constitutional requirement of a balanced budget only with massive and repeated infusions of federal stimulus spending. They are like patients living off blood transfusions.

In 2010, states collectively faced a budget gap of $158 billion, which forced thirty to raise taxes and forty-three to cut services. In 2011, states will face a shortfall of $180 billion.[155]

But these "gaps" are only the tip of the iceberg. The real deficits are much, much bigger, since it is only with massive federal aid—one-shot stimulus spending and regular payments—that most states are able to balance their budgets. If we only look at state and local revenue and compare it with their spending, their combined deficit runs to almost $1 trilllion:

STATE AND LOCAL GOVERNMENT DEFICIT

(in US$ billions)

Year	Revenue	Spending	Deficit
2009	$2,248	$3,016	768
2010	$2,286	$3,209	923

Source: U.S. Government[156]

It would be OK if the states had used federal stimulus money to pay for capital projects. If they had, when the funding stopped, they could have just curtailed their capital programs. Fewer new schools. Cutbacks on highway building. Reduced prison construction.

However, our state and local elected officials have not used stimulus funding primarily for capital improvement projects, but to pay recurring annual expenses. The funds have prevented layoffs of teachers and other public employees.

Of course, the federal stimulus payments are one-shot monies that must be appropriated by Congress each year. Yet states and localities have spent these funds on recurring expenses that automatically come up annually.

While the Obama stimulus has done nothing to regenerate the national economy, it has kept these states from feeling the full impact of the recession as their tax revenues plunged. Like an anesthetic, the cash gifts have cushioned the shock of the state budget deficits and have encouraged continued high and growing spending at the state, local, and school board levels. There has been no reckoning, few cuts, and continued profligacy in state capitals around the nation.

The newly elected House Republican majority is committed to refusing to extend these subsidies and bailouts. Incoming Speaker John Boehner called the 2010 subsidy to the states a "bailout to the teachers unions." He said it is some "of the most irresponsible policy that I have ever seen. The American people are screaming at the top of their lungs 'STOP' and Washington continues to spend, spend, spend." [157]

This attitude of just-say-no is vital to holding the line on tax increases and to slashing government spending. When the states come begging for bailouts, it will be the first real test of the mettle of the Republican House.

Asked if they will bail out California and New York, Congress must not just say "no," it must say "hell no!" These states made their own beds. Nobody made them outspend their revenues or forced them to give in to their unions. Other states resisted and are fiscally solvent. Why should their taxpayers bail out those who were less prudent?

And when the Republican House says "no," it will send tremors through the vast market in municipal and state bonds. This debt, usually backed by the full faith and credit of state governments, has always been seen as secure. But when the Republican Congress refuses to renew the stimulus subsidies, it will be anything but.

There are $2.8 trillion of state, local, county, authority, and municipal bonds outstanding, $470 billion of them issued in 2009. Not only has the amount of debt proliferated, but the number of bond issuers has soared. Now 51,000 public and quasipublic entities issue these bonds. [158]

Strains are already appearing in the municipal and state bond market. In 2009, there were 194 defaults totalling $7 billion. [159] Aware of the danger of default, bond insurers have been raising their premiums on particularly endangered states.

Nationally, since the end of 2009, the cost of insuring state debt for the United States as a whole has risen by only 1%, since most states are not at risk. But the costs for certain states have skyrocketed, reflecting their tenuous financial situation.

INCREASE IN THE COST OF INSURING AGAINST STATE DEFAULT

(price reflects the cost to insure $10,000 of debt for 5 years)

State	% Increase from 12/31/09 to 7/1/10
U.S. Average	1%
Illinois	117%
New York	87%
New Jersey	87%
California	35%

Source: Bloomberg Financial Data[160]

These four states are all judged riskier by the credit markets than either Spain or Ireland, two of the five nations caught in the crosshairs of the European debt crisis. (The others are Greece, Portugal, and Italy.)

Conditions in the state and municipal bond market have steadily deteriorated over the past year, and a crisis is in the offing. On November 18, 2010, state and local governments withdrew $700 million in bonds they had put up for sale because of weak market demand. California postponed a $267.3 million bond offering "in light of market conditions."[161]

"The tax-exempt municipal bond market is a cold, cold world right now for issuers and taxpayers," said Tom Dresslar, a spokesman for the California state treasurer.[162]

After seven months of increasing purchases of municipal bonds, sales dropped by $115 million the week of November 8, 2010—days after the election of a Republican House of Representatives.[163]

The elections likely caused this new trend because it is only one-shot federal stimulus payments that are holding these local and state governments up, and investors fear the Republicans won't continue the subsidies. On average, these grants are now funding 9.4% of state budgets.[164]

When New York and California and some other liberal big-spending states come calling for more aid, the Republican House must hold the line, stopping this raid on the federal Treasury. The cry in the Republican caucus of the House of Representatives must ring loud: "No More Bailouts!"

The spendthrift states will threaten massive closures and predict dire consequences if their path to the Treasury is barred. They will say they will have to close schools and open the prisons! Republicans will be under incredible pressure to cave in. Bondholders will panic and demand federal action.

If Republicans cave in during this first battle, they are doomed. The country will see them as frauds and their own constituents will be revolted. Tea Party–sponsored primaries will not be far behind.

But if they hold their ranks solidly and don't panic in the face of threats of closure of public services in the bankrupt states, they will prevail.

The fact that many of the governors of the more fiscally solvent states will be Republican will help the party hold the line on the demands for state bailouts. These governors will be wrestling with their budget crises and will be largely succeeding without the need for massive federal aid.

Consider the experience of the two Republican governors elected in 2009: Virginia's Bob McDonnell and New Jersey's Chris Christie.

In Virginia, under McDonnell's prodding, the General Assembly slashed state spending to 2006 levels. Delegate Lacey E. Putney, the chairman of the Virginia House Appropriations Committee, said, "In my 49 years in [the House], I've never seen a budget situation like this one this year." [165]

But McDonnell managed to balance the state budget with no new taxes and only about $100 million in new fees, forcing city and county governments to match the state cuts by curbing local spending. The budget cut $250 million from public education, while Medicaid reimbursements were cut by 7%. State workers got no pay raise.[166]

In New Jersey, Governor Chris Christie had to work with a Democratic state legislature but, nevertheless, got through a balanced budget that cut spending by 9% below the previous year. When Democrats passed a one-year surcharge tax on millionaires, Christie vetoed it and the veto stuck. In all, the Democrats were able to restore only $74 million of the $400 million in cuts Christie had wanted.[167]

But, in saying no to state demands for bailouts, the Republican House must give states the same option that private businesses have—go bankrupt and abrogate your union contracts.

It's not as if we don't know what is causing these potential state bankruptcies. There's no mystery. They are due to decades of concessions to public employee unions who multiply their demands for pay raises, benefit increases, and more liberal pension benefits every year.

While only 7% of the national labor force is unionized, 43% of all state, school, and local employees belong to unions.[168] Their wage demands, pension requirements, and work rules are driving their governments over the financial cliff. Many states—notably California, Michigan, and New York—are straining to meet their contracts by raising taxes and driving their economies further down. The familiar death spiral has set in, with ever larger deficits, bigger tax hikes, and slowed economies, which, in turn, lead to even larger deficits.

Like cancer cells multiplying at the expense of their host's health, these union contracts have grown so hefty that they are killing the states that have signed them. Just as the cancer will ultimately strangle the healthy cells, these contracts will doom their governments unless they are stopped.

Already, rabid union demands have led to the death of many American businesses. Unable to meet the stress of foreign competition, the companies have moved offshore, gone bankrupt, or dropped product lines. The cancer kills its host and seals its own fate; the unions that represent these workforces begin the hemorrhaging of jobs. In industry after industry, the unionized workforce has fallen because the union demands have doomed their companies.

But public sector unions, bolstered by their political clout in state and local governments, have avoided this fate. Armed with the power to coerce those who have the power to tax, they have thrived.

In effect, when New York, Illinois, and California come calling for subsidy, the Republican House should say: "No, we won't give you money. But we will give you the way to get yourself out of your financial hole by permitting you to reorganize like any private company can and to free yourself of your union contracts."

If the governors and state legislatures of those states refuse, it's up to them—they can always raise taxes or cut services to make ends meet. That is their option. But if they choose not to do so, the Republicans in the House give them a way out: reorganize in bankruptcy.

Obviously, faced with this choice, the voters of these states will rise and demand that their governments avail themselves of the bankruptcy option. Knowing this likely reaction, Obama will veto the new bankruptcy law and a confrontation will ensue.

The political control exerted by unions such as the National Education Association (NEA), the American Federation of Teachers (AFT), the Service Employees International Union (SEIU), and the American Federation of State, County and Municipal Employees (AFSCME) is so formidable that no local government can stand up to it. When wage demands soar at contract time (even in the face of low or no inflation), state and local governments inevitably cave in. But, even worse, they try to hold wage increases down by expanding pension benefits and agreeing to work rules that make government productivity impossible.

Our entire federal system has been so corrupted by public employee unions that we no longer control our own state and local governments, but find them under the thumb of their unions. No longer do we run schools for the benefit of students. They are operated for the welfare of their teachers. Work rules, pay raises, and union contracts have turned the world upside down. It is now the providers of public services that are themselves served and the public has little control over how its tax money is spent.

PUBLIC EMPLOYEE UNIONS' POLITICAL CLOUT

Union	Membership	Political Spending
NEA	3.2 million	$50 million
AFT	888,000	$19 million
AFSCME	1.5 million	$48 million
SEIU	1.9 million	$58 million

With public employee unions spending almost $200 million each year to influence political decisions, what kind of chance do elected officials have of resisting their demands? The drama has played out in town halls, city halls, state houses, and state legislatures all over America, and the union always wins.

But just as union demands have led to bankruptcies in the private sector, driving jobs overseas, promoting outsourcing, and leading American business to fail in the face of foreign competition, so the moment of truth has come to the public sector.

If Republicans say no to the incessant demands, pleas, and threats from state and local governments and refuse to renew the federal subsidies, these unions and their states will be brought face-to-face—finally—with the consequences of their demands.

Defeating the unions by refusing to bail out the states is also a political necessity in the larger political battle. It is the power of these unions that is bolstering the political fortunes of the Democratic Party.

The elections of 2010 demonstrated their power. In state after state, the vote totals of Democratic candidates, particularly those running for Senate, exceeded the predictions of all pollsters. This gap between preelection anticipation and Election Day results had one main cause: the militancy, money, and manpower of public employee unions. It was the combined efforts of the SEIU, the NEA, the AFT, and AFSCME that preserved the Democratic control of the U.S. Senate.

Nate Silver, writing in the *New York Times*, compared the results of the major public opinion polls for the twenty-one days before the election with the actual results. He found that seven of the eight major polling firms overestimated the Republican vote, some by as much as an average of four points. Silver wrote to criticize the accuracy of these firms and their surveys and, perhaps, to impute a partisan bias to their findings. But it is far more likely that the polls were right and that the Election Day performance of the Democratic Party's ground game overcame even substantial Republican leads in states like Nevada.

Here are Silver's findings.

SIMPLE POLLING ACCURACY ANALYSIS

Senate and Gubernatorial Polls in Final 21 Days of Campaign

Firm	Polls	Average Error	Bias
Quinnipiac	21	3.3	R+0.7
SurveyUSA	30	3.5	R+0.8
YouGov	35	3.5	R+1.1
Public Policy Polling	45	3.8	R+0.3
Mason-Dixon	20	4.6	D+0.4
Marist	14	4.9	R+4.0
CNN/Opinion Research	17	4.9	R+2.1
Rasmussen Reports*	105	5.8	R+3.9

*Includes polls for FoxNews under Pulse Opinion Research brand

Were all these polls wrong? No way. They were right. But they did not take account of the potency of Democratic unions' Election Day efforts to get out their vote.

Almost every poll, for example, had Sharron Angle defeating Harry Reid, usually by three or four points. Her five-point defeat on Election Day can only be attributed to the union-based Democratic effort.

The fiscal crises facing state and local governments and school boards make these unions and their political clout vulnerable, potentially at the mercy of a Republican-controlled House of Representatives. We may, at long last, have a way to liberate our nation from the domination of those who should be our public servants, but instead are frequently our union masters and to free our politics from their financial power.

The House should create a federal bankruptcy procedure for states and require that state governments who are broke abrogate all their union contracts. The new state bankruptcy procedure should offer all states—and through them, their localities, counties, and school boards—the ability to reorganize their finances free of the demands and constraints of their union agreements.

Instead of offering cash or federal guarantees of their debt, offer states the ability to reform themselves by letting them get out of their straitjacket union agreements. The political dynamic in most of these liberal states is such that the voters and their children are the hostages of public employee unions whose voting strength, ability to strike and cripple essential services, and massive cash donations to political campaigns make them invulnerable. The only way to tame the unions and reduce their power is for the House to pass bankruptcy law changes that allow states to escape from their grip.

Then the inevitable shortfall of state revenues will force the issue.

This measure will return our state and local governments to the sovereignty of the people and take them away from the thugocracy of public employee unions.

In doing so, the House will be asking states and their localities to do what private sector corporations like airlines and steel companies did when they went belly-up. They had to sweep aside their union contracts and reorganize themselves into financially viable and going concerns.

Sometimes, the vote of the unions themselves will be legally required in the contract renunciation process. Then, the unions will be face-to-face with a clear choice: no contract or no jobs.

What about Obama's veto—or the Senate's possible refusal to pass—these bankruptcy law changes? Fine. The House should sit back and declare its job done and leave the states to deal with their own financial problems.

When states like California and New York come to Washington begging for relief, they will threaten us with the closure of their schools and the release of their prison inmates if we deny them subsidy. Liberals and President Obama will try to portray the battle as schoolchildren versus niggardly Republican legislators.

But the real fight will be between schoolchildren and citizens on the one hand and unions on the other. The House must shape the issue so that it exposes the real cause of the state shortfalls: the excessive agreements public employee unions have won over the years.

Obama will not be able to stand in the way of reform of the union contracts, nor will state governors be able to dissuade their people from making the needed reforms.

It will be just a matter of time until the House and the Republicans will force Obama and the Senate to give way and pass their bankruptcy law changes.

The unions are about to fall prey to what Margaret Thatcher identified as the terminal drawback of socialism—that eventually one runs out of other people's money! [169]

And how will Republican congressmen, senators, state legislators, and governors from the bankrupt states justify to their electorates such a tough position? Won't their voters hold it against them that they want to turn off the spigot of federal funding? They will succeed because their own voters know how culpable the unions are in their state's financial mess.

The public will side with the Republicans and the House. We are totally fed up with public employee unions and clearly recognize their power and their negative influence over state and local governing bodies.

In California, for example, a Rasmussen Reports poll found that 52% of likely voters agree that "public employee unions place a significant strain" on the state's budget, while only 24% disagree. By 53–43, they oppose unions even existing for public employees! [170] And California is a very blue state!

In 1975, President Gerald Ford came under similar pressure to expand federal aid to New York City, then facing bankruptcy. He refused, leading the New York *Daily News* to run a famous front page headline: "Ford To New York: Drop Dead." [171] The resulting outcry may have cost him New York State in the presidential election.

Not anymore. Now a Congressional decision to demand reform rather than granting a bailout would be greeted with rave reviews by the affected states. Their voters realize—as we all do—that their state legislatures are out of control and that their money is being wasted by greedy public employee unions.

Inevitably, any discussion of state finances will focus on the two key areas that, together, account for the bulk of state spending: education (35%) and Medicaid (17%). [172]

REFORMING PUBLIC EDUCATION AND MEDICAID

Teachers' unions have been especially successful in forcing contracts on their states, localities, and school boards that provide for ever higher wages, benefits, and pensions. Even as the November 2010 election results were being counted, teachers in a Pittsburgh suburb went on strike, claiming that their 4.5% annual wage increase is inadequate!

New teachers and good teachers are not represented by the teachers' unions. In resisting demands for merit pay and offers of truly high salaries in return for demonstrated competence, the unions have shown that their focus is on their oldest and least able teachers.

And why should it not be? Young teachers come and go. One-third of all new teachers quit after two years. One-half leave after five.[173] The stultification of the system, its bureaucracy, and its union-driven refusal to reward ability, dedication, application, and merit drive them away.

In New York State, the union went so far as to get the state legislature to pass a law actually prohibiting the use of student test scores in determining teacher pay. The law, in effect, made it illegal to consider the success or failure of the teacher in deciding how much to pay him or her!

As a result of the union power over education in New York City, it is virtually impossible to fire a teacher for cause. In the past decade, the former schools chancellor Joel Klein has been able to dismiss only two—yes, two—of his 80,000 teachers for cause.[174]

John Stossel, then of ABC News, reported that "it took years to fire a teacher [in New York City] who sent sexually oriented e-mails to 'Cutie 101,' a sixteen year old student." Klein said that, while the teacher was suspended during the proceedings, "we have had to pay him anyway because that's what's required under the [union] contract."[175]

After six years of litigation, the teacher was finally fired but only after he drew $300,000 in compensation while the proceedings unfolded.[176]

Every day, Klein herds principals, assistant principals, and hundreds of teachers into so-called "rubber rooms" where they sit all day, drawing full pay, doing nothing. It costs over $20 million a year.[177] Why? Because the chancellor, in his wisdom, has determined that they are too incompetent, abusive, or insane to risk exposing them to students. But they cannot be fired.

The *New York Post* recently revealed that a "veteran school custodian" in New York City was paid more than $170,000 a year. "Several workers also accuse the Roosevelt HS campus custodian Trifon Radef . . . of splitting school funds with pals for whom he created no-show gigs." Apparently, Radef, who owns ten homes in Queens, New York, also used school employees to fix up his properties. "He renovated all these houses—walls, ceilings, new bathrooms and kitchens—and all the people who did the work are getting paid by the school," a former worker told the *Post*.[178]

The investigation is ongoing, and no charges have been made.

Frequently, the teachers' union squanders public resources on noneducation spending. In Michigan, for example, the union runs its own health insurance company, MESSA, which has a virtual monopoly on providing health coverage for teachers in most of the state's school districts, according to Kyle Olson of the Education Action Group (educationactiongroup .org). The coverage typically costs 20% more than an equivalent private or Blue Cross policy would, and the union pockets the difference to maintain its power. The members don't care. The taxpayers foot the bill.

In 2007, the *Kalamazoo Gazette* reported a school district switched away from MESSA, saved over $200 per student, and the only loss of coverage was for "massages, sex change operations and a treatment for Christian Science practitioners." More recently, the Saugatuck district opted for a MESSA competitor, giving employees similar coverage but saving $3,800 per teacher per year![179]

Governors and localities will also find themselves turning more to contractors instead of unionized employees to perform custodial and transportation services for students. School districts have saved a mint and have found service to be better with private companies, according to Education Action Group. The Grand Rapids district (the third largest in Michigan) hired a private transportation company to bus its students. Over a five-year period, the company saved the district over $18 million.[180] Elsewhere, the Clarenceville district outsourced ten custodial positions, saving $1.2 million over three years.[181]

It is to prevent abuses like these that the House of Representatives must step in and demand reform.

The ultimate solution to the defects in our education system is school choice. We must act to break the monopoly of unionized public schools and enable children of the middle class to do what kids of the wealthy can already do—go to private schools.

We need to expand the number of charter schools dramatically and to create statewide voucher and scholarship systems to let parents choose to send their children to private, charter, or church schools—or to home-school them. And when they do so, the state subsidy—usually about $7,500 per child—needs to follow the boy or girl to the new school.

It is not that these schools are always better than public schools. But parents deserve the right to make the choice and to know that we can close bad charter schools and replace them with good ones, They need not resign themselves to being stuck with bad public schools and their teachers forever.

Many Republican governors and state legislatures will move to programs to encourage school choice, permitting parents to opt for charter schools, private or church schools, or homeschooling instead of high-cost public schools.

Until now, efforts to extend school choice options have been crippled by the political opposition of teachers' unions. But with the states facing draconian budget shortfalls, reforms that have not been adopted in the name of improving education might now see the light of day as part of efforts to trim education spending.

The fact is that private and church schools cost dramatically less than public schools. The Cato Institute researched costs at five municipalities and compared the cost of public and private education.

COST PER PUPIL OF PUBLIC AND PRIVATE SCHOOLS

City	Public	Private
Washington, D.C.	$17,543	$11,032
Los Angeles	10,053	8,378
New York City	17,696	10,586
Chicago	11,536	8,849
Phoenix	9,300	6,770

Source: Cato Institute[182]

With average per pupil spending, nationally, at just over $10,500,[183] the lower average cost of charter schools, only $8,000,[184] gives governors a very attractive alternative.

Of course, higher spending does nothing to guarantee better education. Hobbled by its teachers' unions, New York State spends $17,696 per pupil but has one of the lowest graduation rates in the nation—only 70.8%. And the District of Columbia spends $17,543, but only 56% of its students graduate.[185]

Voucher programs and scholarships that allow students to go to private or church schools at public expense are only just beginning to grow in the United States. Only a handful of students are in such programs while only 1.7 million children go to charter schools.

(Charters are public schools not run by the state or local government, but by the local business, church group, parent association, or even union that set them up. Its teachers are not usually covered by union contracts and, as a result, their administrations are much freer to experiment with merit pay for teachers and innovative methods of instruction.)

CHARTER SCHOOL ENROLLMENT BY STATE

State	Number of Students	State	Number of Students
Alaska	5,300	Idaho	13,812
Arkansas	5,237	Illinois	36,750
Arizona	95,853	Indiana	19,253
California	313,245	Kansas	4,902
Connecticut	4,898	Louisiana	30,405
Washington, D.C.	27,595	Massachusetts	28,247
Delaware	9,141	Maryland	12,249
Florida	128,359	Michigan	104,527
Georgia	62,167	Minnesota	36,404
Hawaii	7,741	Missouri	19,783
Iowa	928	North Carolina	39,033

State	Number of Students	State	Number of Students
New Hampshire	662	Pennsylvania	78,437
New Jersey	22,206	Rhode Island	3,423
New Mexico	13,293	South Carolina	11,142
Nevada	11,827	Tennessee	4,963
New York	42,204	Utah	32,253
Ohio	96,967	Virginia	250
Oklahoma	5,984	Wisconsin	38,005
Oregon	16,725	Wyoming	353 [186]

Several jurisdictions have already enacted full school choice programs that permit students to attend private, charter, or church schools and provide that the funding will follow the children.

Under a program designed by Indiana's Republican governor Mitch Daniels, for example, the state share of school spending would follow the student to the new schools.

School Choice Programs [187]

- Milwaukee: more than 20,000 children participate in this school choice program and each receives a grant of $6,500 for tuition.

- Louisiana: serves 1,250 students in grades K–4 transferred from failing schools. Scholarships average $4,000.

- Cleveland: 6,272 students attend 36 private schools funded by average scholarships of $2,782.

- Ohio: provides 14,000 scholarships of about $5,000 for students in academically failing public schools to go to private institutions.

- Washington, D.C.: 1,700 students get scholarships of up to $7,500.

What governor in his right mind, confronting a budget crisis of the present magnitude, would not opt for replacing public schools with vouchers to private schools to realize these cost savings?

Answer: a committed Democrat.

But with the Republicans taking over eleven governorships and twenty-one state legislative chambers in the 2010 election, GOP states will be flocking to realize these savings.

And those Democratic governors who don't get the message and ask instead for federal bailouts to subsidize their big-spending ways will face irate voters who demand that they cut their costs instead. Both governors, McDonnell in Virginia and Christie in New Jersey, have shown us that it is possible!

For state and local governments, it is not only the cost of education that is driving them over the brink, but the cost of ObamaCare and its plans to expand Medicaid, adding 16 million new patients.[188]

Washington will pick up the full tab in the first two years and 95% of the cost until 2019.[189] But, there are an additional 10 to 13 million people now eligible for Medicaid, but not currently enrolled. As Obama's IRS hounds people to get them to take out insurance, likely a large number of these recalcitrants will sign up. And the federal reimbursement for these new participants will not rise above the 50% to 75% level now in effect. The states will have to pick up the balance.

In Texas, for example, the state Department of Health and Human Services predicts that 800,000 people who are now eligible for Medicaid but haven't enrolled will now join the program.[190] The Texas state government will have to pay 40% of their tab. The total additional cost Texas taxpayers will have to bear will come to $2.4 billion by 2023, raising serious questions about whether or not the state can continue to avoid imposing an income tax.

When you look at the costs of covering those currently eligible for Medicaid who have not enrolled, the fiscal consequences for states will be horrific:

INCREASES IN STATE MEDICAID SPENDING DUE TO OBAMACARE

Florida	$1,200 million (by 2019)
Texas	$2,400 million (by 2023)
California	$2,000 million (by 2020)
Maryland	$829 million (by 2020)
Michigan	$200 million (by 2019)

Source: Congressional Research Service[191]

Between the huge increases in the cost of education mandated by public employee unions and their enormous contracts and the rising cost of Medicaid brought on by Obama's health care changes, states will be in increasingly desperate straits as the decade unfolds.

These states can survive only by reining in the unions.

These battles for our nation's soul make us realize how far we have to go before the threat of Obamaism is lifted from our country. The ultimate answer is to defeat Barack Obama and retake the United States Senate while increasing our margin in the House.

PART FOUR

DEMOCRATS WE MUST DEFEAT

The defeats of 2010 ring like warning bells in the ears of those Democratic senators who are up in 2012. And the narrow escapes from defeat of dozens of other Democratic congressmen who were reelected by hair-thin margins have left them all with cases of PTSD (post-traumatic stress disorder).

Worse for them, they are now outvoted by their radical, leftist colleagues in the Democratic caucuses of the House and the Senate. The Democratic voices of moderation—who generally came from marginal districts—have largely been defeated. A Democratic senator or congressman who is vulnerable in 2012 now finds himself bound by the decisions of a bunch of ultraliberals who, from the comfort of their safe districts, don't mind embracing radical policies that make it even harder for the moderates to get reelected. Indeed, the only way these folks are ever going to lose is if they succumb to liberal primary challenges in the hard-core Democratic districts. This prospect further impels them to move to the left. Not that they need much encouragement!

The opposite is, of course, also true. Republicans now have power in the House. If they cave in or indulge themselves with ethical misbehavior or earmarks or the like, they will lose popular backing and their mandate will be gone.

And, if they disappoint us, many of these Republican congressmen might be gone, defeated in primaries in 2012 by Tea Party–backed true believers. Those who would cave in or compromise prematurely need to be careful lest they throw away the support of their conservative base and endanger their own seats in Congress.

The eyes of the nation are on the Republican House: they had better deliver!

It took the Democrats two cycles—2006 and 2008—to complete their takeover of our government. Republicans made giant strides in 2010, but still need to score impressive gains in 2012 to complete the job.

It will take the same kind of resolve, dedication, unity, and persever-ance that animated our efforts this past year. We dare not let up. The con-sequences of the Democratic revival of 2006–2008 are all too close at hand for us to forget!

DEMOCRATS INVOLUNTARILY RETIRED: A PROGRESS REPORT

In our book *2010: Take Back America—A Battle Plan*, we identified key Democrats, particularly in the House, at whom we urged Republicans to aim in the coming elections. We all did pretty well. In the House, sixty-three seats changed parties!

2010 HOUSE DEMOCRATIC SEATS THAT SWITCHED TO REPUBLICAN

District	Incumbent Democrat	Ran for Reelection	Republican Winner
AL-2	Bright	Yes	Roby*
AR-1	Berry	No**	Crawford
AR-2	Snyder	No	Griffin*
AZ-1	Kirkpatrick	Yes	Gosar*
AZ-5	Mitchell	Yes	Schweikert*
CO-3	Salazar	Yes	Tipton*
CO-4	Markey	Yes	Gardner*
FL-2	Boyd	Yes	Southerland*
FL-22	Klein	Yes	West*
FL-24	Kosmas	Yes	Adams*
FL-8	Grayson	Yes	Webster*
GA-8	Marshall	Yes	Scott*

ID-1	Minnick	Yes	Labrador*
IL-8	Bean	Yes	Walsh
IL-11	Halvorson	Yes	Kinzinger*
IL-14	Foster	Yes	Hultgren*
IL-17	Hare	Yes	Schilling
IN-8	Ellsworth	No	Bucshon*
IN-9	Hill	Yes	Young*
KS-3	Moore	No	Yoder*
LA-3	Melancon	No	Landry*
MD-1	Kratovil	Yes	Harris*
MI-1	Stupak	No	Benishek*
MI-7	Schauer	Yes	Walberg*
MN-8	Oberstar	Yes	Cravaack
MO-4	Skelton	Yes	Hartzler
MS-1	Childers	Yes	Nunnelee*
MS-4	Taylor	Yes	Palazzo*
NC-2	Etheridge	Yes	Ellmers
ND-AL	Pomeroy	Yes	Berg*
NH-1	Shea-Porter	Yes	Guinta*
NH-2	Hodes	No	Bass*
NJ-3	Adler	Yes	Runyan*
NM-2	Teague	Yes	Pearce*
NV-3	Titus	Yes	Heck*
NY-13	McMahon	Yes	Grimm*
NY-19	Hall	Yes	Hayworth*
NY-20	Murphy	Yes	Gibson*
NY-24	Arcuri	Yes	Hanna*
NY-25	Maffei	Yes	Buerkle*
OH-1	Driehaus	Yes	Chabot*

OH-15	Kilroy	Yes	Stivers*
OH-16	Boccieri	Yes	Renacci*
OH-18	Space	Yes	Gibbs*
OH-6	Wilson	Yes	Johnson
PA-10	Carney	Yes	Marino*
PA-11	Kanjorski	Yes	Barletta*
PA-3	Dahlkemper	Yes	Kelly*
PA-7	Sestak	No	Meehan*
PA-8	Murphy	Yes	Fitzpatrick*
SC-5	Spratt	Yes	Mulvaney*
SD-AL	Herseth-Sandlin	Yes	Noem*
TN-4	Davis	Yes	DesJarlais*
TN-6	Gordon	No	Black*
TN-8	Tanner	No	Fincher*
TX-17	Edwards	Yes	Flores*
TX-23	Rodriguez	Yes	Canseco*
TX-27	Ortiz	Yes	Farenthold
VA-2	Nye	Yes	Rigell*
VA-5	Perriello	Yes	Hurt*
VA-9	Boucher	Yes	Griffith*
WA-3	Baird	No	Herrera*
WI-7	Obey	No	Duffy*
WI-8	Kagan	Yes	Ribble*
WV-1	Mollohan	No**	McKinley*

Seat Switch Totals: 68

Democrats: 65

Republicans: 3[1]

*Identified as key races in our last book, *2010: Take Back America—A Battle Plan*
**Lost primary

We should take particular pride in the defeat of Alan Grayson in Florida. This former trial lawyer, the sixth richest member of Congress, achieved notoriety for taking a tape of his opponent, Dan Webster, and editing it so as to twist its context around to mean the exact opposite of what Webster said. He deserved to lose.

The gains of 2010 were huge. There are now fewer Democrats in the House of Representatives than at any time since 1938!

The outcome of the fight for the Senate was less gratifying. While Republicans picked up six seats—seven if you count Scott Brown—we narrowly lost in Washington State and got badly beaten in Nevada, California, Delaware, and West Virginia. And Harry Reid is back!

We have to finish the job in 2012. But we need to learn the lessons of 2010 and work harder in the key states. We need to identify key races earlier and take careful aim for the next two years!

THE SENATE

In 2010, we had to fight for Senate seats in the bluest of blue states like California, West Virginia, Nevada, and Washington State. Republicans did manage takeaways in the usually Democratic states of Pennsylvania, Wisconsin, and Illinois, but it was never easy to turn a blue state red.

The good news is that many of the Democratic senators who are coming up for reelection in 2012 are from states that are far more friendly to Republicans.

In 2010, nineteen Democratic and eighteen Republican Senate seats were up for grabs—a ratio that favored the Democrats. That Republicans held all their own and picked up six Democratic seats (a third of those up) is quite remarkable.

But in 2012, twenty-three Democratic and ten Republican seats are up, with many more vulnerable Democrats than in 2010. (Counted among the Democratic seats are those of Bernie Sanders of Vermont and the just-retired Joe Lieberman of Connecticut, both nominally Independents, who caucus with the Democrats.)

The 2012 class includes a number of freshman senators, elected in the Democratic sweep that gave them control of the Senate in 2006. These new members of the upper chamber are entering their most vulnerable race—

the first one after getting elected. And they will need to swim upstream against a Republican trend.

One of the Democratic senators—Kent Conrad of North Dakota—has followed the example of his buddy Byron Dorgan, who retired in 2010 rather than be beaten. Conrad took himself out of the race for re-election in 2012. In a solidly red state, this seat should go Republican.

Three other Democratic senators, from decidedly red states, will have tough fights:

Ben Nelson, Nebraska—He sold out his constituents by voting for ObamaCare after his state overwhelmingly begged him not to. Now he is among the walking dead. See Blanche Lincoln, who suffered a massive defeat for a similar offense, for details.

Jon Tester, Montana—A freshman elected with only 49.2% of the vote in 2006, he will be in for a tough battle. Montana is a solidly red state that should kick out Tester in 2012. Can his Montana colleague Max Baucus—the father of ObamaCare—be next in 2014??

Jim Webb, Virginia—Another freshman, Webb will be fighting a strong Republican trend in Virginia. The party took over the governor's office in 2009 and three House seats 2010. Webb is an endangered species in 2012.

Then there are seven Democratic senators—including three freshmen—who come from swing states that Republicans carried in 2010:

Sherrod Brown, Ohio—A freshman who first won his seat in 2006, Brown is now running in a state that is becoming redder by the minute. Republicans won the governorship, the other Senate seat, and picked up five new Congressional seats here. Brown is in great danger.

Robert Casey, Pennsylvania—Another freshman from the class of 2006, Casey will have a tough reelection battle. In Pennsylvania, the GOP won the races for governor, senator, both chambers of the state legislature, and took over five new House seats. Casey parades as a conservative because he is pro-life but he has always done what Harry Reid told him to do. His vote for ObamaCare should hurt him badly. His political life expectancy is limited.

Claire McCaskill, Missouri—Another endangered 2006 freshman, McCaskill has to run in a state that went Republican in the Senate race of 2010 by a wide margin. Republican Roy Blunt's Senate win and the defeat of longtime Democratic congressman Ike Skelton do not augur well for her. She is ripe for defeat in 2012.

Herb Kohl, Wisconsin—Wisconsin flipped and became Republican this year. Johnson beat Feingold for the Senate. Walker, a Republican, replaced Doyle, a Democrat, as governor and the GOP picked up two House seats and majorities in the state legislature. Kohl should go back to his department stores.

Jeff Bingaman, New Mexico—Republicans won the governorship and a key House seat here. Bingaman is way too liberal for the state.

Bill Nelson, Florida—Rubio took the Senate seat and five House seats flipped to Republican. The GOP also won the governorship. Can Nelson survive? Probably not.

Debbie Stabenow, Michigan—With the Republicans winning the governorship, both houses of the legislature, and a new House seat here, Michigan might be a takeaway in 2012.

And there are two more Democrats—both freshmen—who could face tough fights in 2012:

Robert Menendez, New Jersey—After Chris Christie's win in 2009 as governor and the defeat of New Jersey Democrat Congressman Adler, Menendez has to be sweating.

Joe Manchin, West Virginia—Just elected in 2010, he will have to run again in 2012 (because he is filling out the term of Robert Byrd, who died in 2010). Manchin ran as something he is not—a Republican. He attacked ObamaCare and cap and trade and boasted of his independence. Now he will have a hard time keeping his promise to oppose Obama. With only a three-vote majority, the Democrats will need him repeatedly to back Obama's programs, votes that could haunt him in West Virginia. With only a 53–47 Senate majority, there is no place for Joe to hide.

Meanwhile, among the ten Republicans up for reelection, most are running in red states. Only Scott Brown of Massachusetts, John Ensign of Nevada, and Olympia Snowe of Maine would seem to be in any jeopardy. Republicans will probably hold the seat now held by Kay Bailey Hutchison of Texas, who has announced that she won't run again. But let's be sure the seat is filled by a true conservative.

But that doesn't mean that conservatives should not try to defeat a RINO (Republican In Name Only) or two! Snowe, Bob Corker of Tennessee, and Richard Lugar of Indiana would be good options. Lugar and Corker toe the liberal line on foreign policy (both backed the START Treaty) and Snowe is the original RINO.

Otherwise, good solid conservatives like Jon Kyle of Arizona, Roger Wicker of Mississippi, Orrin Hatch of Utah, and John Barrasso of Wyoming should have an easy time getting reelected (although Hatch might not run).

Pretty good odds for Republicans, wouldn't you say?

But the Democratic incumbents who are nervous about getting reelected are going to try to fool us with their votes in 2011–12. In 2009–10, we saw their true liberal colors. Senate Majority Leader Harry Reid and President Obama needed every last Democratic senator to toe the line to pass his stimulus spending, and health care changes. And they got them all. Every one of them. They all lined up and voted yes.

In the House, Speaker Nancy Pelosi had a little more leeway and she gave various so-called conservative Democrats a pass to vote no on controversial bills in an effort to fool their constituents into reelecting them. Had she needed their votes, though, she would doubtless have gotten them just like Harry Reid did in the Senate.

But now the political math gives the Democrats an opportunity for chicanery. The senators who are up for reelection in 2012 (and some of the congressmen) may vote with the Republicans on key measures. The likes of Ben Nelson and others may well vote to repeal ObamaCare and against tax increases. And Reid may encourage them to do so in order to get them reelected so he can keep the majority.

After all, even if the Senate passes the conservative legislation sent over by the Republican House, President Obama can veto the bills and the Republicans could not come close to overriding his vetoes. So some of these vulnerable senators will let Obama take the rap with his veto rather than shield him by killing conservative bills in the Senate. Why should they stick their necks out to protect Obama?

Senators Joe Manchin (WV), Ben Nelson (NE), and Jim Webb (VA) followed this reasoning and voted to extend the Bush tax cuts in the lame duck session, joining with the Republicans.

But don't be fooled. If their votes were needed, they would be delivered by the liberals just as they were in 2009 and 2010. Once a liberal Democrat, always a liberal Democrat.

Now let's explore the vulnerable Democrats. It will be fun!

The Most Vulnerable Three

Ben Nelson

Nebraska

Elected 2000

Voted with the Democrats 81% of the time[2]

Appropriations Committee

Armed Services Committee

Agriculture Committee

It's been a long wait since Senator Ben Nelson earned his place in Dante's *Inferno* by voting to pass ObamaCare in the Senate, even though 64% of the voters in his home state of Nebraska are opposed.[3]

In 2010, his fellow turncoat, Blanche Lincoln of Arkansas, paid for her vote with her seat in the Senate, losing to Republican Congressman John Boozman by twenty-one points. Now it's Ben Nelson's turn.

Nelson is one of those senators who masquerades as a conservative Democrat, but when the chips are down, votes as the party leaders tell him to. The stimulus spending package? He wanted it slightly smaller and then he voted for it. ObamaCare? He wanted Nebraska taxpayers to be relieved of paying for Medicaid expansion in their state (the so-called Cornhuskers Kickback) and then he voted for the bill.

Eventually, the stink raised over the deal rose to such heights that Nelson had to surrender and give it up. Now Nebraskans will get soaked for Medicaid increases along with the rest of us (unless we can defund Obama-Care!).

Nelson likely buried his reputation for fiscal conservatism for good when he voted for Obama's stimulus package. He even claimed credit for holding the total price tag under $1 trillion!

Today, Nelson still defends his vote, even after the evidence is tumbling in that the stimulus did not stimulate any growth in the economy, just in the national debt. He points to the tax cuts that constituted one-third of the stimulus, ignoring the two-thirds used to increase government spending. He also neglects to add that the one-shot tax cuts did no good.[4]

Nelson's game—of voting as his party leaders tell him to, but then making a show of holding out for slight moderation in the final bill—is definitely wearing thin. If the party leaders wanted to burn down Washington, he'd probably stipulate that he'd only support it if it were phased in over five years! And then he'd vote yes!

Nebraska voters are catching on to Nelson. Politico.com recounts how "Nelson and his wife were leaving dinner at a new pizza joint near their home in Omaha one night last week when a patron began complaining about Nelson's decisive vote in favor of the Senate's health care bill. Other customers started booing. A woman yelled, 'Get him the hell out of here!' And the Nelsons and their dining companions beat a hasty retreat. 'It was definitely a scene in there,' said Tom Lewis, a 41-year-old dentist and registered Republican who witnessed the incident. A second witness confirmed the incident to *Politico*."[5]

Nelson still doesn't get it. He won't vote to repeal ObamaCare, only to "change" it. How? He's not sure. He told 1290 KKAR radio that "I'm perfectly prepared to join with others and I started on my own in two or three areas to develop legislation that would make some changes. But you don't throw it all out just because there are some pieces of it, or parts of it, that aren't working as good as some others are working."[6]

(Translation: he won't change the individual mandate provision, won't vote for repeal of ObamaCare, and won't eliminate the cuts in Medicare. In other words, he'll just talk and do nothing).

But Nelson's conduct on the financial regulation bill that passed in 2010 was outrageous, even for him.

One of the few good provisions of the bill required companies that hold derivative contracts to put up collateral to shield them in the event of big losses.

Derivatives are essentially bets on the future prices of commodities or stocks. Like any bets this side of Vegas, you can win big or lose your shirt.

The American Insurance Group, AIG, lost big and needed $182 billion in TARP bailout funds.[7]

The *Los Angeles Times* reports that "the goal of the provision [requiring collateral for derivatives] is to force companies to provide a capital buffer for themselves in case of heavy losses on derivatives."[8]

Ben Nelson objected to the provision and held up passage of the entire bill to insist on its deletion. Why? Well, Warren Buffett and his Berkshire Hathaway Company happen to be big contributors to his campaign. And the *Wall Street Journal* reported that Berkshire "extensively uses derivatives in its financial dealings, despite the billionaire's [Buffett's] now-famous 2003 warning about derivatives being 'financial weapons of mass destruction.' Berkshire has been able to use its strong financial position to post little collateral against its big derivatives portfolio, freeing up capital for investing elsewhere."[9]

Why was Nelson so sensitive to the needs of Warren Buffett and Berkshire Hathaway? It wasn't only that he got their campaign contributions. The *Washington Post* reports that "Nelson's most recent financial disclosure form, filed last year, shows that he and his wife owned between $1.5 million and $6 million in Berkshire stock in 2008—by far Nelson's largest listed asset."[10]

The *Post* also reports that "Berkshire Hathaway or individuals associated with the company have contributed $75,550 to Nelson's campaign *war chest* since 2000, according to records filed through the end of March and analyzed by OpenSecrets.org, a project of the Center for Responsive Politics. One Berkshire company, MidAmerican Energy, also contributed $9,600 to Nelson's Nebraska Leadership *PAC*."[11]

The *Post* reported that, on April 26, 2010, Nelson voted to block debate on the regulation bill. He "protested that he was looking out for Main Street's interests, but earlier in the day the Democrats had stricken a special provision from their bill that would have created a loophole for the wealthiest Nebraskan of them all, Warren Buffett. The loophole would have exempted Berkshire Hathaway, Buffett's company, from having to pay the fees on derivatives it already holds—fees that all other derivative-holders would be compelled to pay under the terms of the bill. The Democrats sensed, correctly, that this one carve-out was hard to justify as a matter of policy and harder still as a matter of politics, a move that apparently left Nelson so peeved that he voted to keep the financial reform debate from beginning."[12]

Eventually, as he always does in the end, Nelson caved in and the financial derivative regulation provision passed.

If Nebraska is truly disenchanted with a senator who sells himself as a conservative to the voters in one of the most conservative states in the nation and then enables all kinds of radical, socialist measures to pass in Washington, they will throw Nelson out in 2012.

In fact, Nebraska Democrats may beat us to it! Because he opposed the creation of a government-owned insurance company and kept the stimulus spending package down in cost, liberals are criticizing him. Obama recently claimed that he wanted a larger stimulus package—which he says would have worked—but couldn't get it passed.

"I mean," the president said, "if folks think that we could have gotten Ben Nelson, Arlen Specter and Susan Collins to vote for additional stimulus beyond the $700 billion that we got, then I would just suggest you weren't in the meetings."[13] Hey! We weren't invited!

Only in the Alice-in-Wonderland world of Washington, D.C., would a president be able to say, with a straight face, that the stimulus would have worked had it been larger, and that the likes of Ben Nelson made it too small. Some of us, less attuned to the ways of Washington, believe wasting $780 billion was quite enough!

Ben Nelson will lose in 2012. A Rasmussen Reports poll reports that Republican governor Dave Heineman would defeat him by 61–30 if the election were held now.[14] And if Nelson loses the Democratic primary, we will likely defeat any Democrat who takes his place on the ballot. After fooling the voters of Nebraska into electing him and reelecting him, his time has run out!

Jon Tester

Montana

Elected 2006

Votes with the Democrats 89% of the time[15]

Appropriations Committee

Banking Committee

Homeland Security Committee

Committee on Indian Affairs

Committee on Veterans Affairs

Montana has two of the most liberal senators in America, Max and Max Jr., despite being one of the reddest of states. Max, of course, is Max Baucus, who wrote the ObamaCare bill, and Max Jr. is his colleague (aka Jon Tester), who follows Big Max everywhere he goes and votes the way he is told to. Max Jr. voted down the line with Big Max and with Obama and Reid—backing the stimulus, health care changes, financial regulation, and all their other initiatives.

It's time Montana voters woke up. They elected Tester by fewer than 4,000 votes in the anti–Iraq War, anti-Bush sweep of 2006, when the Democrats won the Senate. They sent their message. Now it's time to get serious and get rid of Tester and elect a conservative in his place!

But Tester has another problem, besides liberalism: a certain lack of intelligence. Read his interview with Alexis Glick of FoxNews.com on July 18, 2008. Senator Tester was pushing his bill to limit speculation in oil futures to hold down gasoline prices.

Glick threw him a curveball to start the interview. She asked what his bill would do. He couldn't handle a trick question like that!

"Well, I think basically, what it will do is exactly what—what you said, is it will put more transparency in the marketplace and really deal with the folks on Wall Street who are—are putting the boots to the people on Main Street, and, you know, come forth with that bill, and it's a part of the puzzle."

Told by Glick that the U.S. only has jurisdiction over one-third of the oil futures' trade, Tester didn't cover himself with glory in his comeback: "Well, I think—I think—you know, it's a big puzzle, obviously. And—and we're a part of that puzzle. And I think that anything we can do to help is a step in the right direction."

Then he clarified himself, sort of. "I'm not saying the speculation thing is an end-all to the cost of high price of oil, absolutely not. But neither is drilling. Neither is putting all our eggs in the renewable energy basket.

I think it's—it's a big puzzle, and we—we put forth every piece we can to help knock down oil prices . . ."

Tester's best answer of the day came when Alexis said: "Senator Tester, thanks so much for joining us this afternoon. We appreciate it."

Without hesitation, Tester shot right back: "It indeed is a pleasure. Thank you, Alexis."[16]

Since his election by a hair in 2006, Tester has followed a very simple rule: follow Max. Anything Baucus, the senior senator, did, do the same! Nobody in Washington would give Baucus much credit for brilliance. But, in the world of the blind, the one-eyed man is king!

Tester describes himself as "a pioneer in ethics reform." His website boasts that his "first act in Congress was passing the most sweeping ethics overhaul since the Watergate scandal" and notes that Tester "is also the first U.S. Senator to post his daily schedule online and to conduct a self-imposed ethics audit of his office."[17]

Really? His ethics "audit" apparently didn't turn up that he has been getting federal earmarks at our expense and then turning around and hitting up the lobbyists whose clients got them for big campaign donations.

Tester, who sponsored 95 earmarks in 2010, costing us $138 million (38th in the Senate), took $1,618,500 in campaign contributions from the lobbyists for those who got earmarks. This handy sort of campaign cash has, thus far, accounted for 23% of the $6.9 million he has raised for his 2012 election campaign.[18]

Here are the campaign contributions he got in exchange for earmarks:

TESTER'S EARMARKS AND DONATIONS

Earmark Recipient	Amount	Campaign Donation
FLIR Systems MA; MT	$4,000,000	$620,000
Federal Technologies Group	$2,400,000	$170,000
University of Montana	$2,000,000	$154,500
Montana State University	$1,600,000	$250,000

University of Idaho	$547,000	$130,000
HomeWORD	$487,000	$20,000
Missoula County, MT	$400,000	$84,000
Montana State University/Bozeman	$133,000	$190,000
	Total	**$1,618,500**[19]

Quite a little racket he has going—donations for earmarks. Unfortunately, we end up paying the tab.

Montana has a good alternative: Steve Daines, a fifth-generation Montanan, is the general manager and vice president of the Asia-Pacific region for RightNow Technologies, a publicly traded software company based in Bozeman, Montana. When Steve joined RightNow in 2000, they had 100 employees. Now they are up to 900, including 500 in Montana. Their average wage: $70,000 a year. A businessman who knows how to create jobs will be quite an improvement over the intellectually challenged Jon Tester.

Jim Webb

Virginia

Elected 2006

Voted with the Democrats 91% of the time[20]

Committee on Foreign Relations

Committee on Veterans' Affairs

Joint Economic Committee

Ah! The anguish of the moderate Democrat! We might call it the "Revolt of the Rubber Stamps."

Suffering buyer's remorse after handing the keys to the treasury over to the big spenders, moderates like Jim Webb are giving interviews to allude—discreetly—to how they really had doubts all along.

But what Nelson, Webb, and all the other so-called moderates have in common is this: they all cave in to the liberal leadership when the chips are down. They all voted for the stimulus. They all voted for financial regulation. They all voted for ObamaCare.

But, if Webb did not have the integrity to say no on the Senate floor, he did have the starch to kvetch to Obama in private. David Paul Kuhn, writing for realclearpolitics.com, recounts how "Jim Webb went to the White House last September. The Virginia senator was meeting with the president to discuss Guantanamo detainees. The conversation soon shifted to healthcare. 'I told him this was going to be a disaster,' Webb recalls. 'The president believed it was all going to work out.'" [21]

And, as Kuhn noted, "Democratic leaders broadly believed it was all going to work out. The stimulus, healthcare, cap and trade. Americans were to come around to the left side." [22]

The only problem, of course, is that they didn't. "'I've been warning them,' Webb says, sighing, resting his chin on his hand. 'I've been having discussions with our leadership ever since I've been up here . . . I'm very concerned about the transactional nature of the Democratic Party. It's evolved too strongly into interest groups rather than representing working people, including small business people.'" [23]

Webb, who served as Ronald Reagan's secretary of the Navy, mutters to himself about the direction of his party as he marches in lockstep over the cliff with them. Kuhn notes: "His criticism [of the Democratic Party] is discernibly girdled. He begins to tell a story about a conversation with a Democratic leader and pulls back. 'I don't want to talk about that,' he said. 'I have had my discussions. I've kept them inside the house. I did not want to have them affect this election, quite frankly. I didn't want to position myself in the media as a critic of the administration.'" [24]

And there you have the reason to get rid of Jim Webb. Virginia—having just ousted three liberal Democratic congressmen—needs a senator who votes his conscience, not the party line. Webb's musings are all very interesting, but when it comes time to vote, he eats his words and votes the way Harry Reid tells him to.

The fact is, of course, that this public Hamlet act is all a put-on. Webb is a Democrat. A liberal Democrat. In Washington, you are how you vote. His misgivings, premonitions of disaster, and squeamishness are all an act to convince a red state that he is with them, even though he is true blue on the Senate floor.

Ambivalent though he likes to think he is, Jim Webb has learned to play the corrupt game of earmarks-for-donations as well as anyone in Washington. He's gotten $129 million in 85 separate earmarks and gotten $2,516,168 in campaign contributions from lobbyists of these projects,[25] more than a quarter of the $9.6 million he has raised for his campaign so far.[26]

JIM WEBB: EARMARKS FOR CAMPAIGN CONTRIBUTIONS

Earmark	Amount	Campaign Contribution
National Rural Water Assn.	$13,000,000	$ 679,916
Hampton University	$ 4,000,000	$ 10,000
Kitco Fiber Optics MA; VA	$ 2,000,000	$ 45,000
KSARIA MA; VA	$ 2,000,000	$ 20,000
Dynamic Animation Systems	$ 2,000,000	$ 360,000
Curtiss-Wright Corp.	$ 1,600,000	$ 420,000
Moog Inc. CA; NY	$ 1,600,000	$ 70,000
Old Dominion University	$ 1,200,000	$ 50,000
Soluble Systems OH; VA	$ 800,000	$ 90,000
University of Cincinnati OH; VA	$ 800,000	$ 120,000
An Achievable Dream Inc.	$ 600,000	$ 120,000
George Mason University	$ 550,000	$ 160,000
Conservation Fund	$ 500,000	$ 271,252
Virginia Community College System	$ 350,000	$ 100,000
	Total	$2,516,168

Source: opensecrets.org[27]

Webb may be reading the handwriting on the wall. He is undecided about running for reelection and the highly popular former governor Republican George Allen may take him on in 2012. Webb narrowly beat Allen after the governor called a Democratic heckler *macaca* at a campaign rally.

George Allen is a solid conservative who led the fight against earmarks and is particularly outspoken about the drawbacks of taxing carbon and strangling our domestic energy potential. We should beware of sending relative newcomers to face the likes of Jim Webb. This is no place for on-the-job training in the art of candidacy and Allen is a master.

Asked if he is going to run again, he said he was "still sorting that out."[28] Ambivalence, irresolution, weakness define him.

It might as well have been for him that Shakespeare wrote in *Hamlet*, Act III, Scene 1:

> And thus the native hue of resolution
> Is sicklied o'er with the pale cast of thought,
> And enterprises of great pitch and moment
> With this regard their currents turn awry
> And lose the name of action.[29]

Other Vulnerable Democratic Senators from States Republicans Carried in 2010

Sherrod Brown

Ohio

Elected: 2006

Voted with the Democrats 96% of the time[30]

Committee on Appropriations

Committee on Agriculture, Nutrition, and Forestry

Committee on Banking, Housing, and Urban Affairs

Committee on Veterans' Affairs

Select Committee on Ethics

Sherrod Brown is the single most liberal member of the United States Senate—or at least tied for that honor, according to the *National Journal*, with Rhode Island's two Democratic senators—Jack Reed and Sheldon Whitehouse—and Maryland Democrat Ben Cardin. The *Journal* based its rankings on their 2009 voting record.[31]

Ohio, traditionally a swing state, will find him way too liberal for its taste in 2012.

The stimulus package? It was too small, Brown says. It was no failure. But they do "need to speed it up a bit . . . to help create demand for autos and houses and everything else."[32]

ObamaCare? Good idea, but too limited. Brown thinks we need a public option—a government health insurance company to compete with the private sector. "So eager was Brown to further Obama's full-blown takeover of the health care system," wrote the *Intelligencer*, "that the bill . . . did not go far enough for the Ohio Democrat. It lacked the so-called 'public option,' setting up a single-payer plan in which the government would provide insurance directly. Brown said . . . that if the public option was not included in the bill—as it was not—he would push for it through separate legislation."[33]

Cap and trade? Most Ohio lawmakers have been cautious given the state's heavy dependence on coal-fired power plants. Not Brown! Writing in *Roll Call* in 2009, Brown said "we must craft an aggressive strategy to combat global warming and we must do it now."[34]

Jobs? Brown focuses his fire on "tax breaks for corporations that ship jobs overseas." He complains that "now large multinational corporations are doing everything possible to beat us [Democrats]."[35]

The facts are that companies that operate overseas pay their foreign taxes in the host country and then their U.S. corporate taxes. But they can now defer payment of the U.S. taxes until they bring money back into the country. Democrats like Sherrod Brown want to end that deferral and make them pay it right away.

Why are Republicans so concerned about foreign operations of U.S. companies? Because when a company operates internationally, we may see it as two companies, but the company itself does not. The profits from one sector—in a foreign country—are often key to generating jobs in the United States. According to William Melick, a professor of economics at

Kenyon College, a 2009 study determined that "elimination of [tax] deferral would cost 159,000 in U.S. multinational corporations" translating to a
loss of 17,633 in Ohio. From 1997 to 2007, American corporations created
2.1 million American jobs in part because of their profits from overseas
operations.[36]

But Brown's aversion to American companies that operate overseas
does not include the General Motors Corporation, even though it is one
of the biggest companies shipping jobs overseas. General Motors employs
205,000 worldwide,[37] but only 68,000 of them are in the United States.[38]
Despite GM's record of shipping jobs overseas, he voted to pump $50 bil-
lion of tax money into the ailing company. Perhaps the fact that GM donated $5,000 to his campaign smoothed the way for this vote.[39]

Brown was also a key beneficiary of ACORN's efforts in the 2006 election. According to a report by the Republican members of the House
Committee on Oversight and Government Reform, "ACORN provided
contributions of financial and personnel resources to . . . Ohio Senator Sherrod Brown." The Committee called ACORN's political activities
"a scheme to use taxpayer money to support a partisan political agenda,
which would be a clear violation of numerous tax and election laws."[40]

But Brown also used public funds to advance his campaign. After he
was elected to the Senate in 2006, Brown worked overtime to earmark federal funds for projects in Ohio and to collect campaign donations from the
lobbyists for those who benefited.

Brown spent $121 million of our money to make 74 earmarks. But—
more important to him—he collected $4,507,101 from the lobbyists for
those who got the money.[41] In the past five years, Brown has collected a
total of $12.6 million[42] for his campaign, so more than one-third of his
campaign is being financed by those who got earmarks at our expense!

SHERROD BROWN: EARMARKS FOR CAMPAIGN CONTRIBUTIONS

Recipient	Amount	Campaign Contribution
American Burn Assn CA	$4,500,000	$ 140,000
Steris Corp.	$4,500,000	$ 625,000
American Engineering & Manufacturing	$3,200,000	$ 60,000
TechSolve Inc.	$2,400,000	$ 40,000
Water Environment Research Foundation	$2,000,000	$ 190,000
Edison Welding Institute	$2,000,000	$ 80,000
Edison Materials Technology Center	$2,000,000	$ 60,000
University of Akron	$1,600,000	$ 130,000
Alliant Techsystems	$1,200,000	$ 2,020,000
Moog Inc.	$ 800,000	$ 70,000
City of Cincinnati	$ 625,000	$ 120,000
University of Toledo	$ 825,000	$ 130,000
Bowling Green State University	$ 500,000	$ 80,000
Cuyahoga County Board of Commissioners	$ 300,000	$ 300,000
Starr Commonwealth	$ 200,000	$ 120,000
Ohio State University	$ 160,000	$ 262,101
	Total	$ 4,507,101 [43]

Now we can expect him to use that $4.5 million he got for his campaign from the earmark lobbyists to tell us how honest he is and how he fights for us!

Ohio's ideological centrism is not served by having a left-wing zealot like Brown in the Senate. He was elected because Ohioans wanted to vote against Bush. Now Bush has gone and so should Brown.

Robert Casey Jr.

Pennsylvania

Elected: 2006

Voted with the Democrats 95% of the time[44]

Foreign Relations Committee

Agriculture Committee

Health, Education, Labor and Pensions Committee

Joint Economic Committee

Dick used to work for Robert Casey Jr.'s father. The original Bob Casey became famous as auditor general for Pennsylvania unearthing scandals, wastes of funds, corruption, bribes, and kickbacks at the highest levels of Pennsylvania politics. Without regard for party, he would follow the evidence. Based on his performance as auditor general, he was elected governor of Pennsylvania in 1986, where he was just as unrelenting in holding down wasteful spending as he had been as auditor.

Then along came Junior. He ran for four state offices in six years and finally cashed in on his father's reputation to become a U.S. senator. His dad was seen as a conservative Democrat not only for his fiscal restraint, but for his strong pro-life views. An old-school Catholic Democrat, the governor would not cotton to the increasingly pro-choice views of his party. He was barred from speaking to the 1992 Democratic National Convention for his apostasy.[45]

The Senate used to be filled with sons and daughters of famous fathers—or spouses of famous husbands—who parlayed their last names into seats in the upper chamber. But most have gone from the scene. Al Gore, son of Senator Al Gore, is gone. Senator Chris Dodd, son of Senator Thomas Dodd, is out. Elizabeth Dole has departed. Hillary Clinton is at the State Department. Mrs. Jean Carnahan, widow of Governor Mel, has left the Senate, and Robin, his daughter, just lost a bid for the Missouri Senate seat. Evan Bayh has retired. Only Mark Pryor (D-AR), Jay Rockefeller (D-WV), Mary Landrieu (D-LA), Lisa Murkowski (R-AK), and Casey Junior remain in the Senate. Voters increasingly understand that if you have hereditary Senate seats, you end up with senators as intellectually feeble as the monarchs of Europe became.

Junior shares his dad's pro-life views, sort of. And, as a result, he has tried to portray himself as a conservative. But, unlike Pop, he is a fraud. He is about as conservative as Obama himself. Look at the record:

- Junior endorsed Obama early in the Democratic nominating process, one of the few Pennsylvania Democrats to do so.[46]

- Junior voted for the $787 billion stimulus package, a vote that probably made his father roll over in his grave!

- Junior only backs pro-life legislation one-third of the time and got a 65% favorable rating from the National Abortion Rights League (NARAL) in 2007.[47] "He voted against barring federal funds to organizations that provide abortion services, though such services may not be central to the organization's chief purpose."[48]

- Junior was one of only seven senators to vote against cutting off funding to ACORN, the radical-left group that has been accused of promoting voter fraud. ACORN came "under fire after hidden-camera videos show ACORN workers in Baltimore giving financial advice to individuals posing as a pimp and a prostitute; they were actually conservative activists."[49] Casey's spokesman said "he did not want to punish the organization for the actions of 'a few employees' rather than prematurely target an entire organization . . ."[50]

- Junior backs a path to citizenship for illegal aliens now living in the U.S., a proposal many consider the same as amnesty.

- Despite having attended church schools as a child, Casey opposes school vouchers, though they would give poor children the opportunity to have the same kind of excellent education his parents could afford to give him.[51]

- Even though tort reform could save the country $54 billion over ten years, Junior is opposed and said that a $250,000 cap on damages was "insulting to our system of justice."[52]

- Junior voted down the line for ObamaCare. After initially objecting that funds could go for abortion, he danced a little two-step on the issue. First he voted in committee for the Stupak amendment, which would have barred any funds from being used for abortion in the ObamaCare program. Then the president attacked the Stupak amendment, saying it went too far. And Junior caved on the issue.

Lifenews.com reported that Junior's "office has released a statement that appears to go along with comments from President Barack Obama saying that the Stupak amendment goes too far in banning abortion funds, even though the analysis is off base." [53]

Casey's spokesman said he "thinks that health care reform should not be used to change longstanding policies regarding federal financing of abortion which have been in place since 1976." [54] Deciphering the double-talk, Lifenews.com wrote that "the comments [by Junior's spokesman] make it appear Casey would side with the Stupak amendment, but with President Obama and abortion advocates saying it changes the status quo on abortion funding—by going further than the Hyde amendment—that leaves the door open to Casey voting against a Stupak-type amendment." [55] Got it?

Now Obama's people are walking through the door left open by Junior and are planning to include abortion funding in the health insurance policies being offered by the state exchanges they are establishing.

If there is one illustration of how far Junior has strayed from his dad, consider that he has sponsored 137 earmarks that cost the taxpayers $144 million.[56] Even less like his father is the fact that he collected $5.9 million in campaign donations from the lobbyists for those who got the earmarks, almost a third of the total of $20.2 million he has raised.[57] Dad would not approve.

Here is the list of earmark recipients whose lobbyists gave money to Casey in return.

BOB CASEY: EARMARKS FOR CAMPAIGN CONTRIBUTIONS

Earmark Recipient	Amount	Campaign Contribution
National Rural Water Assn.	$13,000,000	$ 679,916
Piasecki Aircraft	$ 5,000,000	$ 92,500
SCHOTT North America	$ 3,200,000	$ 484,000
Rajant Corp.	$ 3,200,000	$ 170,000
Power & Energy Inc.	$ 2,400,000	$ 80,000
LORD Corp.	$ 2,400,000	$ 80,000
MaxPower Inc.	$ 2,400,000	$ 40,000
V System Composites	$ 2,400,000	$ 180,000
CHI Systems CA; PA	$ 2,000,000	$ 50,000
South Carolina Research Authority	$ 2,000,000	$ 240,000
KCF Technologies	$ 1,600,000	$ 50,000
Converteam Inc.	$ 1,600,000	$ 120,000
Arkema Inc.	$ 1,600,000	$ 731,598
Sechan Electronics	$ 1,600,000	$ 30,000
NanoBlox Inc.	$ 1,600,000	$ 60,000
Accipiter Systems	$ 800,000	$ 40,000
ProModel Corp.	$ 800,000	$ 100,000
INRange Systems	$ 800,000	$ 230,000
PPG Industries	$ 800,000	$1,109,367
Eaton Corp.	$ 600,000	$ 674,942
Findlay Township Municipal Authority	$ 500,000	$ 80,000
Philadelphia University	$ 500,000	$ 120,000
East Stroudsburg University	$ 500,000	$ 40,000
City of Philadelphia, PA	$ 987,000	$ 300,000
Rape, Abuse & Incest National Network	$ 300,000	$ 60,000

Lower Providence Township	$200,000	$ 70,000
Pittsburgh Life Sciences Greenhouse	$100,000	$ 30,000
Total		**$5,942,323**[58]

Bob Casey is a perfect illustration of the Peter Principle, which happens when hereditary politics is at work: he has risen to the level of his own incompetence and it's time to send Junior home.

Claire McCaskill

Missouri

Elected: 2006

Voted with the Democrats 84% of the time[59]

Armed Services Committee

Commerce, Science and Transportation Committee

Homeland Security Committee

Claire McCaskill thinks we voters need more education. She believes that the reason Americans lurched to the right in 2010 was that we were uninformed, ignorant, and need more information.

In a recent interview in *The Oregonian*, she blamed Americans for being "wrapped around this notion that things have gone crazy in Washington."[60]

Well, when the deficit is tripled and the national debt increased by $3.8 trillion in two years, how could we have gotten that misguided impression?

She is convinced that the reason we disapprove of ObamaCare, legislation that she loyally supported, is that we are not well informed.

When voters in her home state voted three-to-one in favor of Proposition C in August 2010, which attacked the individual mandate that lies at the heart of ObamaCare, McCaskill said it was just a matter of their needing more information. "I certainly noticed the vote on Prop C, the healthcare law, and: message received," she said. "I think there has been . . . a lot of noise about the mandate that people have gotten so focused on that they don't realize that there's going to be more access and affordability and more choices."[61]

She also "declared that Democrat losses [in 2010] were the result of failed communication rather than a failed agenda, and she argued that she wasn't going to have to 'pivot.'"[62]

Our abysmal lack of education and information extends to our objections to intrusive body searches and pat-downs by the Transportation Safety Administration. She says that TSA's groping are just "love pats." In a Capitol Hill hearing, McCaskill said, "I'm wildly excited that I can walk through a machine instead of getting my dose of love pats."[63] She suggested "that the public outcry was a problem of education: if Americans learned more about the TSA's new procedures, they wouldn't object to the new searches."[64]

Our propensity to be misinformed extends also to our concerns about closing Guantánamo and transferring the prisoners there to the United States to stand trial. At a town hall meeting in Sedalia, Missouri, she said, "everybody needs to take a deep breath" about Guantánamo.[65] She said we need to close the prison and dismissed claims that the terrorists couldn't be tried in the United States. She "compared terrorists to violent criminals, saying that they could be successfully tried and jailed in Missouri."[66]

McCaskill misses the point. If we try terrorists before civilian courts in the United States, much of the evidence we have gathered cannot be admitted under U.S. judicial rules. It was the inability to get a confession obtained by "enhanced interrogation techniques" that led a New York jury to dismiss 284 out of 285 charges brought against terrorist Ahmed Ghailani.

And, as former attorney general Michael Mukasey wrote, "Terrorism prosecutions in this country have unintentionally provided terrorists with a rich source of intelligence."[67] We invite discovery and cross-examination in our criminal trials. If the prosecution withholds evidence that might tend to exculpate the defendant, they can be subject to court-ordered sanctions. A civil trial in the United States opens up a treasure trove for the terrorists and a Pandora's Box for the government.

Sometimes, when we vote wrong, McCaskill feels it is her duty to correct us. So when Congress rejected the cap and trade legislation, she voted to let the EPA impose by regulation what Congress had turned down.

She knew better, in this case, than the legislature of Missouri, which voted overwhelmingly to pass a resolution calling on the "Environmental Protection Agency to rescind its formal endangerment finding on greenhouse gases."[68]

Claire knows best. We voters, obviously, do not!

McCaskill very recently demonstrated that she had learned nothing at all from the repudiation of the Obama agenda. Facing the issue of whether or not to renew the Bush tax cuts, she told FoxNews.com that she wanted them to be extended for everyone but millionaires,[69] upping the $250,000 level that Obama has set in his speeches. But Americans understand that tax increases on anyone hurt us all.

And even when she seems to understand the concerns of Americans, she ends up veering to the left anyway.

She goes to great pains to assure us that she grew up with guns in rural Missouri. She told the *Kansas City Star* that "whenever Mom got out a can of Campbell's cream of mushroom soup, we knew that Daddy had killed something."[70] She told the *St. Louis Post-Dispatch*, "Dad was shooting things all the time, and we had to eat them. I'm not interested in taking away anyone's guns."[71]

She told the *St. Louis Beacon* that she strongly endorsed gun owners' rights: "She said she would never vote to curb Americans' access to guns."[72]

But then she did. Not just once, but again and again. When the Senate rejected, 67–29, a bill to let states decide whether or not their citizens could carry guns on federally owned land within their borders, she voted no, leaving the blanket federal prohibitions intact.[73]

In 1995, she lobbied against state-level concealed weapons legislation, telling the *Kansas City Star* that "no one will ever convince me that more guns will mean more safety."[74]

In 1996, she told the *Star* that "this country continues to pay a tremendous price for its love affair with guns."[75]

And, in 1999, when Missouri voters decided not to allow concealed weapons, she said that she agreed that "guns are not the answer for safety."[76]

That's why Missouri Republicans have taken to calling her "Chameleon" Claire McCaskill!

There is, however, one area in which she does not believe we need more information: her tax shelter in Bermuda, which cuts her liability to the IRS. She refuses to release her income tax returns and has stubbornly maintained her refusal ever since she entered public life.

But we do know that she and her husband own a reinsurance company based in Bermuda, which, says David Cole, chairman of the Missouri Republican Party, "is valued at up to $1,000,000 . . . according to her own estimates."[77]

McCaskill says that it all belongs to her husband, not to her.

Her office said, "Like Warren Buffett, Claire's husband has an investment in a reinsurance company in a foreign country." The spokesman went on to say that there "has never been a tax benefit to him nor will there ever be a tax benefit for this investment."[78]

But, in 2004, McCaskill scoffed at the idea that the "assets of my family don't belong to me. That notion is pretty archaic." She said that "my husband and I are a team . . . We are married and we share everything—assets, children and a house."[79]

She also seems to have implied, in an earlier statement, that the investment was indeed a tax shelter. Responding to attacks from Senator Jim Talent, whom she defeated in 2006, she told the *Kansas City Star*, "There is absolutely no tax sheltering that is occurring that is not part of a tax code that Senator Talent embraces."[80]

That's a bit different from her subsequent statement that there is "no tax sheltering" going on. Now she seems to be saying that it is a tax shelter, but she defends it as a legal part of the tax code. That's quite different!

The *New York Times* sheds light on what is probably going on with her Bermuda investment. In a March 6, 2000, article headlined "Bermuda Move Allows Insurers to Avoid Taxes," the paper wrote that reinsurance company "profits come from investing the premiums their customers pay from the time they are collected until they are paid out in claims. In the United States these investment earnings are subject to the 35% corporate income tax and about 5% in state taxes. But Bermuda does not tax corporate profits. By moving its headquarters there, an insurer can put the investment income on the books of its Bermuda offices, beyond the reach of the Internal Revenue Service."[81]

Or maybe McCaskill's company liked the pink beaches!

Senator McCaskill could end the discussion by releasing her and her husband's tax returns to demonstrate that she is telling the truth when she says that there is no tax sheltering going on. But she won't. That would be TMI (too much information).

Polls in Missouri show the senator with a 53% disapproval rating,[82] likely because of her vote for ObamaCare. But she actually wanted to go further than Obama did and set up a government-owned insurance company. On ABC's *This Week*, she "reiterated her support for the public option and predicted that her party would pass it over the objections of Missourians."[83]

The "public option" was a proposal embraced by liberals to have the government establish an insurance company to compete with private firms. The idea was that it would offer comprehensive coverage at reasonable premiums and would, through competition, force private firms to do likewise. Opponents of the idea were concerned that the public company—which would receive a lot of direct and indirect government subsidy—would put private firms out of business and lead to a single-payer system, as in Canada, where the government pays for all care.

The public option was slated to pass the Senate—as it did in the House—until Connecticut's Independent Senator Joseph Lieberman said he would not support legislation that included it.

McCaskill told FoxNews.com, "I have gone against my party more than almost anyone else in the Democratic caucus."[84] But she didn't mention that when she does, she's usually to the left of it!

Jim Talent, the former senator whom McCaskill defeated in 2006, may run again and would be a worthy and strong candidate. But we like Sarah Steelman, the former Missouri state treasurer who pioneered the way toward effective sanctions against Iran. She was the first state official in the nation to insist that none of her state's assets be invested in companies that do business with Iran or North Korea. In doing so, she was really the first person to demonstrate how really to hurt Iran and force it to make hard decisions about which it values more—it's economy or the bomb. Other states and, belatedly, the Feds have followed suit. Sarah would make a great senator.

Let's hope Missouri voters, who went overwhelmingly Republican in 2010, repeat the trend in 2012.

Herb Kohl

Wisconsin

Elected 1988

Voted with the Democrats 96% of the time[85]

Appropriations Committee

Banking Committee

Judiciary Committee

Wisconsin is changing from blue to red. In 2010, Republicans elected a U.S. senator, Ron Johnson, who replaced the ultra-ultra-liberal Senator Russ Feingold. Republicans also elected a new governor, Scott Walker, a conservative dedicated to educational choice, lower taxes, and cuts in spending. They swept both houses of the legislature and picked up a seat in Congress. Nice work.

Herb Kohl is next on the list. He ought to be. What does Wisconsin need a senator for? Kohl votes the way the party tells him to 96% of the time. Save the money on his salary and just elect a voting machine instead!

Kohl is one of the richest members of the Senate. FoxNews.com reports that he "listed numerous investments [on his disclosure form], including stock in the Milwaukee Bucks valued at more than $50 million, the highest category on the forms. Kohl owns the Milwaukee Bucks professional basketball team, which *Forbes* magazine valued at $260 million this year." [86]

That's OK. He earned his money. But he is also very fond of spending our money as freely as he may choose to spend his own. He uses his seat on the Senate Appropriations Committee and his extensive seniority to promote all kinds of spending projects. He authored 69 earmarks in 2010, costing a total of $95 million.[87]

As the *Wisconsin State Journal* noted, Kohl has certainly brought home the bacon for Wisconsin. But, "by playing the earmark game, he's also helped to shell out billions to other states. Some of this spending may be justified. But earmarks dodge the normal review process that requires evidence of need. Congressional leaders also use earmarks as bait to get uncooperative colleagues to support legislation they would otherwise oppose." [88]

And consider some of the earmarks he has made us pay for: [89]

- Corrosion Control Hangar at General Mitchell Airport—$5 million

- Dairy Forage Agricultural Research Center in Prairie du Sac, Wisconsin—$4 million

- Dairy Forage Research in Marshfield, Wisconsin—$2.5 million

- Water Environment Research Fund—$2 million

- Shipyard Repair Facility, Superior, Wisconsin—$2 million

- Dairy Market Development—$2 million

- Henry Avenue Bridge reconstruction—$974,000

- Nutrition Enhancement Public Institute—$950,000

- Marquette University Rural Dental Health—$850,000

- Grazing Lands Conservation Institution $835,000

Sometimes Kohl is so anxious to appease the special interests in his state that he hurts us all. For example, he recently lobbied Agriculture Secretary Tom Vilsack to increase the purchase price for products under the federal Dairy Price Support program, a move that would trigger higher milk prices.

Kohl wrote that "a meaningful but temporary increase in the Dairy Price Support program will begin to restore farm level prices and help restore producers' ability to produce basic cash flow for their operations during these difficult financial times." [90]

If Herbert Kohl lavished the same kind of attention on protecting taxpayers that he used on serving customers in his famous chain of stores, he would make a much better senator.

Jeff Bingaman

New Mexico

Elected: 1982

Voted with the Democrats 96% of the time[91]

Chairman, Energy and Natural Resources Committee

Armed Services Committee

Finance Committee

Health, Education, Labor, and Pensions Committee

Joint Economic Committee

Jeff Bingaman was Dick's client when he was first elected in 1982. That was when they were both liberal Democrats. Bingaman still is.

He voted against the Bush tax cuts (back in 2001 and 2003, and against extending them now). He backed ObamaCare, the stimulus, the financial regulation, the GM bailout, etc., etc. He backs immigration reform, cap and trade, and any other liberal initiative.

But he's been forthright about his views and kept to a high standard of personal ethics.

His wife is another story. Anne Bingaman was appointed to head the antitrust division of the Justice Department by President Bill Clinton. While the appointment may appear to smack of nepotism (possibly a blind spot in a president who helped his wife's career along a time or two), those who know Anne all say she is highly competent, aggressive, and able. She was a strong enforcer of antitrust laws under Clinton.

Then she went through the revolving door and took a $2.5 million fee from Global Crossing Limited as a lobbyist.[92] Her representation was perfectly legal, since she had been out of office the requisite amount of time required by law, but it was disappointing nonetheless.

BusinessWeek noted that "Global Crossing's adventures in Washington make for an . . . audacious—and cautionary—tale of influence buying. Global Crossing, which [has] filed for bankruptcy, became a lobbying powerhouse . . . as it sought help from lawmakers and regulators to expand its international cable network." [93]

In 1998, Global Crossing wasn't much interested in politics and gave only $34,000 to candidates and parties. But, in 2000, when they needed favors in Washington, they coughed up $2.9 million—including money for Anne Bingaman. [94] "They came out of nowhere and papered the town with money," says Larry Makinson, executive director of Citizens for Responsive Government. [95]

BusinessWeek reports that "in 1999, Global Crossing was planning to lay a transpacific fiber-optic cable and faced competition from a powerful consortium of companies, including AT&T and WorldCom."

[Global Crossing CEO Gary] Winnick hired Anne Bingaman, former Justice Dept. antitrust chief from 1993–96, and Greg Simon, a former domestic policy adviser to Vice President Al Gore, to lobby the Federal Communications Commission. Global Crossing paid Bingaman, now chairman of Valor Communications in Irving, Texas, an unprecedented $2.5 million for six months' work. The company failed to block the rival group from getting a license, but did force it to modify its proposal in ways so it couldn't dominate the market. [96]

When Jeff Bingaman went to Washington, it was after a distinguished tenure as New Mexico's attorney general. But he clearly has benefited financially from his wife's passage through the revolving door that separates government officials from lobbyists. Now, after thirty years in Congress, maybe his Mr.-Smith-Goes-to-Washington credentials are a bit rusty.

Bill Nelson

Florida

Elected in 2000

Voted with the Democrats 92% of the time [97]

Budget Committee

Armed Services Committee

Finance Committee

Intelligence Committee

Senator Bill Nelson has a problem. He voted to cut Medicare by $500 billion. And he comes from Florida, the state with the highest percentage of elderly in the nation. While 12.4% of the U.S. population is 65 or over, 17.6% of Floridians are.[98]

So how does he explain that he not only voted for the Medicare cut, but that his was the deciding vote that let it pass? Tough question.

He had high hopes that he would be able to buy his way out of political trouble when he got a special interest carve-out that exempted most Floridians from losing their Medicare Advantage benefits—a largesse that was not extended to any other state's elderly. Through Medicare Advantage, seniors can get expanded benefits like dental and eye care at a federally subsidized premium. It also provides for better coordination of their care among their doctors and a managed care approach to their treatment. The elderly like it so much that almost 10 million have enrolled. They're now out of luck, but Nelson preserved the benefits for most of Florida's elderly.

Big deal! The Feds will still cut $500 billion from Medicare—Nelson's amendment notwithstanding—and the cuts will fall disproportionately on Florida because of its large senior population, who are well aware that substantial cuts in Medicare mean one thing for them: rationing.

Already, with the sharp cuts in fees to doctors for treating Medicare patients, it has become increasingly difficult for those in the program to see a specialist. One GI doctor told me that he gets less than half as much per colonoscopy from Medicare as from private insurance. "I have to quota my practice so that no more than fifteen percent is under Medicare. I can't afford any more."[99] When a Medicare patient calls for an appointment, he schedules them for three or four months hence. But a privately insured patient gets seen right away. It's not that he isn't conscientious, it's that he needs to feed his family!

Increasingly, because of ObamaCare, elderly Medicare patients will not be able to see specialists under the program. Those doctors won't be accepting Medicare patients with the drastically limited reimbursement rates the government will offer. Oncologists, cardiologists, GI specialists, OB-GYN doctors, dermatologists, and the like will only be accessible if the elderly have private insurance, just as when they were under sixty-five. Not the Medigap insurance most elderly have, but full private insurance so they can see the specialists they'll really need when they get very sick.

Will the elderly forgive Nelson? No way!

Nelson tries to dress the cuts up as a way to "save" Medicare by "extending its life" for additional years. The theory is that if it offers fewer benefits, it will last longer. By that logic, eliminating all the benefits would permit it to last indefinitely!

The fact is, the money that is saved by cutting Medicare is not going into the Medicare fund, it is being used to subsidize insurance for younger people, who don't have it, whether they want it or not.

But the elderly need the medical care more. After all, those who are now uninsured are, by definition, not old (they get Medicare), not children (they get State Children's Health Insurance Program coverage), and not poor (they get Medicaid). Also remember that noncitizens who are here legally are a large proportion of those whose coverage will be paid by cutting Medicare benefits.

Nelson's attempts to slash Medicare spending are doomed to fail in any case. With the elderly population of the United States likely to rise by 37% by 2020 and by 80% by 2030,[100] who is Nelson kidding that we can cut the cost of Medicare? Its cost will inevitably rise as the elderly population increases. These cuts will not eliminate these increases, they will just hurt elderly medical care.

The elderly don't want their benefits cut. Having paid into Medicare for forty years, they want to be able to see an oncologist when they get cancer and a cardiologist when they have a heart attack.

Nelson thinks they are being "intolerant." He says "what we are seeing is an intolerance of ideas, an intolerance of attitudes. We're seeing an intolerance of anyone who is different from the people who are so intolerant."[101]

The senator, safe behind the generous government insurance policy he has as a member of Congress, can well afford to be glib about "intolerance."

He frankly admits that "the president cannot win Florida today."[102] Why not? Because "the White House staff has not done a good job reflecting the president's desires and wishes," Nelson said. "When your two friends go to be president and vice president, what you quickly learn is that a palace guard forms around them and it becomes almost impenetrable," [103] he said.

Gainesville.com notes that Nelson "put part of the blame on communication failures, such as a misconception that Obama wants to eliminate the manned space program. The White House also needs to do a better job explaining things like the fact that tax cuts made up 40% of the stimulus bill, Nelson said." [104]

Does the $500 billion Medicare cut bear any of the blame for Obama's political fall? Are the president's misguided policies—not just his communications—part of the problem? Apparently not in Senator Nelson's opinion. Even allowing for the myopia and astigmatism that afflicts U.S. senators, Bill Nelson's analysis is unbelievably out of touch.

Aware that he is on thin ice as the 2012 elections approach, he has amassed a massive campaign fund to try to get us to ignore his Medicare cuts. But he has gathered it largely by getting earmarks into the federal budget and then collecting big campaign contributions from the lobbyists for those who got the money. He has collected $8.2 million in donations from lobbyists for whose clients he secured earmarks! Here's the list.

BILL NELSON: EARMARKS FOR CAMPAIGN CONTRIBUTIONS

Earmark	Amount	Campaign Contribution
Arkansas State University	$4,800,000	$ 160,000
Florida A&M University	$4,800,000	$ 90,000
Florida State University	$7,700,000	$ 180,000
Alliant Techsystems	$4,000,000	$2,020,000
Columbia Group	$2,880,000	$ 16,000
University of South Florida	$7,700,000	$ 380,000
University of Florida	$2,200,000	$ 70,000
ADA Technologies CO	$2,000,000	$ 30,000
Jackson Health System	$2,000,000	$ 250,000

Florida Atlantic University	$2,000,000	$ 50,000
Rockwell Collins FL; IA; KS; OR; UT	$1,600,000	$740,138
Mainstream Engineering	$1,600,000	$ 40,000
Nanotherapeutics Inc.	$1,600,000	$200,000
University of Central Florida	$1,820,000	$100,000
Conservation Fund	$1,500,000	$271,252
City of Jacksonville, FL	$1,250,000	$400,000
Space Florida	$1,100,000	$ 50,000
Mikros Systems	$1,000,000	$ 50,000
Alachua County, FL	$ 900,000	$ 70,000
Collier County, FL	$ 800,000	$120,000
Lake County, FL	$ 800,000	$ 10,000
University Community Hospital	$ 800,000	$ 70,000
CHI Systems	$ 800,000	$ 50,000
Burnham Inst. for Med. Research CA; FL	$ 800,000	$ 45,000
City of Doral, FL	$ 750,000	$ 80,000
City of Palm Bay, FL	$ 600,000	$120,000
City of Miami Beach, FL	$ 500,000	$100,000
City of Homestead, FL	$ 500,000	$ 80,000
Orange County, FL	$ 400,000	$120,000
City of Maitland, FL	$ 400,000	$ 90,000
Forever Family	$ 400,000	$ 30,000
Space Florida	$ 400,000	$ 50,000
City of Tamarac, FL	$ 300,000	$ 80,000
Rape, Abuse & Incest Ntnl. Network	$ 300,000	$ 60,000
Embry-Riddle Aeronautical Univ.	$ 300,000	$100,000
A Child Is Missing	$ 300,000	$ 60,000
Orlando Health	$ 450,000	$ 90,000
City of Jacksonville Beach, FL	$ 250,000	$ 80,000
St Johns County, FL	$ 250,000	$ 40,000
Tallahassee Community College	$ 245,000	$ 90,000

Santa Rosa County, FL	$ 220,000	$242,000
Nova Southeastern University	$ 200,000	$250,000
Marion County, FL	$ 200,000	$ 80,000
School District of Palm Beach County	$ 200,000	$ 90,000
Ohel Children's Home & Family Services	$ 200,000	$ 70,000
Leon County, FL	$ 200,000	$ 80,000
KidsPeace	$ 200,000	$100,000
Miami-Dade County	$ 150,000	$ 54,000
Florida International University	$ 100,000	$325,000
Barry University	$2,180,000	$ 80,000
	Total	**$8,153,390**[105]

In all, Nelson put 164 earmarks into the federal budget in 2010, costing us $172 million.[106]

When Marco Rubio, newly elected Republican senator from Florida, voted to ban earmarks, Senator Nelson leapt to their defense. Thestatecolumn.com reports that he "said Florida has benefited from the use of earmarks." So has he![107] It's a win-win situation, unless you happen to be a taxpayer!

Taking donations from those whose clients got earmarks is relatively clean money compared to some of Nelson's early fund-raising exploits. When he ran for reelection to the Senate in 2006, the *Orlando Sentinel* reported that he got $62,000 from Riscorp, the company whose CEO "pleaded guilty to felony counts involving illegal campaign donations and conspiracy and served prison time. The Riscorp scandal involved dozens of Florida state legislators and was among the largest scandals in recent Florida history."[108] Some estimates of the amount Nelson got from Riscorp go up to $80,000.[109]

Nelson's 2006 opponent, Katherine Harris (of 2000 election count fame), also got money from Riscorp. But she returned it. He didn't. According to the *Sentinel*, "Sen. Nelson has never repaid the funds he received [from Riscorp] and used in his campaign."[110]

All of these campaign funds, whether from Riscorp or from lobbyists whose clients got earmarks, are being used, presumably, to tell us how honest Nelson is!

> Debbie Stabenow
>
> Michigan
>
> Elected: 2000
>
> Voted with the Democrats 95% of the time [111]
>
> Budget Committee
>
> Agriculture Committee
>
> Energy Committee
>
> Finance Committee
>
> Democratic Steering Committee

More than any other state, Michigan has been destroyed by a combination of unions and the Democratic Party. Like parasites, they have fed off the state until large parts of it are a hulking, empty shell.

The parasitic UAW (United Auto Workers) has destroyed its host, America's automobile industry, while the MEA (Michigan Education Association) has eaten state and local governments alive.

The results are dire. Michigan entered the recession years before any other state, and it now has the second highest unemployment rate in the nation. And Debbie Stabenow is an integral member of the parasitic clan that has destroyed much of the state. (Some senators, like Casey of Pennsylvania, Brown of Ohio, or McCaskill of Missouri, are tangential to the decay of their states. But Stabenow is front and center.)

Compare Pittsburgh and Detroit. In 2000, Pittsburgh had an unemployment rate of 5.1%, while Detroit's was only 4.0%. Now the roles are reversed. Pittsburgh is at 7.4% and Detroit is stuck at the bottom, with 13.4%. Why? Because Pittsburgh—led by its political, labor, and business establishment—adjusted to the loss of the steel industry, while Detroit kept betting on the car companies to come back. And the politicians found it politically useful to peddle that delusion rather than make their constituents face the facts.

The UAW pushed wages and benefits to such heights that the car companies couldn't compete and crashed. The MEA forced up teacher pay, insurance costs, pension deals, and other expenses, to a point where Michigan is dying because of tax increases.

Meanwhile, in Washington, Debbie Stabenow and her liberal colleagues voted in mileage efficiency standards that made Detroit uncompetitive and gave foreign cars a huge advantage.

Meanwhile, Stabenow helped to maintain the illusion that the car industry was coming back, finally orchestrating the deal in which the UAW and Washington combined to take over GM, defraud the people who had lent it money, and try to make a go of it. The recent IPO for GM does not even begin to repay the $50 billion American taxpayers have invested in this moribund company.[112] And, even if it recovers, GM now employs two-thirds of its labor force abroad.

Stabenow is very good at getting earmarks for Michigan. She lives off the campaign contributions her earmarks generate. In 2010, we paid for $235 million in 208 different earmarks.[113] For Debbie, they generated $5 million in campaign contributions from lobbyists for those who got earmarks, more than a third of the $12.4 million her campaign has raised in this cycle to date![114]

DEBBIE STABENOW: EARMARKS FOR CAMPAIGN DONATIONS

Earmark	Amount	Donation from lobbyists
National Rural Water Assn.	$13,000,000	$679,916
Karmanos Cancer Institute	$ 4,760,000	$120,000
Cybernet Systems	$ 3,200,000	$108,000
Michigan State University	$ 2,800,000	$330,000
Bosch Rexroth Corp.	$ 2,800,000	$ 50,000
A123 Systems	$ 2,400,000	$110,000

Eaton Corp.	$2,000,000	$ 674,942
South Carolina Research Authority	$2,000,000	$ 240,000
SYS-TEC Corp.	$2,000,000	$ 30,000
Lawrence Technological Univ.	$1,600,000	$ 109,053
Michigan Technological Univ.	$1,600,000	$ 50,000
IQ Technologies NY; OH	$1,200,000	$ 10,000
Consortium for Plant Biotech Research	$1,000,000	$ 33,000
Starr Commonwealth	$ 876,600	$ 120,000
ProModel Corp.	$ 800,000	$ 100,000
Calumet Electronics	$ 800,000	$ 40,000
Mott Community College	$ 800,000	$ 40,000
Third Wave Systems	$ 800,000	$ 80,000
Wayne State University	$ 840,000	$ 200,000
Wayne County, MI	$1,100,000	$ 390,000
Eastern Michigan University	$ 500,000	$ 140,000
City of Detroit, MI	$1,250,000	$ 240,000
Detroit Economic Growth Corp.	$ 500,000	$ 110,000
Automation Alley	$ 394,800	$ 70,000
Buena Vista Charter Township	$ 389,600	$ 80,000
Rape, Abuse & Incest Ntnl. Network	$ 300,000	$ 60,000
Wayne County, MI	$ 300,000	$ 390,000
United Way for Southeastern Michigan	$ 250,000	$ 250,000
Starr Commonwealth	$ 200,000	$ 120,000
Detroit Renaissance	$ 200,000	$ 60,000
Ducks Unlimited	$ 155,000	$ 165,000
Cleary University	$ 100,000	$ 80,000
	Total	**$5,029,000**

Source: opensecrets.org[115]

Stabenow added insult to injury this year when she accepted a $5,000 donation from General Motors, right after she voted to make us invest $50 billion of our money in the company.[116]

Michigan voters began to see the light in 2010, when they reversed their habit of electing Democrats who kept promising salvation. They turned the state over to a free-market, business-oriented, pro-growth Republican governor—Rick Snyder—and elected GOP majorities in each house of the legislature. They even ousted one of their Democratic congressmen.

But now the time has come to get rid of the establishment itself, as embodied in Stabenow and, in 2014, her colleague Carl Levin. Rarely has a pair of senators served as better enablers of a destructive addiction to unions, government, wage raises, and pork.

Vulnerable Democrats from States We Lost in 2010

Joe Manchin

West Virginia

Elected: 2010

Even though Manchin was just elected in 2010, he has to run again in 2012 since he is filling the seat vacated by Senator Robert Byrd, who died in 2010.

Manchin has a problem. He's a Democrat. Even though West Virginia voters knew him as a pro-gun, pro-life conservative, he had to run in 2010 as the candidate of the party of Harry Reid and Barack Obama. Elected governor in 2004 and reelected to the post in 2008, he was expecting an easy run for the Senate. But West Virginia does not like Obama. His Republican opponent, John Raese, instead began to close the gap and the governor's lead vanished by early October.

Then Manchin made a fundamental—and brilliant—strategic decision. He would remain a Democrat, but run as a Republican. In his ads, he began to criticize ObamaCare, the stimulus spending, and cap and trade legislation. It worked. He pulled ahead of Raese and won handily.

Now he has to pull off an encore.

But the encore has to come in 2012, after two years of service in the

Senate. With only a 53–47 majority, the Democratic majority doesn't have a lot of votes to spare. Harry Reid is likely to need Manchin's vote on a host of issues. If Manchin reveals his true colors and votes like a Democrat, approving Obama's programs, the voters of West Virginia will not be pleased. They will remember the saying: "Fool me once, shame on you. Fool me twice, shame on me!"

Of course, Manchin may just vote Republican on the key issues, knowing that even if the Senate passes a conservative Republican bill that comes over from the House, Obama will veto it and there will be no override. He did just that on December 4, 2010, when he voted to defeat the Democratic bill that would have extended the Bush tax cuts only to those making under $250,000. Will that fool West Virginia voters?

Meanwhile, federal investigators are closing in on the West Virginia state government. Nobody knows who they are after, but the subpoenas are falling uncomfortably close to Manchin. There are at least four investigations under way.

In the months before the 2010 election, federal probers began looking at the $150 million Fairmont Gateway project, particularly a $1.3 million four-lane section of it that has been under construction for years. Governor Manchin's former chief of staff, Larry Puccio, has a real estate business in Fairmont, West Virginia, and $57.6 million of the project's cost is for buying properties and relocating utilities.[117] Did he profit from any of that money?

In a second probe, the Feds recently subpoenaed the flight logs of official state aircraft, including those of the State Aviation Division's hangar at Yaeger Airport, where Manchin leases space for his personal airplane.[118] Could there have been misuse of the state plane?

The third probe centers around Clark Diehl, a contractor who wallpapered the governor's reception room and Puccio's office. He pled guilty to bypassing the regular contract bidding process to get the job. Diehl is cooperating with prosecutors.

A fourth investigation concerns possible help Manchin may have given his daughter to help her get an MBA degree from the University of West Virginia, a state school. She apparently did not meet the requirements for getting the degree, and some question was raised as to whether she had been granted favoritism at the institution because of her father's position.

After the matter became public, following an investigation by the *Pittsburgh Post-Gazette*, a university committee led by Provost Gerald Lang and the dean of the College of Business and Economics, R. Stephen Sears, found that she was, indeed, entitled to the degree and awarded it to her.

After a public outcry, a special independent investigation found that the process by which she got her degree was "seriously flawed." Lang and Sears resigned, and university president Michael Garrison was given a vote of no confidence by the faculty senate.[119]

So far, Manchin has skated away from all these scandals, but his luck might be running out as the federal investigation spreads.

In any event, Manchin was elected as an opponent of Obama's programs. It remains to be seen whether he turns out to be that or just a faker.

Our money's on the latter.

Robert Menendez

New Jersey

Elected 2006

Voted with the Democrats 96% of the time[120]

Banking Committee

Finance Committee

Foreign Relations Committee

Energy Committee

There is no doubt in our minds who is the single sleaziest member of the United States Senate: Robert Menendez of New Jersey, hands down! Let's throw him out of public office in 2012!

Here is a partial—very partial—list of the scandal charges that have been lodged against him. Some triggered prosecutorial attention. Others didn't. But let's all remember that there is a vast difference between innocent and not guilty!

- On July 21, 2009, Senator Menendez wrote Ben Bernanke, chairman of the Federal Reserve Board, asking him to grant permission for JJR Holdings to acquire First BankAmericano of Elizabeth, New Jersey. He noted that the Fed was about put the bank into receivership in three days. He said that the failure of a "minority-owned" bank "would send yet another negative message to consumers and investors and further impact our fragile economy."[121]

The senator neglected to mention that the bank's president, Joseph Ginarte, and the vice president, State Senator Raymond Lesniak, were prominent contributors to his campaign.[122]

Bernanke didn't intervene and the Fed closed the bank. Why? Because Lesniak and five other directors "received more than $2 million in mortgages and commercial loans, some made even after the bank was warned that its banking practices were unsound," according to *The Record*.[123] In 2007, the FDIC had ordered the bank to " 'cease and desist' from its loan practices. It described inadequate supervision and management of its loans and corner-cutting on anti-money-laundering regulations, among other faults. Yet the insider loans continued even after the bank received this order . . ."[124]

Menendez claims he was just helping a constituent in trouble. Right.

· Menendez's friends, contributors, and political allies are all profiting handsomely from a 437-acre waterfront development in Bayonne, New Jersey, being built with $30 million in federal money that Menendez helped to get.[125] The *New York Times* reports that "the first major contract to develop the site went to a company that hired a Menendez friend and political confidant, Donald Scarinci, to lobby for it. The obliging developer later took on Mr. Menendez's former campaign treasurer, Carl Goldberg, as a partner. Bonds for a portion of the project were underwritten by Dennis Enright, a top campaign contributor, while Kay LiCausi, a former Menendez Congressional aide and major fund-raiser, received lucrative work lobbying for the project."[126]

Scarinci, who lobbied for the contractor in the Bayonne project, has donated "more than $250,000 to [New Jersey] Democrats and helped raise millions more; he and his wife and members of his law firm have contributed more than $40,000 to Menendez's . . . campaigns." [127]

Of Scarinci, the *Times* writes, "perhaps no one has done more to foster Mr. Menendez's political success than Mr. Scarinci, a childhood friend . . . [He] has won millions of dollars in state and local contracts for his law firm, many of them with government entities over which Menendez and his allies hold immense influence." [128]

- Menendez got Scarinci a legal contract with the Casino Reinvestment Development Authority in New Jersey. Scarinci's firm has made $2.8 million in fees from the Authority since 2002. [129]

- When Mayor Rudy Garcia of Union City fired Scarinci as city attorney, Menendez led what the *Times* calls "a fierce recall effort" against him that led to his resignation. Garcia's successor saw the light and rehired Scarinci. [130]

- During Menendez's campaign for the Senate in 2006, Scarinci was heard on an audio tape advising a client to hire someone as a "favor" to Menendez. The *Times* reported that the client said "Scarinci's message was clear: hire Mr. Menendez's friend or risk losing the contracts" he had with Hudson County. [131]

- The *New York Times* reported that while serving as U.S. attorney, future New Jersey governor Chris Christie "subpoenaed the records of a Hudson County social services agency that leased a building, for $300,000 over nearly ten years, from Mr. Menendez while, as a House member, he helped it win millions in federal financing." [132]

- Randy Bergmann, editorial page editor of the *Asbury Park Press*, wrote that Menendez "wrote a letter to federal prison officials asking that a father and son who were in jail on racketeering and drug charges be allowed to transfer to a facility closer to home, allowing them to be reunited . . . A Menendez spokesman said that [he] had no relationship with the mobsters" and that he sent the letter just so visitation would be more convenient.[133] How very considerate of him!

Menendez says that he is innocent of all accusations and that he is being labeled as "guilty by geography," referring to the corrupt reputation of Hudson County, his home turf.[134]

Menendez is up to his old tricks in the Senate, where he ranks ninth in the amount of earmarks he got passed in 2010, to the tune of $239 million in 206 separate earmarks. But more important than what he gave is what he got. Menendez's campaign benefited from $8.1 million of campaign donations from the lobbyists employed by those who got federal earmarks—that's enough to fund an entire campaign! (Even allowing for ads to tell the voters how honest he is.)[135]

Here is a list of the 2010 earmark recipients who anted up campaign money for Senator Menendez.

ROBERT MENENDEZ: EARMARKS FOR CAMPAIGN CONTRIBUTIONS

Recipient	Amount	Campaign Contribution
National Rural Water Assn.	$13,000,000	$ 679,916
Stevens Institute of Technology	$ 5,600,000	$ 350,000
New Jersey Institute of Technology	$ 4,500,000	$ 250,000
American Burn Assn.	$ 4,500,000	$ 140,000
Imperial Machine & Tool	$ 3,840,000	$ 130,000
Dynamic Animation Systems	$ 3,500,000	$ 360,000
Ocean Power Technologies	$ 3,200,000	$ 331,918
Alliant Techsystems	$ 3,200,000	$2,020,000
Monmouth County	$ 750,000	$ 80,000

Drexel University	$3,040,000	$242,614
LGS Innovations	$4,000,000	$ 90,000
Robert Wood Johnson Univ. Hosp.	$2,400,000	$130,000
Hackensack Univ. Med. Center	$2,400,000	$280,000
Rutgers University	$2,000,000	$280,000
LifeCell Corp.	$2,000,000	$ 70,000
Hycrete Inc.	$1,680,000	$ 80,000
Drakontas LLC	$1,600,000	$ 60,000
Frontier Performance Polymers	$1,600,000	$ 80,000
II-VI Inc.	$1,600,000	$350,000
ID Systems	$1,600,000	$ 60,000
Englewood Hospital & Med. Center	$1,492,800	$ 29,000
Curtiss-Wright Corp.	$1,200,000	$420,000
Bergen County	$ 900,000	$ 68,000
Thermo Fisher Scientific	$ 800,000	$675,000
Passaic Valley Sewerage Commission	$ 750,000	$120,000
Woodbridge Township, NJ	$ 500,000	$ 80,000
City of Jersey City	$ 400,000	$ 10,000
City of Newark	$ 400,000	$120,000
City of Trenton	$ 610,000	$ 80,000
Rape, Abuse & Incest Ntnl. Network	$ 300,000	$ 60,000
KidsPeace	$ 250,000	$100,000
Georgian Court University	$ 200,000	$ 30,000
Ohel Children's Home & Family Services	$ 200,000	$ 70,000
180 Turning Lives Around	$ 200,000	$ 80,000
Generations Inc.	$ 200,000	$120,000
	Total	**$8,126,448**[136]

You read some of these earmark recipients and the senator's humanitarian impulse warms your heart until you consider that he even requested campaign contributions from charitable organizations for whom he got earmarks.

Consider the $250,000 in federal earmarks he got for the KidsPeace Cumberland County Therapeutic Foster Care Program in Hoboken. They gave him $100,000 in donations.[137]

Or the $200,000 he got for "at risk youth and child abuse prevention" for Ohel Children's Home and Family Services in Teaneck. They donated $70,000 to his campaign.[138]

Or the $200,000 he had the Feds pay to the 180 Turning Lives Around program in Hazlet, New Jersey. They gave him $80,000.[139]

When we hear some grateful testimonial ad from one of these groups, praising Menendez for coming through for our kids, let's remember the price they paid to get his attention . . . and our money!

The money Menendez got in campaign contributions from the lobbyists for those who received earmarks amounted to more than half of the total he has raised for his reelection campaign so far.[140] As a taxpayer, we'll bet you didn't realize that you are one of Menendez's best fund-raisers!

THE HOUSE OF REPRESENTATIVES

In the House, the same incumbents whom we failed to beat in 2010 will again be up for reelection. But there will be one crucial difference: they will have to run in new districts.

The census of 2010 will have kicked in, and the 2012 House elections must be waged in the newly drawn districts. In many key states, it is the Republicans who will do the drawing.

After the capture of 11 new governorships and 21 new legislative chambers in 15 states, Republicans control the reapportionment for 17 states with 196 seats in the new Congress. Democrats control only 7 states with 49 seats.[141] The results could be significant.

REPUBLICAN STATE GAINS, 2010

State	Gains
Alabama	House, Senate
Colorado	House
Indiana	House
Iowa	Governor, House
Kansas	Governor
Louisiana	House
Maine	Governor, House, Senate
Michigan	Governor, House
Minnesota	House, Senate
Montana	House
New Hampshire	House, Senate
New Mexico	Governor
New York	Senate
North Carolina	House, Senate
Ohio	Governor, House
Oklahoma	Governor
Pennsylvania	Governor, House
Tennessee	Governor
Wisconsin	Governor, Assembly, Senate
Wyoming	Governor

These are huge gains. Even though Republicans lost governorships in Connecticut, Hawaii, California, and Minnesota, their domination of state legislative processes will be formidable.

The Census Bureau has announced that twelve House seats will switch states with eight states gaining and ten states losing them. The following table indicates the shifts:

GAINS AND LOSSES IN HOUSE SEATS, 2012

Gains	Losses
Arizona	Illinois
Florida (2)	Iowa
Georgia	Louisiana
Nevada	Massachusetts
South Carolina	Missouri
Texas (4)	Michigan
Utah	New Jersey
Washington	New York (2)
	Ohio (2)
	Pennsylvania [142]

Among the states gaining members of Congress, the Republicans control the redistricting in Texas, Florida, Georgia, South Carolina, and Utah. Control of the reapportionment in Nevada is divided between the parties. In Arizona and Washington State, the lines will be drawn by an independent commission.[143]

Among those that will lose Congressional seats, Republicans control the reapportionment in Pennsylvania, Ohio, and Michigan. Democrats control it in Massachusetts and Illinois. Control is divided in Louisiana and New York. New Jersey and Iowa use an independent commission to draw their lines.[144]

In our 2003 book, *Off with Their Heads!*, we urged all states to adopt independent commissions to draw their district lines. At the time, only two states had them. Now seven do.

Even in states that neither gain nor lose seats, population shifts will require that new lines be drawn. In many cases, the lines were controlled by Democrats after the 2000 election and the Census that followed it (remember that Gore won the popular vote that year). Now the gerrymandering that helped secure these districts for the Democrats will be overridden by Republican legislatures.

After all, it is Democratic, inner-city districts that are losing the most population, and this makes it more likely that blue seats are eliminated. On the other hand, the constraints of the Voting Rights Act push in the other direction to maintain, as far as possible, minority representation in Congress.

Drawing on the work of Sean Trende, realclearpolitics.com's brilliant analyst, here is the scoop on what is likely to happen:

Arizona Gains a seat, but an impartial commission will draw the lines. Since Republicans currently predominate on the delegation 5–3, Trende bets that the new seat will lean Democratic.[145]

California Democrats and Republicans conspired in 2001 to draw Congressional lines that favored both party's incumbents. Republican voters were put into Republican districts and Democrats into Democratic ones. This incumbent protection program worked perfectly. In 2008, only one Congressional seat changed parties and in 2010 none did. In the rest of the nation, almost one seat in six changed parties, but in California, there were no changes at all. That's how good the gerrymandering was!

The incumbents will have a rougher time in 2012 because now the lines will be drawn by an independent (very independent!) commission. Since Republicans get about 45% of the vote in the state, but have only 35% of the Congressional delegation, Trende predicts Republican gains.[146] And a 10% swing on a delegation of 53 seats can be pretty big!

After the 2001 gerrymandering, California voters had finally had enough of this bilateral incumbent protection deal and took matters into their own hands. In 2008, the voters decided to set up an independent non-partisan commission to draw state legislative districts and, in 2010, they expanded their mandate to drawing Congressional boundaries.

But the commission is not like any you have ever seen! The ballot initiative voters approved requires that it be manned by private citizens who are chosen through a lottery—just like a jury. So, as the *Los Angeles Times* reports: "A bookstore owner from Yolo County, a retired engineer from Claremont, an insurance agent from San Gabriel and an attorney from Norco are among those who will determine how legislative districts are drawn as part of an experiment that promises to drastically change the state's political landscape."[147]

The new California system also eliminates primaries for each party. Instead, all candidates will run in one primary and the top two will face each other in the general election, whether they are from opposite parties, the same party, or no party at all. As the *Los Angeles Times* pointed out, "These two changes together will rattle a system that for decades has protected incumbent officeholders."[148]

Now there is a good chance of a fair reapportionment, which will put lots of California seats up for grabs for the first time in a decade. Since 2012 looks like a Republican year, this can only help our cause.

Florida gains two seats in the reapportionment. Republicans control the governorship and both houses, but a recently passed ballot initiative limits how they can draw the districts (and a liberal State Supreme Court will decide any lawsuits). Hard to tell what will happen.

Georgia gains a seat and Trende thinks it will be in the "heavily Republican Atlanta suburbs."[149]

Illinois loses a seat, but the Democrats will decide which one.

Iowa also loses a seat and Trende thinks it will be a Democratic one.[150]

Louisiana loses a seat, but Trende thinks the Republicans will suffer because of the mandates of the Voting Rights Act to preserve minority districts.[151]

Massachusetts loses a seat and it has to be a Democrat because that's all they've got.

Michigan also drops a seat and most of the population loss has been in Democratic districts. Trende thinks a Democratic seat will be eliminated.[152]

Missouri The Republicans have a veto-proof majority in both houses and Trende thinks that they will use it to eliminate a Democratic district.[153]

Nevada gains a seat and Trende thinks it will be a Democrat.[154]

New Jersey loses a seat and an independent commission makes the decision. Trende thinks the deleted seat will be a Democratic one.[155]

New York If New York loses two seats, Trende thinks one will be a Democratic seat and one a Republican.[156]

North Carolina Did you notice on election night of 2010, how the Democrats got clobbered in Virginia, but not in North Carolina? Republicans got 55% of the vote that night, but won only 45% of the seats. While North Carolina is slated to neither gain nor lose seats, Trende thinks that the legislature will redistrict to switch three and possibly four seats from blue to red.[157]

Ohio will lose two seats. After knocking off five Democrats, the Republican governor and legislature will probably give a priority to making their new members more secure. But Trende thinks one Democrat and one Republican district are likely to go.[158]

Pennsylvania loses one seat and it will probably be a Democratic one.

South Carolina gains a seat. It will probably be a Republican one unless, as Trende points out, the courts demand that it create an additional minority-controlled seat.[159]

Texas is the big winner in the reapportionment derby. In 2001, Republicans were vicious in their gerrymandering and produced a top-heavy GOP delegation. Since, as Trende points out, Texas will pick up four seats, two in Houston, one in Dallas and one in Austin, look for them to do it again. Most of the population growth is in heavily Republican districts.[160]

Utah gets a new seat and it will probably be Republican.[161]

Washington State's new seat will probably be Democrat.[162]

Putting all these estimates together, it seems likely that Republicans can gain between 10 and 15 seats as a result of reapportionment. After the 2010 elections, Republicans control 242 seats and Democrats 193 seats in the current House. The shift stemming from reapportionment would expand the GOP margin to between 252–182 and 257–177. An additional gain of 33 additional seats would give the Republicans a veto-proof majority—not an inconceivable outcome.

Everywhere, Republican legislators, strategists, and governors are going to face a critical choice: do they reapportion so as to strengthen the party's hold on the seats we have just won in the 2010 election, or do they focus on making marginal Democratic districts more ripe for the picking? Do they bend the district lines so that they put more Republicans and Independents into districts GOP candidates have just won or do they go out of their way to put them into districts still represented by Democrats— whom we might beat in 2012?

They should go for the extra seats. While newly elected Republican congressmen will howl and moan and plead to get more GOP-friendly districts, legislative leaders should shunt aside those pleas and put the friendly precincts into swing Democratic districts in an effort to win them in 2012.

If things go right, we will win the 2012 election nationally and our presidential victory will carry over to reelecting the freshman Republican congressmen who won in 2010. If 2012 is a Republican year, these new members will be safe regardless of whether or not their districts are improved. Meanwhile, we have a chance to pick up two dozen or more new seats in the House by giving the Democrats who escaped defeat in 2010 more competitive districts.

And, after the elections of 2012, the class of 2010 will have two election victories under their belts and will have enough strength in their districts to keep on winning, barring a pro-Democratic tsunami. But if we mess up and lose that badly, good district lines won't be enough to save them anyway.

But let's choose the key races carefully.

MEMBERS OF CONGRESS WE MUST DEFEAT

In fifty House districts, the Democratic incumbent won with 55% of the vote or less. In fourteen of them, the Democrat won by three points or less. These districts deserve our special focus in the 2012 election. Here they are.

DEMOCRATS WHO WON WITH LESS THAN 55% OF THE VOTE

State	Democratic Winner	Republican Loser
MA	Bill Keating (47%)	Jeff Perry (42%)
CA	Jerry McNerney (48%)	David Harmer (47%)
IN	Joe Donnelly (48%)	Jackie Walorski (47%)
NY	Bill Owens (48%)	Matthew Doheny (46%)

MN	Tim Walz (49%)	Randy Demmer (44%)
AZ	Raul Grijalva (49%)	Ruth McClung (45%)
WA	Adam Smith (24%)	Dick Muri (20%)
IA	Bruce Braley (49%)	Benjamin Lange (48%)
MO	Russ Carnahan (49%)	Ed Martin (47%)
VA	Gerry Connolly (49%)	Keith Fimian (49%)
KY	Ben Chandler (50%)	Andy Barr (50%)
MI	Gary Peters (50%)	Rocky Raczkowski (47%)
WI	Ron Kind (50%)	Dan Kapanke (47%)
IA	Dave Loebsack (51%)	Mariannette Miller-Meeks (46%)
IA	Leonard Boswell (51%)	Brad Zaun (47%)
GA	Sanford Bishop (51%)	Mike Keown (49%)
OR	Kurt Schrader (51%)	Scott Bruun (46%)
PA	Jason Altmire (51%)	Keith Rothus (49%)
PA	Mark Critz (51%)	Tim Burns (49%)
RI	David Cicilline (51%)	John Loughlin (45%)
UT	Jim Matheson (51%)	Morgan Philpot (46%)
WA	Rick Larson (51%)	John Koster (49%)
CA	Loretta Sanchez (52%)	Van Tran (41%)
NM	Martin Heinrich (52%)	Jonathan Barela (48%)
NY	Maurice Hinchey (52%)	George Phillips (48%)
TX	Lloyd Doggett (53%)	Donna Campbell (45%)
OH	Dennis Kucinich (53%)	Peter Corrigan (44%)
MO	Emanuel Cleaver (53%)	Jacob Turk (44%)
CO	Ed Perlmutter (53%)	Ryan Frazier (42%)
CT	Jim Himes (53%)	Dan Debicella (47%)
HI	Colleen Hanabusa (53%)	Charles Djou (47%)
MI	Dale Kildee (53%)	John Kupiec (44%)
NJ	Rush Holt (53%)	Scott Sipprelle (46%)

NC	Mike McIntyre (54%)	Ilario Pantano (46%)
NC	Heath Shuler (54%)	Jeff Miller (46%)
CT	Chris Murphy (54%)	Sam Caligiuri (46%)
MA	Barney Frank (54%)	Sean Bielat (43%)
NY	Carolyn McCarthy (54%)	Francis Becker (46%)
OH	Timothy Ryan (54%)	Jim Graham (30%)
OR	Peter DeFazio (54%)	Art Robinson (45%)
OR	David Wu (55%)	Rob Cornilles (42%)
MA	Niki Tsongas (55%)	Jon Golnik (42%)
KY	John Yarmuth (55%)	Todd Lally (44%)
MN	Mike Michaud (55%)	Jason Levesque (45%)
MN	Collin Peterson (55%)	Lee Byberg (38%)
OH	Betty Sutton (55%)	Tom Ganley (45%)
NC	Brad Miller (55%)	William Randall (45%)
NJ	Frank Pallone (55%)	Anna Little (44%)
WV	Nick Rahall (55%)	Elliott Maynard (45%)

A word about some special races. Dick worked with eight of the narrowly defeated candidates on this list. Each has a special place in our hearts, and we want to call your attention to the need to continue to battle in these districts.

CA	Jerry McNerney (48%)	David Harmer (47%)

In one of the closest races in the nation, David Harmer lost by one point to Democrat Jerry McNerney. Harmer is an extraordinary candidate and, with fairer district lines, he should win in 2012.

IA	Leonard Boswell (51%)	Brad Zaun (47%)

Boswell, a thirteen-year incumbent, won with the dirtiest campaign we've seen in a long time. Brad Zaun, a hardworking conservative in Iowa, deserves another shot and a victory next time.

| PA | Mark Critz (51%) | Tim Burns (49%) |

Burns lost by seven points in the special election early in 2010 to succeed the late John Murtha. He whittled Critz's lead down to two in the 2010 election. Burns is a real comer and should win with better lines this time.

| UT | Jim Matheson (51%) | Morgan Philpot (46%) |

Nobody gave Philpot a chance. Nobody gave him money. No independent expenditures were waged on his behalf. Yet he almost defeated Utah's lone Democratic congressman. Now that Philpot has shown his credibility, he should be able to win. With Utah gaining a seat in the House, he should have better lines this time.

| CO | Ed Perlmutter (53%) | Ryan Frazier (42%) |

Ryan Frazier is the Republican, conservative answer to Obama. A brilliant, articulate African-American, he has a great future!

| CT | Jim Himes (53%) | Dan Debicella (47%) |

A few thousand paper ballots suddenly showed up in Bridgeport, Connecticut, and defeated Debicella. Himes, lately of Goldman Sachs, deserves defeat and this time, with an honest election, he may meet it.

| CT | Chris Murphy (54%) | Sam Caligiuri (46%) |

A last-minute surge by Murphy won this seat, although the polls had Caligiuri leading. He should win this seat next time.

| AR | Mike Ross (58%) | Beth Anne Rankin (40%) |

Some of the defeated Republican challengers in these districts are licking their wounds in the aftermath of their losses. A few of the defeated Republican challengers are still hurt and bitter. They frequently bemoan the lack of party support and feel thoroughly battered by their opponents' negative ads. Many need to go back to making a living and feel they have neglected their jobs and their families long enough.

But they need to get back in the game! Their investment of time, talent, energy, and money is too extensive for them to quit now. A tough district often takes two or even three shots before being won. Defeating an incumbent congressman is often not a one-shot battle. Former House Speaker Newt Gingrich, for example, loves to regale people with the story of how he lost twice to Democratic incumbent Georgia congressman Jack Flynt before he finally won the seat on his third try!

Flynt had been in Congress since 1955. Newt first took him on in 1974 and lost (it was the Watergate year and no Republican won). He tried again without success in 1976 (Georgia governor Jimmy Carter was getting elected and the state went solidly Democratic). By 1978, Flynt had gotten tired of defending his seat and chose to retire. Too much money. Too much work. Too much hassle. Newt walked into the seat winning by nine points!

In some cases, the 2010 Democrats, facing tough challenges in 2012, may follow Flynt's example and opt to pull out and not go through the wringer again. The 2010 campaign was exhausting, even for the winners, and required Herculean outpourings of effort, time, and money. It is the rare incumbent who doesn't mind going through it all again two years later.

Many Democrats, reading the handwriting on the wall after narrowly turning back challenges in 2010, will simply call it quits, and some will seek higher office. After all, the Democrats are now in the minority in the House and are likely to remain so after the 2012 election. Being in the House minority is a little like being a well-dressed hostage. The smaller party in the Senate has great power due to the possibility of a filibuster. But House minority party members have no such consolation. Retirement beckons.

If their Republican challengers make it clear that they are coming again—this time with more money, more experience, more name recognition, and (maybe) more favorably reapportioned district lines—many

Democrats will find better things to do than to seek another term. Our persistence can cause their retirements!

The novelist Jack London said it best in *The Call of the Wild*: "The patience of creatures preyed upon is a lesser patience than that of the creatures doing the preying."

The defeated Republicans of 2010 have lots of work to do to remain viable. They enter the races of 2012 with more advantages than just better districts. They already have their donor base secured. Most have raised up to or more than $1 million. They have the names, addresses, e-addresses, and phone numbers of their past donors.

Use them! Stay in touch with your base! Send them regular updates, keep them current on the misguided votes your Democratic opponent is casting. Keep them up on your views on the issues. And with each mailing, each phone call, each e-mail, you will send an unmistakable message: "I will be back!"

The hardest thing for an insurgent candidate to achieve is credibility. The incumbent seems far too formidable to defeat and the challenger too puny, too new, to be up to the task. It is a long, hard haul to get the funding, the standing in the polls, and the presence in the district to be considered viable. But the 2010 insurgents who lost, but then choose to run again in 2012, start off their new races with instant credibility. Their narrow margins of defeat in 2010 and their success in mobilizing, funding, and generating a campaign speak volumes to potential new donors and oddsmakers. They don't have to prove themselves. They've already done the hard homework.

In the 2012 cycle, the Republican Party leadership and other independent expenditure groups don't have to spread themselves thin over scores of House races. Assuming Obama is on the ropes, we can concentrate on the districts we narrowly lost in 2010. Now that these Republican candidates have shown their mettle and demonstrated their political abilities, they deserve full support and funding from the party and its allies. And they likely will get it!

Finishing the unfinished business of 2010—winning those districts that were within reach, but where Republicans fell just short—deserves a high priority in the elections of 2012!

Republicans who would run in 2012 need to get busy right now!

Use each fight in Congress to rally and expand your base. When state bailouts or the federal debt limit or the budget come up for votes, hold rallies throughout the district to battle against taxes, cap and trade, card checks, and ObamaCare. Work closely with Tea Party groups and with organizations like Americans for Prosperity and 60 Plus to galvanize your base to a fever pitch! Keep touring the district. Keep meeting with voters.

Don't stop campaigning. Wage a permanent campaign. Nonstop. Your defeat in 2010 was an episode in your political ascent, not the end of the road. It was a midterm, not the final exam!

But as we enter the elections of 2012, let's learn what lessons we can from 2010. We don't want to make the same mistakes twice.

LESSONS LEARNED

A lot went right with the Republican campaigns of 2010, but a lot went wrong too. We lost some House seats we should have won and, obviously, fell short of a Senate majority. It's important to recount where we fell short and do better next time.

Always, Always, Always Answer Negatives

The Democratic Congressional campaigns of 2010 were particularly vicious. In politics, one gets used to negative ads, but theirs was the first campaign to consist *exclusively* of negative ads. Never a positive. Not even a biographical spot. Just wall-to-wall negatives.

The key Democratic consultants were not the pollsters or the media creators or the strategists, but the private detectives, the negative researchers who pried open the lids of their opponents' private, personal, and business lives to find anything they could use or distort to fling at them in the closing days of the campaign.

Everything was fair game.

- Jim Renacci, running in Ohio against freshman Democrat John Boccieri, had appealed an IRS ruling, which made his business pay more taxes than he thought were due. He lost the appeal and promptly paid up. The Democrat branded him a tax cheat in a vicious negative ad. Renacci won nonetheless.

- Tom Ganley, also of Ohio, wasn't so lucky. He was well on his way to defeating Democratic freshman Betty Sutton when a woman accused him of rape. Later she said it was really just groping. Then she dropped the charges. But it cost Ganley the election.

- Brad Zaun, who ran against Leonard Boswell, a fourteen-year Democratic incumbent from Iowa, had a fight with his girlfriend twenty years before. The cops came. No charges. No indication of abuse. And the former girlfriend was backing Brad for Congress. But the Democratic negative ad made him look like a serial wife beater and he lost a race he would otherwise have won.

- Tom Marino, opposing freshman Democrat Chris Carney of Pennsylvania, had recommended his employer for a casino license. The Democrats found out that his boss had been arrested and convicted of a misdemeanor forty years before. Since then, no record—and he was a major donor to the area's charitable enterprises. With a clean record after the earlier misstep, he got his casino license. But since both Marino and his former boss were Italian, the entire campaign was filled with unjustified innuendo implying a mob connection. Marino won when he effectively answered the ad.

- Morgan Griffith's sin was that he lived a foot—literally twelve inches—outside the Congressional district represented by twenty-eight-year Democratic incumbent Rick Boucher of Virginia. Boucher made it seem like Griffith was from another planet and said he did not share "southwest Virginia values." Griffith ran a rebuttal with a tape measure showing how far outside the district he really was and won.

- Steve Palazzo, who defeated twenty-two-year Democratic incumbent Gene Taylor in Mississippi, was accused of favoring big developers who were trying to take an old lady's home. The facts? Palazzo supported a ban on the use of eminent domain for private purposes, but voted against a watered-down version of the ban backed by the industry and Taylor was trying to use his vote against the weaker bill against him. Steve answered, revealing the facts, and won.

There's a lesson here. The candidates who answered the Democratic negatives won. The nominees who let the attacks go without a rebuttal lost. You can't just sit there and let the Democrat hit you. It's not enough to just hit him back. You've got to explain away the attacks one by one.

Republican consultants and political leaders generally don't get it. They never answer. They never rebut. They just throw their own negatives. They feel that answering is going over to the defense. But it's not. It is just giving the voters the accurate facts with which to make a decision.

Where Democrats couldn't find any personal garbage to bring up, the Democrats ran "issue-oriented" negative ads. Two were most prominent:

- Since most Republicans signed the tax pledge promoted by Americans for Tax Reform (ATR) not to vote for a tax increase, the Democrats charged that this meant that they would not vote to terminate tax benefits for firms that move offshore. This flimsy charge—used in dozens of campaigns—laid the basis for claiming that the Republican would ship jobs overseas!

- Many Republicans had signed onto Congressman Paul Ryan's (R-WI) "roadmap" of fiscal and economic reforms. These included letting those under 55 divert a portion of their Social Security tax payments to their own individual retirement accounts. There, they could invest the funds in one of a number of investment vehicles approved by the government. Agreeing with Ryan subjected scores of Republican candidates to the charge that they favored privatizing Social Security, aired in ads featuring outraged old people pleading for us not to cut their Social Security.

These negative ads were fanciful to be sure, but they had to be answered. Unless you explain the facts to the voters, they have no way of knowing them. It's not just good politics to answer, it's your duty.

Adjust Your Strategy When Your Opponent Does

We lost two Senate seats because our candidates' campaign operatives wouldn't change course when they needed to adjust to effective Democratic campaigns. In both cases—Dino Rossi, who was defeated by Senator Patty Murray of Washington State and John Raese, who lost to Governor Joe Manchin of West Virginia—the Republican candidate was persuaded by his consultants to stay the course when a strategic adjustment could have saved the day.

In Washington State, Rossi opened with a strong campaign against Murray powered by a great message—that she was no longer the "little lady in tennis sneakers" she ran as when she was first elected eighteen years ago, but that now she was more into Washington, D.C., than Washington State. Smart opening.

Amazingly, Rossi took the lead in a race few thought would be in play. But then Murray came back with two devastating negative ads—one accused Rossi of being a corrupt banker who made fraudulent loans and the other used his opposition to abortion to paint him as anti-women.

Both charges were ridiculous, but Rossi never told his side of the story.

Patty Murray's negative ad made these accusations: [163]

- Rossi "hid a personal loan given by a businessman now under federal investigation."
  FACT: he got the loan in 1997 and did not disclose it until 2001. He says it was an oversight. But he admitted it ten years ago. Hardly a timely accusation. Now, thirteen years later the businessman who lent the money is under investigation for things that have nothing to do with Rossi. So what? How was Rossi to anticipate that thirteen years ago?

- Rossi "co-founded a bank together with business lobbyists. That bank is now under federal investigation."
FACT: Rossi was one of 37 founders who invested $10,000 each. Two of them were lobbyists.

- "Auditors found Rossi's bank made unsafe and unsound loans and lost millions of dollars."
FACT: Rossi was neither a director nor an officer of the bank and had no decision-making power there.

- "No wonder Dino Rossi wants to repeal tougher regulations on Wall Street."
FACT: Rossi objected to the supervision of small banks, not of Wall Street.

Rossi could have answered the charges and destroyed the whole basis of Murray's negative campaign. But he never did.

And Murray ran a second ad, just as inaccurate, criticizing Rossi over women's issues.

Murray's ad said: "Rossi voted to allow insurance companies to refuse to pay for contraception."[164]
FACT: Rossi opposed making everyone pay for policies that covered birth control. If you had a vasectomy or a hysterectomy why should you have to pay for the added coverage? Those who wanted coverage for birth control could get it without those who didn't need it or want it subsidizing them.

- "Rossi opposes a woman's right to choose."
She's right on that one.

- "Rossi voted to deny unemployment benefits to domestic abuse victims who flee their homes and jobs for safety."
FACT: Rossi backed the benefits. He just wanted the state to pay for it, not the small business owners.

Again, Rossi could have answered the ad (not the choice issue, but the other two charges). He could have survived being pro-life, but letting the contraception and abuse charges stand killed his chances.

Rossi's people wouldn't change course to answer the ads. They just ran ads saying that Murray was lying and left it at that. They never set out the facts before the voters.

Rossi lost his lead and lost the race by less than one point.

In West Virginia, John Raese, the Republican, started with a big advantage: everybody liked Joe Manchin as governor and wanted him to stay there. In the State Capitol in Charleston, Joe was a solid conservative. The voters feared that, in the U.S. Senate, he would turn liberal. These apprehensions powered Raese to an early lead.

Then Manchin put on a skillful ad. Dressed up in his hunting outfit, he calmly loaded his rifle, aimed it, and fired while the announcer said that he was for gun rights, wanted to "repeal the bad parts of ObamaCare," and would "oppose cap and trade because it's bad for West Virginia." With that Manchin pulled the trigger and shot a dead bull's-eye on a target pasted to a tree labeled "cap and trade."

Manchin, a Democrat, was running as a Republican!

Raese kept pounding away at the issues, talking about how Manchin wouldn't repeal ObamaCare and was not opposed to higher taxes, but the attacks had stopped working. He fell behind and then fell further behind.

He should have adjusted. Raese should have pointed out that it didn't matter how Manchin voted in Washington. His election would keep Harry Reid and the Democrats in power and once in power, Obama could pass anything he wanted, Joe Manchin or no. Manchin could vote against cap and trade all day, but with a Senate majority, Obama could pass it anyway. Manchin's very election would spell the end of West Virginia's coal industry.

The lesson is obvious. When your opponent makes a skillful adjustment, you must do so too. Consistency is, as Ralph Waldo Emerson wrote, "the hobgoblin of little minds." [165] In both campaigns, the consultants running the show assured Dick that there was no need to change course. Just like the captain of the *Titanic*!

For candidates, there is a broader message: you are not the hired help. Don't just trust your advisors to steer you. Get involved, know the issues, weigh in on the strategy.

Bill Clinton was Dick's co-consultant on all his own campaigns. He knew as much as any political advisor did and had as much experience. He participated in every decision and every nuance of each of his campaigns. Had Rossi and Raese used their excellent minds to alter their campaign's direction, they might both be in the Senate today.

Target Your Vote Better on Election Day

The Democrats clearly outclassed the Republicans on Election Day in 2010. Every poll had Republican Sharron Angle defeating Democrat Harry Reid in Nevada's Senate race, but she lost by five points.

Republicans watched their leads evaporate entirely during the last week in the Senate races in Washington State, West Virginia, and Colorado and dwindle alarmingly in Pennsylvania.

What happened?

John Zogby's post-election polling reveals that voters who made up their minds about how to vote within the last week voted Democrat by 57–31 while those who made up their minds earlier backed the Republican candidate, 53–44. Zogby's data indicated that it made no difference whether the voter decided for whom to vote two or three weeks before the election or more than a month before. Both groups backed Republicans by 10 points. But those who decided in the voting booth or in the week immediately before voting backed the Democrat by large margins.[166]

Fortunately for the GOP, only 8% of the electorate were late deciders.

These Democratic late deciders were all straight from the party's base:

- 15% of single voters decided late, and singles voted 64% Democrat.

- 14% of under-$25,000-income voters decided late, and voters in this income category voted Democrat by 59–36.

- 20% of voters 18–29 decided late, and this group backed Obama by 56–37.[167]

So Obama's appearances on *The Daily Show* and in youth-oriented media in the last week before the 2010 election worked well.

Historically, Democrats "come home" as Election Day approaches, and those whose involvement in politics is most marginal—who tend to be poorer, less educated, and more Democrat—make late decisions to support Democrats. The 2010 election was no exception to this trend.

We thought that it would be different this time. Based on the solid Republican trend that continued well into October, we believed that the late deciders would tend to side more with the GOP than usual. We felt that those who normally voted Democrat would stay at home. They didn't. And Obama's last-minute campaigning had a lot to do with it.

But it was not just Obama's presence at campus campaign rallies or his pushing the immigration issue among Latinos (who voted Democrat by 58–37) [168] or his stoking racial fears of the Tea Party to hype black turnout that helped him move voters in the last week. The Democrats just did a better job on Election Day itself.

Leading up to that day, the Republicans seemed to have the better field organization. The Tea Party routinely drew thousands to its many rallies and the enthusiasm on the stump was incredible. States where politics had been a spectator sport watched on television were suddenly ablaze with rallies and banners.

The Democrats had none of that. They watched enviously as Republicans drew thousands out to the streets and they muttered to themselves that the Tea Party must be racist to have such appeal.

But, on Election Day, the Democratic machines delivered. The party apparatus, long rusted and decayed, wasn't worth much. But the unions were another matter. They were very disciplined in turning out their vote. Republican losses in Nevada and West Virginia were partially due to the huge union organizations that dominate each state's major industry (entertainment in Nevada and coal mining in West Virginia). These unions knew how to pull out voters.

By contrast, the field efforts of the organized Republican Party were pathetic. In one state, for example, the national party cut its field budget from $400,000 to $200,000 right before Election Day, leaving the party scrambling for resources.

Vast amounts were spent on television advertisements, most by independent expenditure groups, but the field organization was sadly deficient. There was too much reliance on robo-calls—taped messages to voters asking them to turn out—and not enough on door-to-door solicitation of previously identified Republican supporters.

The various Tea Party groups concentrated too much on hoopla and rallies, while their silent Democratic opponents quietly went down their pulling lists and made sure their union members voted.

In 2012, we will need to professionalize our Election Day operation, using our vast pool of excited and energetic volunteers in a more systematic way, better directed by experienced political operatives.

Former senator Eugene McCarthy said when he ran for president in 1968 that he felt that his grassroots activists were like Irish troops while his opponent Bobby Kennedy's skilled managers were like German generals. In 2012, we need a combination!

Run Better Candidates

We strongly supported Senate candidates Sharron Angle in Nevada and Christine O'Donnell in Delaware after they won their primaries. Both were treated shabbily by a sexist media. But let's face it, O'Donnell was a lousy candidate and Angle was an inexperienced one!

Their campaigns had to spend most of their resources putting out fires their own candidate had started. When Angle said she wanted to "phase out Social Security and Medicare," it took $1 million to explain that she wasn't going to cut out the programs, just reform them to make them better. When Christine O'Donnell spent $1 million telling Delaware voters that "I am not a witch," her campaign was headed nowhere. (A better approach would have been to run an ad written by skilled Republican media expert Rick Wilson that attacked the "real witchcraft going on in Washington, D.C.— voodoo budgets, a demonic deficit, and a coven of three witches brewing up tax increases." But O'Donnell wouldn't run the ad).

In Nevada, Senator Harry Reid actually intervened in the Republican primary to help to pick Angle as his opponent. His allies—through independent expenditures—attacked Sue Lowden, the establishment candidate, during the primary and helped Angle beat her.

On the day she won her primary, Angle had no headquarters, no media consultants, and, really, no campaign. She had won the primary by a combination of Democratic attacks on Lowden and the grassroots enthusiasm of the Tea Party people. Through a Nevada PAC, Americans for New Leadership, we tried to help her campaign (and spent upwards of $200,000 to do so), but Angle kept tripping over her own feet.

By October, Angle had gotten it together and beat Reid decisively in the debate, but her rocky start showed that she had not been ready for prime time in the early going. She's got a lot to offer. Hopefully, she'll be back and do better next time!

O'Donnell faced a firestorm of media mockery when she won the primary. Bill Maher, the Democratic comedian-at-large now that Al Franken is in the Senate, replayed her episodes on his old show *Politically Incorrect* and the sarcasm doomed her campaign. Probably there was nothing O'Donnell could have done to defend herself. But wouldn't it have been better to vet her before she won the primary, not after?

The message here is that political experience is not a bad thing in choosing a Republican candidate. The enthusiasm and commitment of the Tea Party people made the victories of 2010 possible in the first place, but we should have been more careful not to sweep out candidates who had run before and knew how to handle themselves on the stump. You don't want to run men and women who are so professional that they are captured by the corruption of Washington, but Senate races against the likes of Harry Reid are not really places for amateurs to get on-the-job training.

WHY WE NEED TO CLOSELY MONITOR THE MEMBERS OF CONGRESS AND MAKE THEM ACCOUNTABLE TO THE VOTERS . . . AND HOW TO DO IT

PART FIVE

WHY WE NEED TO
CLOSELY MONITOR
THE MEMBERS
OF CONGRESS
AND MAKE THEM
ACCOUNTABLE TO
THE VOTERS . . .
AND HOW TO DO IT

"KNOWLEDGE IS POWER"

In the late sixteenth century, Sir Francis Bacon, the British philosopher, first articulated the idea that knowledge is the basis of all power.[1] More than four hundred years later, Bacon's concept that information and education are the roads to empowerment is still timely. For those of us who are determined to elect Congressional candidates who embrace our conservative values and support our insistence on transparency in all aspects of government, Bacon's theory is critical.

It's equally important for developing a strategy to throw out those countless self-serving incumbents who have used their privileged positions as members of Congress to enrich themselves and their donors, to the detriment of the voters, yet still managed to get reelected last November. They escaped this time, but we'll have another chance to defeat them in two years.

It will be impossible to defeat them without diligently collecting and disseminating information about their votes, their donors, and their personal finances.

But we can do it. Now is the time to begin to orchestrate a citizen's coup for 2012.

It's a serious mission. We need to learn everything we can about the people we elect—before we elect them—and then we need to monitor everything they do after we elect them. Everything.

Our late friend Sy Syms, a discount clothing store owner, always said that "an educated consumer is our best customer." To paraphrase Sy, a knowledgeable voter is the best citizen patriot.

Because the only way to reform Congress and save America from Obama's overreaching agenda is to elect people who have a solid commitment to the issues that are important to us and who are strongly supportive of changing the old-boy-business-as-usual system that has completely failed us. And the only way to accomplish that is to first understand exactly where each candidate stands on important public policies—taxes, the deficit, etc.—and then make sure that they are held responsible for their votes and actions.

We're the only ones who can do this.

The process was started in the 2010 Congressional elections when we defeated—or forced out—a record number of incumbents who had routinely ignored the concerns of the voters. It was an upheaval that was long overdue.

The Tea Party taught us how to do it, but now we must go further. We still have a lot more work to do and many more Democrats to send home. Because it's painfully clear that, for too long, the Democratic Congress has shown little interest in what the voters think. Instead, they've been more concerned about what the lobbyists and their donors think.

That's why we're now revolting and refusing to accept the status quo. No more. No way.

They've given us no choice.

From now on, it's our way or the highway.

Just remember how they handled the health care reform debate.

THE HEALTH CARE DEBACLE AS A METAPHOR FOR WHAT'S WRONG WITH WASHINGTON

If there was ever a single issue that highlighted every evil tradition inherent in the way that Washington does business, it was the health care debacle of 2010. That process was nothing less than a metaphor for everything that's wrong with Washington. The appalling way in which Congress handled this process—most of it on display for all of us to see—illustrates exactly why voters have such a low regard for Congress.

To begin with, the bill was drafted in secret by the White House and the Democratic leadership. Throughout the process, there was no transparency at all—even members of Congress were denied adequate time to even read the final bill before it came to the floor for a vote.

How crazy is that? The final health care bill was more than two thousand pages long and affected an estimated 16% of our GDP.[2] (*Note:* The average Senate bill is only fifteen pages long.[3]) Moreover, the legislation drastically changed the delivery of health care and the costs of coverage. Yet it was presented to lawmakers at the very last minute—literally. As for the public, the voters, we were completely kept in the dark. In fact, the whole reason for the secrecy was to prevent us—the people whom members of Congress represent and the people whose lives would be drastically changed—from knowing the details of the final version of a bill. That way we would have no time to lobby against specific provisions.

That's what passed for democracy in 2010.

Although Republicans protested, Democrats refused to change the rules and allow for more time. One congressman, John Conyers of Detroit, sarcastically ridiculed those who pressed for additional time to read the bill before the vote: "I love these members, they get up and say, 'Read the bill,'" said Conyers. "What good is reading the bill if it's a thousand pages and you don't have two days and two lawyers to find out what it means after you read the bill?"[4]

Conyers voted for the bill, of course.

To truly understand his arrogance (or stupidity), go to the Sunlight Foundation blog to see the video of Conyers speaking those words at a luncheon:

http://blog.sunlightfoundation.com/taxonomy/term/John-Conyers/

As Paul Blumenthal points out, it was apparently not the first time that Conyers voted on a major bill without reading it. He views that as standard operating procedure for a member of Congress. In Michael Moore's film *Fahrenheit 911*, Moore and Conyers have the following exchange:

Moore: "How could Congress pass the Patriot Act without even reading it?"

Conyers: "Sit down, my son. Do you know what that would entail if we were to read every bill that we passed?"[5]

To truly appreciate Conyers's incredulous response, go watch the amazing conversation on YouTube.

http://www.youtube.com/watch?v=2Zf2nCiBJLo

So Conyers never read the Patriot Act either. Sounds like he never reads anything. That's not surprising. He probably doesn't have much time in between visiting his wife in federal prison (bribery charges) and rescuing his son who was driving around Detroit in Conyers's $77,000 car (paid for by the taxpayers) when a thief took an Apple computer and $27,000 worth of concert tickets. Let's face it—there are only so many hours in a day.

Is this responsible government? Of course not. But, regrettably, it wasn't the end of the chicanery that surrounded passage of the bill.

REID BRIBES SENATORS FOR THEIR VOTES

There was also the tawdry and expensive deals by Harry Reid to actually buy the votes of recalcitrant senators on the health care bill.

John McCain was outraged by the special deals and named a few of them, including the "Cornhusker kickback," the "Louisiana purchase" and the "Florida Flim-Flam."[6]

What were they?

The "Cornhusker kickback" was especially designed to convince Senator Ben Nelson (D-NE) to vote for the bill. The enticing provision would exempt Nebraskans from paying for any expansion of Medicaid, shifting that burden to the rest of us. It was reportedly worth $45 million in the first ten years alone.

Nelson voted for the bill, of course.

The "Louisiana Purchase" was meant to convince Senator Mary Landrieu (D-LA) to join the party. It provided an additional $100–$300 million for Medicaid recipients in Louisiana.

Landrieu voted for the bill, of course.

The "Florida Flim-Flam" protected Medicare Advantage subsidies for Florida residents—at an estimated cost of $5 billion. (Special protections for New York and Pennsylvania were also offered, but they didn't warrant a special name.)

Florida Senator Bill Nelson (D-FL) supported the bill, of course.

Pennsylvania Senators Specter and Casey supported the bill. Dodd supported the bill. Of course.

Chris Dodd (D-CT) also negotiated another expensive deal—a $100 million grant for a new medical center in a state that just might be Connecticut.[7] And was the plan to name it after the retiring senator?

This was a new low even for Congress—bribing its own members!

Not to be outdone, the White House granted exemptions to more than a hundred of its special corporate and union friends so that they did not have to comply with the provisions of the new law for at least another year.

Ultimately, some of the special deals were removed from the bill in conference after loud protests from voters in states that did not receive special treatment. So, for once, senators were treated much like any other citizen in dealing with the Democratic leadership. Reid's word (fortunately in this case) meant nothing. Perhaps the most egregious part of the process was the total disregard of the wishes of the American people.

WHO CARES WHAT THE VOTERS THINK?

During the entire health care debate, the Democrats in Congress and in the White House simply did not care about what their constituents thought. Not for a minute.

They thought that they could just ram their health care plan through Congress, despite the obvious widespread opposition, and control the fallout later. Amazingly, they seriously believed that voters would eventually get used to it and approve it. If they liked it, we'd like it.

They were not only wrong, they were stupid. They didn't get the revolution that had started outside their very doors. They were also arrogant. Instead of listening to their troubled constituents, who could have taught them a thing or two, they went into hiding and blissfully listened only to each other, creating a flawed but consistent echo of bad ideas.

Instead of reading the polls, they convinced themselves that they knew better than the voters, that they were not hostages of public opinion polls.

One of those who showed utter disdain for the opinions of the voters was former senator Chris Dodd, who wisely decided against running for another term because of strong—and understandable—voter animosity at home. Dodd, one of the Senate leaders on health care, was particularly clueless on just how much Americans—his constituents—abhorred the health care bill. Clueless? Or was it contemptuous?

In early March, when 53% of Americans were opposed to the legislation, Dodd told the press that he "sensed a mood change" in the country in support of the bill.[8] Sensed a mood change? Was he kidding? It was just one more very clear sign of just how seriously out of touch Dodd had become.

Dodd's "mood change" has still not materialized. By late November 2010, opposition to health care reform had increased. According to Rasmussen Reports, 57% of Americans support a repeal of the health care bill.[9]

No doubt Dodd is still feeling that mood change.

Fortunately, Dodd is gone, but many of his like-minded buddies are, regrettably, still around. But not all of them. Many of the supporters of Obama's health care reform who refused to listen to the voters were voted out of office with the help of the Tea Party.

And good riddance to them.

The White House was similarly ignorant. Months after the passage, when public opinion polls showed continuing antagonism to the plan, White House officials still ignored it.

"I think that health care, over time, is going to become more popular," said David Axelrod, Obama's political guru in September 2010.[10]

Axelrod's stellar political instincts may explain why he headed back to Chicago—and why his boss has tanked in the polls.

Consider this. For the six months immediately preceding the health care vote in the House of Representatives, the majority of Americans opposed the legislation, according to Rasmussen Reports:

PUBLIC OPINION ON HEALTH CARE "REFORM" DURING SIX MONTHS BEFORE PASSAGE

Date	Favor	Oppose
Mar 19-20	41%	54%
Mar 17	45%	52%
Mar 13-14	43%	53%
Mar 5-6	42%	53%
Feb 27-28	44%	52%
Feb 21-22	41%	56%
Feb 9-10	39%	58%
Jan 20-21	40%	58%
Jan 16-17	38%	56%

Jan 8-9	40%	55%
Jan 3	42%	52%
Dec 29	39%	58%
Dec 27	40%	55%
Dec 18-19	41%	55%
Dec 12-13	40%	56%
Dec 4-5	41%	51%
Nov 29	41%	53%
Nov 21-22	38%	56%
Nov 13-14	47%	49%
Nov 7-8	45%	52%
Oct 30-31	42%	54%
Oct 24-25	45%	51%
Oct 16-17	42%	54%
Oct 10-11	44%	50%
Oct 2-3	46%	50%
Sep 24-25	41%	56%
Sep 16-17	43%	56%

Source: Rasmussen Reports, March 21, 2010. http://www.rasmussenreports.com/public_content/politics/current_events/healthcare/september_2009/health_care_reform

During the week that the bill passed the House in March 2010, 54% of Americans opposed the bill, as indicated above. Yet the majority of House and Senate members completely ignored the will of the voters, and, instead, responded only to the will of their party, its leaders, and its core constituents—a minority of Americans.

What they did care about was what the health care industry unions wanted. And the health professionals pulled out all the stops to let members know and understand their positions. In 2010, the industry spent more than $66,000,000 on lobbying![11] And, according to opensecrets.org, the top recipients of campaign donations from all lobbyists were

CAMPAIGN CONTRIBUTIONS
FROM LOBBYISTS, 2010

Harry Reid	$551,286
Blanche Lincoln	$399,189
Chuck Schumer	$395,584
Kristin Gillibrand	$300,721
Patty Murray	$303,355
Steny Hoyer	$172,378
James Clyburn	$87,859
Nancy Pelosi	$81,750

Source: opensecrets.org[12]

Many members of Congress simply feel that they know best what should be done. We, the voters, couldn't possibly be as well informed as they, the high and mighty congressmen. No way. Representative Anthony Weiner (D-NY) articulated this somewhat arrogant theory:

There are, however, issues where I seek to lead my neighbors rather than follow. There is simply no playbook for this. But [if] I feel—on a substance, gut, or ethical level—that there are some issues on which I have more information at hand than my constituents. On these issues I'll incorporate what they've said to the best of my ability with my own instincts, vote accordingly, and then work as hard as I can to explain my decision to them.[13]

Translation: I know best.

What Weiner—and many others—didn't seem to understand is just how much contempt voters have for people like him who are in Congress and think that they know better.

In a ranking of all American institutions in June 2010, voters had less confidence in Congress than in any other major institution.[14] They had

more confidence in the medical profession, banks, newspapers, and organized labor, among others.

Americans don't think very highly at all about the work Congress is
doing (or not doing) . . . and with good reason. Over the past years, our
elected representatives in Washington proved over and over again that they
weren't looking out for our interests. Not at all. Instead, they were busy
looking out for their own interests, the special interests, and Obama's interests.

But this time, many of them didn't get away with it. Voters understand
what they did and threw many of them out.

According to both FoxNews and Gallup polls released in March 2010,
when health care reform was debated, 80% of all Americans disapproved
of the job being done by Congress—and only 16% gave our senators and
congressmen a positive job rating.[15] To put this in perspective, the Gallup
Poll in February 2009—just weeks after Obama'a inaguration—showed a
39% approval rating for Congress.[16]

Since then, ratings have declined even further. Immediately following
the November elections, voters gave Congress a 17% job approval rating.

Congressional Job Approval, Trend Since January 2009

Do you approve or disapprove of the way Congress is handling its job?

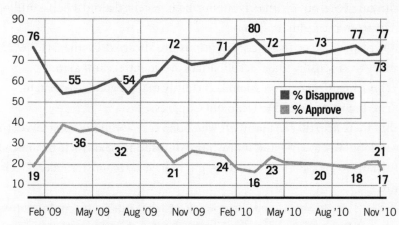

Source: http://www.gallup.com/poll/144419/Congressional-Approval-Elections.aspx

These stunningly high negative numbers reflect the contempt that
most voters now feel when they watch a body that has morphed from a

do-nothing Congress into a rubber-stamp Congress. As Congress brazenly passed unpopular legislation, ramming it through in the middle of the night using arcane procedures and buying off votes with special favors, voters were understandably angry. And it's showing in the polls. In fact, there's been only one other time since 1974 that showed lower job approval ratings for Congress. And things are not getting better. In April 2010, the Harris poll showed a slightly higher disapproval rate of 84%.[17]

Those folks just can't catch a break, can they?

The fact is that they don't deserve one.

HELP FROM THE HEALTH CARE INDUSTRY

It's not surprising that many of the biggest proponents of ObamaCare benefited from the largesse of the health care industry, which made massive donations in the 2010 elections, favoring incumbents and donating to more Democrats than Republicans.[18] The leadership of both houses were special favorites of the industry, with Harry Reid receiving more than any other incumbent or candidate and Nancy Pelosi and Steny Hoyer each pulling in tens of thousands of dollars.[19]

Former senator Blanche Lincoln of Arkansas, who wavered on the health care vote, but ultimately supported it, received almost half a million dollars from the industry group.[20]

Of course, all of those contributions are dwarfed by the $11,739,231 given by the industry to Barack Obama's presidential campaign.[21]

Those health care professionals certainly made a good investment.

The Tea Party helped to clean out Congress.

But there are still too many left who don't care about the voters. We still have a long way to go—and many more unresponsive and self-promoting politicians to get rid of before can begin to have a responsive federal legislature.

So let's get to work. Let's keep track of what our own representatives are doing. It doesn't matter whether they're Republicans or Democrats— they're all incumbents and bear watching!

In order to do that, each of us needs to have access to the essential information that will enable us to make intelligent choices in the voting booth and ensure accountability in the Congress. This chapter will provide you with the tools to accomplish this.

A CITIZEN-PATRIOT'S GUIDE TO EVERYTHING CONGRESS DOESN'T WANT YOU TO KNOW

Let's start with what we need to know about every candidate. The prerequisite for supporting any candidates should be a clear understanding of their position on issues that we care about—*before we elect them*. But there's a lot more that we also need to know before we can possibly make an informed decision. We also need to understand:

- their professional backgrounds and experience

- their voting records

- their financial history (*and their spouse's!*)

- whether they or their family have ever received federal funds

- their supporters and donors

- their relationship to lobbyists and special interests

- any travel paid for by private organizations or the government

But it doesn't stop there. In fact, that's only the beginning. Once we elect our representatives and senators, we need to know more. Because the only way to ensure that the people that we send to Washington are accountable to us—their constituents—and not just lobbyists and donors is to watch everything that they do. And it's not just what they do that matters; we also need to know and watch what they *don't* do.

And when we find that they're not doing their job or they're not keeping their word, we need to confront them. They need to know that we're watching them and keeping track. Every day. That's the only way to keep them honest.

Our obligations and rights as citizens and patriots don't end on Election Day. Yes, we've elected a new Republican House of Representatives. And yes, these new members are committed to change in Washington. But that's not enough.

If we don't make sure that they keep their promises, if we don't make sure that they remember why we elected them, if we don't stop them from becoming mute sheep who blindly follow their leaders, then we will have squandered the election of 2010.

But it's not just the new members that we have to monitor. They're on our side! We need to watch all of our individual representatives. We need to keep track of their votes, their absences, the bills that they sponsor, the people that they take money from, the lobbyists that they meet with, and the people who employ their spouses. And we have to keep in touch with them and let them know how we feel about how they're doing their jobs.

In the information age of the twenty-first century, the data that we need is definitely available, even though Congress tries hard to make it difficult for us to access it. So let's use it. Knowledge and information will lead us to power.

Think about it. These 535 people have the ultimate ability to control our future—our finances, our taxes, our health care choices, our businesses, our privacy, and almost every other aspect of our lives. And they do! They've even dictated what kind of lightbulbs we can use!

We need to keep them from encroaching any further. We need to stop them from raising taxes to pay for ridiculous programs. We need to force them to focus on how to turn around our economy.

Without knowledge, without information about what they are doing, how can we possibly make informed decisions? And how can we make sure that they keep their promises?

The answer is simple: we can't.

Before we can cast a rational vote for any of our representatives, we need to know exactly how they've performed. It's not enough for them to broadly tell us what they support and what they oppose. We need to be able to review their records and judge for ourselves how they act—in committee and on the floor. We need to see what their relationships are with the special interests. In short, we need to make them accountable and their transactions transparent and we can only do that based on information in public records.

All of that data is available. We'll teach you how to find it and use it. It's crucial. Yet for more than two hundred years, the American Congress has maintained a deliberate policy of limiting information on how it operates, how members vote, how members and their wives make money, and everything else that is essential to voters in making intelligent electoral choices.

And the media haven't helped much either. Not only does the mainstream media bend over backward to try to shield liberal Democrats from criticism, but newspapers just don't devote much space to covering Congress anymore. Too many murders and celebrity doings to cover. Very few newspapers routinely publish roll call votes. The information is available on the Internet, but there are still many people—especially the elderly—who have no access to the Internet. For years, for example, the *New York Times* published a weekly summary of all roll call votes by members of Congress from New York, New Jersey, and Connecticut along with their vote. That practice was quietly terminated several years ago. Now they don't even list the roll call votes on controversial or critical issues such as the expiration of the Bush tax cuts.

Even with the proliferation of political coverage on the Internet, very little space is devoted to the specifics of actual votes in Congress.

So we are just going to have to do this job ourselves. Don't worry; you won't have to become experts on parliamentary procedure. You just need to spend some time getting familiar with the public records that are most relevant.

In recent years, under pressure from voters and civic groups, Congress has made more information available, but still not nearly enough. But let's go through what *is* available and learn how to access it and use it.

First, we need to routinely check voting records—for both policy positions and for attendance.

CONGRESSIONAL VOTING RECORDS

Don't be intimidated—it's easy. Once you do it a few times, you'll be checking the votes every day. (Although, of course, members of Congress don't work every day like the rest of the workforce does.)

U.S. Senate

To access voting records for the Senate, go to http://www.senate.gov.

Once you've opened the site, click on the Legislation and Records banner across the top.

This will bring you to the 112th Congress, First Session.

Go to the bottom right column and click on **Roll Call Votes**.

This will bring you to a summary of the most recent vote, but you can also scroll up and down for previous votes. (You can also access previous sessions of Congress.)

For each roll call vote, you will see columns identifying the Roll Call Vote number, the House or Senate Bill Number, and the procedural question to be considered, such as passage of the bill, a vote on an amendment, or a vote on cloture. Normally, senators may debate as long as they want on a bill and this has often led to a filibuster, a prolonged debate to deliberately delay or prevent a vote. But there is a way around that.

Cloture is a procedural motion in the Senate to stop all debate and move a bill to a floor vote. Cloture requires sixty votes and, if it passes, prevents a filibuster. It's often used to kill an amendment or bill because it's clear that there won't be sixty votes.

You will also see a short description of the legislation, as well as the outcome—Agreed to, Passed, or Rejected.

Here's an example of the summary.

Question: On the Amendment (McCain Amdt. No. 3724 As Modified)

Vote# 00115

April 15-   *H.R. 4851*   On the Amendment *S.Amdt. 3724*
Agreed to   McCain Amdt. No. 3724 As Modified; Expressing the sense
of the Senate that the Value Added Tax is a massive tax increase that will
cripple families on fixed income and only further push back America's economic recovery and the Senate opposes a Value Added Tax.

This is a summary of a roll call vote on April 15, 2010, on a McCain amendment that expressed the "sense of the Senate" and its disapproval of the value-added tax, known as VAT. Often called a hidden tax, the VAT is imposed at each stage of production instead of just on the end product, like a sales tax. At the time, the Obama administration was floating the idea of a 5% VAT, which would likely have been passed on in a 5% price hike to the consumer.

Sense of the Senate resolutions are not binding, but can be used to show support for a position and to notify the president of opposition to his policies.

If you want to see the actual text of the resolution, click on Amendment 3724. That will also provide you with the names of the sponsors, the cost projections, and all previous actions on the bill. In this case, the resolution was attached to a bill to continue spending on numerous programs and departments.

No doubt Senator McCain strategically chose April 15 as the date to indicate to the president the Senate's unhappiness with an unpopular tax plan.

For the actual roll call vote, click on the first column, Vote 00115. The following will appear:

U.S. SENATE ROLL CALL VOTES 111TH CONGRESS—2ND SESSION

as compiled through Senate LIS by the Senate Bill Clerk under the direction of the Secretary of the Senate

Vote Summary

Question: On the Amendment (McCain Amdt. No. 3724 As Modified)

Vote 115   Date: April 15, 2010, 05:00 PM

Required For Majority: ½   Vote Result: Amendment Agreed to

Amendment Number: *S.Amdt. 3724* to *S.Amdt. 3721* to *H.R. 4851* (Continuing Extension Act of 2010)

Statement of Purpose: Expressing the sense of the Senate that the Value Added Tax is a massive tax increase that will cripple families on fixed income and only further push back America's economic recovery and the Senate opposes a Value Added Tax.

Vote Counts: YEAs 85   NAYs 13   Not Voting 2

Alphabetical by Senator Name

Akaka (D-HI), Nay	Cornyn (R-TX), Yea
Alexander (R-TN), Yea	Crapo (R-ID), Yea
Barrasso (R-WY), Yea	DeMint (R-SC), Yea
Baucus (D-MT), Yea	Dodd (D-CT), Yea
Bayh (D-IN), Yea	Dorgan (D-ND), Nay
Begich (D-AK), Yea	Durbin (D-IL), Yea
Bennet (D-CO), Yea	Ensign (R-NV), Yea
Bennett (R-UT), Yea	Enzi (R-WY), Yea
Bingaman (D-NM), Nay	Feingold (D-WI), Yea
Bond (R-MO), Yea	Feinstein (D-CA), Yea
Boxer (D-CA), Yea	Franken (D-MN), Yea
Brown (D-OH), Nay	Gillibrand (D-NY), Yea
Brown (R-MA), Yea	Graham (R-SC), Yea
Brownback (R-KS), Yea	Grassley (R-IA), Yea
Bunning (R-KY), Yea	Gregg (R-NH), Yea
Burr (R-NC), Yea	Hagan (D-NC), Yea
Burris (D-IL), Yea	Harkin (D-IA), Yea
Byrd (D-WV), Nay	Hatch (R-UT), Yea
Cantwell (D-WA), Yea	Hutchison (R-TX), Yea
Cardin (D-MD), Nay	Inhofe (R-OK), Yea
Carper (D-DE), Yea	Inouye (D-HI), Yea
Casey (D-PA), Yea	Isakson (R-GA), Yea
Chambliss (R-GA), Yea	Johanns (R-NE), Yea
Coburn (R-OK), Yea	Johnson (D-SD), Yea
Cochran (R-MS), Yea	Kaufman (D-DE), Nay
Collins (R-ME), Yea	Kerry (D-MA), Yea
Conrad (D-ND), Yea	Klobuchar (D-MN), Yea
Corker (R-TN), Yea	Kohl (D-WI), Yea

Kyl (R-AZ), Yea

Landrieu (D-LA), Yea

Lautenberg (D-NJ), Yea

Leahy (D-VT), Yea

LeMieux (R-FL), Yea

Levin (D-MI), Nay

Lieberman (ID-CT), Yea

Lincoln (D-AR), Yea

Lugar (R-IN), Yea

McCain (R-AZ), Yea

McCaskill (D-MO), Yea

McConnell (R-KY), Yea

Menendez (D-NJ), Yea

Merkley (D-OR), Yea

Mikulski (D-MD), Yea

Murkowski (R-AK), Yea

Murray (D-WA), Yea

Nelson (D-FL), Not Voting

Nelson (D-NE), Yea

Pryor (D-AR), Yea

Reed (D-RI), Nay

Reid (D-NV), Yea

Risch (R-ID), Yea

Roberts (R-KS), Yea

Rockefeller (D-WV), Yea

Sanders (I-VT), Yea

Schumer (D-NY), Yea

Sessions (R-AL), Yea

Shaheen (D-NH), Yea

Shelby (R-AL), Yea

Snowe (R-ME), Yea

Specter (D-PA), Yea

Stabenow (D-MI), Yea

Tester (D-MT), Yea

Thune (R-SD), Yea

Udall (D-CO), Yea

Udall (D-NM), Nay

Vitter (R-LA), Yea

Voinovich (R-OH), Nay

Warner (D-VA), Not Voting

Webb (D-VA), Nay

Whitehouse (D-RI), Nay

Wicker (R-MS), Yea

Wyden (D-OR), Yea

Grouped by Vote Position

YEAs—85

Alexander (R-TN)

Barrasso (R-WY)

Baucus (D-MT)

Bayh (D-IN)

Begich (D-AK)

Bennet (D-CO)

Bennett (R-UT)

Bond (R-MO)

Boxer (D-CA)

Brown (R-MA)

Brownback (R-KS)	Hatch (R-UT)
Bunning (R-KY)	Hutchison (R-TX)
Burr (R-NC)	Inhofe (R-OK)
Burris (D-IL)	Inouye (D-HI)
Cantwell (D-WA)	Isakson (R-GA)
Carper (D-DE)	Johanns (R-NE)
Casey (D-PA)	Johnson (D-SD)
Chambliss (R-GA)	Kerry (D-MA)
Coburn (R-OK)	Klobuchar (D-MN)
Cochran (R-MS)	Kohl (D-WI)
Collins (R-ME)	Kyl (R-AZ)
Conrad (D-ND)	Landrieu (D-LA)
Corker (R-TN)	Lautenberg (D-NJ)
Cornyn (R-TX)	LeMieux (R-FL)
Crapo (R-ID)	Leahy (D-VT)
DeMint (R-SC)	Lieberman (ID-CT)
Dodd (D-CT)	Lincoln (D-AR)
Durbin (D-IL)	Lugar (R-IN)
Ensign (R-NV)	McCain (R-AZ)
Enzi (R-WY)	McCaskill (D-MO)
Feingold (D-WI)	McConnell (R-KY)
Feinstein (D-CA)	Menendez (D-NJ)
Franken (D-MN)	Merkley (D-OR)
Gillibrand (D-NY)	Mikulski (D-MD)
Graham (R-SC)	Murkowski (R-AK)
Grassley (R-IA)	Murray (D-WA)
Gregg (R-NH)	Nelson (D-NE)
Hagan (D-NC)	Pryor (D-AR)
Harkin (D-IA)	Reid (D-NV)

Risch (R-ID)

Roberts (R-KS)

Rockefeller (D-WV)

Sanders (I-VT)

Schumer (D-NY)

Sessions (R-AL)

Shaheen (D-NH)

Shelby (R-AL)

Snowe (R-ME)

Specter (D-PA)

Stabenow (D-MI)

Tester (D-MT)

Thune (R-SD)

Udall (D-CO)

Vitter (R-LA)

Wicker (R-MS)

Wyden (D-OR)

NAYs—13

Akaka (D-HI)

Bingaman (D-NM)

Brown (D-OH)

Byrd (D-WV)

Cardin (D-MD)

Dorgan (D-ND)

Kaufman (D-DE)

Levin (D-MI)

Reed (D-RI)

Udall (D-NM)

Voinovich (R-OH)

Webb (D-VA)

Whitehouse (D-RI)

Not Voting—2

Nelson (D-FL)

Warner (D-VA)

You can see that the resolution passed at 5:00 by a margin of 85–13, with two senators absent—Nelson (D-FL) and Warner (D-VA). Twelve Democrats voted against the bill, along with one Republican.

It's safe to say that the thirteen senators who voted against the resolution—on April 15, no less—would support just about any tax. Watch them in the future. Twelve of them were Democrats, but George Voinovich is a Republican. So why would he vote against a bill that criticizes a VAT? Probably because he's a liberal at heart and was not running again. With no more elections to win and nothing to lose, Voinovich was showing his true colors.

The roll call votes also give you attendance information. You can track those members who don't even show up for work. But note that most members of Congress know that attendance is closely tracked and so they show up, at the very least, for roll call votes.

But during election season, the temptation is often too great. Incumbent members want to be out in their district. So keep checking. Remember, we're not paying them to run for office.

During the 2008 presidential race, Barack Obama, Hillary Clinton, and John McCain broke all records for absenteeism. Of the Senate's fifty-nine voting days in the first six months of the year, they were at work in the Senate only nine days. They all simply stopped working to campaign for a better job, while still drawing their $165,000-a-year paycheck. Their reward: election as president, appointment to secretary of state, and reelection to the Senate.

How would your boss react to your taking almost two years off—with pay—to try to get a better job?

As we pointed out in our 2008 book, *Fleeced*: "If they want to take almost two years away from their responsibilities as elected officials, they should resign from the Senate. They're fleecing us."

So keep track of them and let them know how you feel about their votes—and their attendance.

House of Representatives

Go to http://clerk.house.gov/legislative/legvotes.html.

On the right, you will see the heading **Roll Call Votes**. Click on the session that you want to research. The current Congress is the 112th, First Session, 2011.

Scroll through the vote summaries to the vote you want (or look at all of them).

THIS IS THE SUMMARY OF THE OBAMA HEALTH CARE BILL THAT PASSED THE HOUSE

To see the actual roll call vote, click on the number 165.

Here is the Roll Call:

FINAL VOTE RESULTS FOR ROLL CALL 165

H R 3590 RECORDED VOTE

21-Mar 2010 10:49 PM

QUESTION: On Motion to Concur in Senate Amendments

BILL TITLE: Patient Protection and Affordable Care Act

	Ayes	Noes	PRES	NV
Democratic	219	34		
Republican		178		
Independent				
TOTALS	219	212		

—AYES 219—

Ackerman	Blumenauer	Carnahan
Andrews	Boccieri	Carney
Baca	Boswell	Carson (IN)
Baird	Boyd	Castor (FL)
Baldwin	Brady (PA)	Chu
Bean	Braley (IA)	Clarke
Becerra	Brown, Corrine	Clay
Berkley	Butterfield	Cleaver
Berman	Capps	Clyburn
Bishop (GA)	Capuano	Cohen
Bishop (NY)	Cardoza	Connolly (VA)

Conyers	Frank (MA)	Johnson (GA)
Cooper	Fudge	Johnson, E. B.
Costa	Garamendi	Kagen
Costello	Giffords	Kanjorski
Courtney	Gonzalez	Kaptur
Crowley	Gordon (TN)	Kennedy
Cuellar	Grayson	Kildee
Cummings	Green, Al	Kilpatrick (MI)
Dahlkemper	Green, Gene	Kilroy
Davis (CA)	Grijalva	Kind
Davis (IL)	Gutierrez	Kirkpatrick (AZ)
DeFazio	Hall (NY)	Klein (FL)
DeGette	Halvorson	Kosmas
Delahunt	Hare	Kucinich
DeLauro	Harman	Langevin
Dicks	Hastings (FL)	Larsen (WA)
Dingell	Heinrich	Larson (CT)
Doggett	Higgins	Lee (CA)
Donnelly (IN)	Hill	Levin
Doyle	Himes	Lewis (GA)
Driehaus	Hinchey	Loebsack
Edwards (MD)	Hinojosa	Lofgren, Zoe
Ellison	Hirono	Lowey
Ellsworth	Hodes	Luján
Engel	Holt	Maffei
Eshoo	Honda	Maloney
Etheridge	Hoyer	Markey (CO)
Farr	Inslee	Markey (MA)
Fattah	Israel	Matsui
Filner	Jackson (IL)	McCarthy (NY)
Foster	Jackson Lee (TX)	McCollum

McDermott	Peters	Sires
McGovern	Pingree (ME)	Slaughter
McNerney	Polis (CO)	Smith (WA)
Meek (FL)	Pomeroy	Snyder
Meeks (NY)	Price (NC)	Speier
Michaud	Quigley	Spratt
Miller (NC)	Rahall	Stark
Miller, George	Rangel	Stupak
Mitchell	Reyes	Sutton
Mollohan	Richardson	Thompson (CA)
Moore (KS)	Rodriguez	Thompson (MS)
Moore (WI)	Rothman (NJ)	Tierney
Moran (VA)	Roybal-Allard	Titus
Murphy (CT)	Ruppersberger	Tonko
Murphy (NY)	Rush	Towns
Murphy, Patrick	Ryan (OH)	Tsongas
Nadler (NY)	Salazar	Van Hollen
Napolitano	Sánchez, Linda T.	Velázquez
Neal (MA)	Sanchez, Loretta	Visclosky
Oberstar	Sarbanes	Walz
Obey	Schakowsky	Wasserman Schultz
Olver	Schauer	Waters
Ortiz	Schiff	Watson
Owens	Schrader	Watt
Pallone	Schwartz	Waxman
Pascrell	Scott (GA)	Weiner
Pastor (AZ)	Scott (VA)	Welch
Payne	Serrano	Wilson (OH)
Pelosi	Sestak	Woolsey
Perlmutter	Shea-Porter	Wu
Perriello	Sherman ·	Yarmuth

No one missed that vote in the House!

ATTENDANCE RECORDS

In addition to each roll call vote, the Washington Post provides attendance records of all members of Congress in its Votes Database, http://projects .washingtonpost.com/congress/111/

In the last Congress, the 111th, only thirteen of the 100 senators and 5 of the 435 members of the House had perfect attendance record:

SENATE PERFECT ATTENDANCE

John Barasso (R-WY)

Michael Bennett (D-CO)

Scott Brown (D-MA)

Ben Cardin (D-MD)

Susan Collins (R-ME)

Al Franken (D-MN)

Carte Goodwin (D-WV)

Chuck Grassley (R-IA)

Paul Kirk(D-MA) (temporarily filled Ted Kennedy seat)

Ben Nelson (D-NE)

Harry Reid (D-NV)

Kenneth Salazar (D-CO)

Olympia Snowe (R-ME)

Source: http://projects.washingtonpost.com/congress/111/senate/perfect-voters/

HOUSE PERFECT ATTENDANCE

Jason Altmire (D-PA)   Frank LoBiondo (R-NJ)

Tom Graves (R-GA)   Thomas Reid (R-NY)

Lynn Jenkins (R-GA)

Source: http://projects.washingtonpost.com/congress/111/house/perfect-voters/

According to the *Post*, the following members of the Senate missed 10% or more of the votes:

SENATE WORST ATTENDANCE

Member	Votes missed	%
Mark Kirk (R-IL)	75	10.8
Johnny Isaacson (R-GA)	72	10.4
Jay Rockefeller (D-WV)	71	10.3

Source: http://projects.washingtonpost.com/congress/111/senate/vote-missers/

HOUSE WORST ATTENDANCE

Member	Votes missed	%
J. Gresham Barrett (R-SC)	696	42.1
Peter Hoekstra (R-MI)	460	27.8
George Radanovich (R-CA)	434	26.2
Zachary Wamp (R-TN)	434	26.2
Pete Stark (D-CA)	342	20.7

Bill Young (R-FL)	319	19.3
Mary Fallin (R-OK)	278	16.8
Bill Delahunt (D-MA)	270	16.3
John Sullivan (R-OK)	263	15.9
Linda Sanchez (D-CA)	202	15.8
Luis Gutierrez (D-IL)	253	15.3
Roy Blount (R-MO)	252	15.2
John Lewis (D-GA)	226	13.7
Steve Buyer (R-TN)	221	13.4
John Conyers (D-MI)	210	12.7
Gary Miller (R-CA)	202	12.3
Mike Capuano (D-MA)	202	12.2
Mark Kirk (R-IL)	75	10.8

Source: http://projects.washingtonpost.com/congress/111/house/vote-missers/

So, peruse the roll call votes every few weeks. In addition to providing the policy position of each of the members and showing attendance records, the voting records afford us an opportunity to see how very *little* they accomplish. Too much of their time is spent renaming post offices and courthouses and congratulating sports teams.

We've covered this ridiculous practice in our other books—*Outrage* (2007), *Fleeced* (2008), and *Catastrophe* (2009). It is a waste of time and resources as well as taxpayer money. If this inane custom cannot be stopped, then, at the very least, it should be confined to one calendar day a month.

Unfortunately, we don't have statutory term limits in the United States, but we can certainly impose them ourselves. If our elected representatives won't listen to us, won't commit to us, won't even meet with us, then let's get rid of them and start all over again with people who understand what they are supposed to be doing in Washington. Because too many of the folks who are there now don't have a clue.

That's why they deserve to go. Many of them are self-serving, self-important, and self-indulgent people who don't reflect the work ethic of this country and don't even respect the voters who elected them. They spend a minimal amount of time working on legislation and maximize the time they spend campaigning and fund-raising—while they are on the public payroll! We're constantly paying them to run for reelection.

Consider this: in January 2010, when the unemployment rate was close to 10%, there was absolutely no consideration of anything concerning jobs, unemployment, banking issues, or the economy. This is truly amazing. The country was in a monumental crisis and the Congress totally ignored the problems. Very little substantive work was accomplished. The House was in session for only seven days and the Senate was in session for five days. The average American worker showed up for work on twenty days during that same time period. And the average worker wasn't paid the $174,000 that was paid to members of Congress. And on the days when the members did show up, they spent very little time doing actual work—sometimes mere minutes.

During the first week of the Second Session of the 111th Congress, in the week of January 12, the House considered one bill to override the president's veto. It failed, as they knew it would. Aside from that, all of its other work concerned proclamations, renaming of post offices, and congratulations to sports teams and athletes. The only exception was a consideration of several Native American water rights bills and the creation of a national park in St. Croix.

During January 2010, the House was in roll call session for less than five hours over the course of seven days. Then they adjourned and held roll call votes on seven days in February.

Here's some of what we are paying them over $174,000 to do.

HOUSE OF REPRESENTATIVES SCHEDULE

JANUARY 2010

January 1–11	**no work**
Tue 12	**less than 10 minutes in session**

Roll Call 1. Quorom call 7:07 p.m

61 members absent[22]

Wed 13   **less than 40 minutes in session**

Roll Call 2, 3:59 p.m. failed attempt to override the President's appropriation veto:

44 absent,[23] including Jerry Lewis, (R-CA) Ranking Member, Appropriations Committee and Reps. Kirk (R-IL), Crenshaw (R-FI), and Wamp (R-TN), all members of the Committee that crafted the bill that was vetoed. *But they didn't have time to vote on the override*!!

Roll Call 3. 3:59 Honoring the life and work of Dr. Martin Luther King, Jr. and encouraging the continued commitment to the Martin Luther King, Jr. Day as a national day of service.

54 absent,[24]

Roll Call 4.[25] 4:09 Supporting the initiatives of Chicago Wilderness and the Children's Outdoor Bill of Rights:

63 absent

Roll Call 5. To designate the facility of the United States Postal Service located at 101 West Highway 64 Bypass in Roper, North Carolina, as the "E.V. Wilkins Post Office"

76 absent[26]

But that's not really all that they did. Let's give them some credit: the House also passed the following resolutions without a roll call vote:

- Supporting continued political and economic development in Ukraine

- H. Res. 970, to congratulate Flint native, University of Alabama sophomore, and running back Mark Ingram on winning the 2009 Heisman Trophy and to honor both his athletic and academic achievements

- H. Res. 862, amended, to congratulate the staff, student, and faculty at the Illinois Mathematics and Science Academy for winning the 2009 Star Innovator in the Intel Schools of Distinction competition

- H. Res. 1001, to congratulate North Central College on winning the 2009 NCAA Division III men's cross country championship

- Sergeant Matthew L. Ingram Post Office Designation Act: H.R. 4139, to designate the facility of the United States Postal Service located at 7464 Highway 503 in Hickory, Mississippi, as the "Sergeant Matthew L. Ingram Post Office."

After completing that exhaustive agenda, the House adjourned for a week until January 19, 2010.

You get the picture, don't you?

They returned to complete the following:

January 19   **16 minutes in session**

Roll Call 6: Congratulating the Northwestern University Feinberg School of Medicine for its 150 years of commitment to advancing science and improving health

Roll Call 7: Congratulating the Penn State women's volleyball team on winning 2009 NCAA Division 1 National Championship

Roll Call 8: Commending the University of Virginia men's soccer team for winning 2009 Division 1 NCAA National Championship

January 20   **27 minutes in session**

Roll Calls 9, 10, 11: Rule for Native American Water Rights and National Park in St. Croix

January 21   **24 minutes in session**

Roll Calls 12, 13, 14: Native American Water Rights

Roll Call 15 :Expressing condolences to and solidarity with the people of Haiti in the aftermath of the devastating earthquake of January 12, 2010

January 26   **16 minutes in session**

Roll Call 16: Sense of Congress that president should create a Nuclear Forensic program (nonbinding)

Roll Call 17: Expressing support for designation of January 2010 as National Mentoring Month

Roll Call 18: Recognizing the importance of cervical health and of detecting cervical cancer during its earliest stages and supporting the goals and ideals of Cervical Health Awareness Month

Roll Call 19: Expressing support for the designation of January 10, 2010, through January 16, 2010, as National Influenza Vaccination Week

January 27   **2 hours and 56 minutes in session**

Roll Call 20: Rule for Tribal Rights Bill & Historic Site Bill (St. Croix)

Roll Call 21: Expressing support for designation of January as Poverty in America Awareness Month

Roll Call 22: Idaho Wilderness Water Facility

Roll Call 23: Creation of the Castle Nugent Historic Site in St. Croix, a $50 million program to purchase 2900 acres of privately owned oceanfront property to create a national park and "preserve a Caribbean cultural landscape."

Roll Call 24: Extension of SBA programs (8 minutes)

Roll Call 25: Honoring the 95th anniversary of the signing of the Rocky Mountain National Park Act

Source: U.S. House of Representatives Roll Call Votes, http://clerk.house.gov/evs/2010/ ROLL_000.asp

Are we really paying them to honor NCAA champions or celebrate the anniversary of national parks or designate poverty awareness months? Is that what this country needs from its Congress?

It's no wonder that Americans don't think very highly of the work Congress is doing (or not doing). Our elected representatives in Washington have proven over and over again that they aren't looking out for our interests. Not at all.

But from now on, we can't let them get away with that anymore. We showed them in 2010 that we're not just going to ignore what they're doing. We made them understand that they're accountable to us. That we're watching them and that voters understand what they're doing and don't like it at all.

FOLLOW THE MONEY

But it is only when you get to the money—the campaign donations, assets, liabilities and investments—that you can really understand the men and women who represent you in Congress.

It's not financial voyeurism. We are entitled to know what is influencing the votes of our representatives. In the section of this book on Nebraska's Democratic senator Ben Nelson, for example, we describe how he blocked a bill regulating investments in derivatives. And how it turned out that his largest personal investment was in Warren Buffett's company, which was directly affected by and strongly opposed to the legislation.

The best source of information about money and Congress is the Center for Responsive Politics and its website, www.opensecrets.org. The Center analyzes and disseminates invaluable information—the kinds of things that many members of Congress would prefer to keep secret. Much of their work involves going through thousands of paper documents that are housed in Washington and not available to the people who need the information. The organization does a great job and deserves all of our support. Without them, we would still be in the dark about much of what is going on in Washington and they depend on our contributions to do their important work.

Through its website, you can find out about campaign contributions, donors, PACs, the personal finances of members of Congress, earmarks, and travel by members.

To get started, go to www.opensecrets.org. On the left side of the home page, you will see a heading labeled "Politicians and Elections." Click on that to open a menu and then scroll down to "Congress." Click on that and then click on the "112th Congress," or, to see members of the last Congress, click on "111th Congress."

Let's start with a look at some overall financial information. On the left, click on "Net Worth," which you'll find in red about halfway down.

Net Worth

This section provides information on the assets and liabilities of each member of Congress. You might be interested in taking a look at the chart in the center of the summary page. It lists the richest members of Congress—and there are lots of them!

RICHEST MEMBERS OF CONGRESS

Name	Minimum Net Worth	Average	Maximum Net Worth
Darrell Issa (R-CA)	$156,050,022	$303,575,011	$451,100,000
Jane Harman (D-CA)	$151,480,522	$293,454,761	$435,429,001
John Kerry (D-MA)	$182,755,534	$238,812,296	$294,869,059
Mark Warner (D-VA)	$65,692,210	$174,385,102	$283,077,995
Jared Polis (D-CO)	$36,694,140	$160,909,068	$285,123,996
Herb Kohl (D-WI)	$89,358,027	$160,302,011	$231,245,995
Vernon Buchanan (R-FL)	$69,434,661	$148,373,160	$366,180,982
Michael McCaul (R-TX)	$73,685,086	$137,611,043	$201,537,000
Jay Rockefeller (D-WV)	$61,446,018	$98,832,010	$136,218,002
Dianne Feinstein (D-CA)	$46,055,250	$77,082,134	$108,109,018

Source: opensecrets.org

As a group, members of Congress are much wealthier than the rest of America. In fact, 237 of the 535 members are millionaires. In general, senators are wealthier than their House counterparts. In 2008, they had a median net worth of $1.79 million, while the House median net worth during the same period was just over $600,000.[27] Whereas about 1% of Americans are considered millionaires, 44% of members of Congress were in that category. Fifty members had wealth topping $10 million.[28] But most of them are well below that: 95% of the Congressional millionaires are between 1 million and 10 million.[29]

As you can see from the chart above, there are ten members with an average net worth of more than $75,000,000! Darrell Issa (R-CA) is the wealthiest member, with an average net worth of $303,575,011, according to the Center for Responsive Politics. Jane Harman (D-CA) is second, with $293,454,761, followed by John Kerry at $238,812,296. Herb Kohl is sixth, with $160,302,011 and Jay Rockefeller is ninth at $98,832,010. Dianne Feinstein is tenth at $77,082,134, and Nancy Pelosi is twelfth at $58,436,537.[30]

Why so many rich senators and congressmen? It is a direct consequence of campaign finance reform. This legislation, enacted to curb special interest donations and fat cat sponsorship of political candidates, limits all campaign contributions to fixed maximum amounts—except for money a candidate gives to his own campaign.

Congress intended to limit that, too, but the Supreme Court wouldn't let them and ruled that it violated that individual's right of free speech. So really rich candidates are free to spend whatever they want of their own money. Candidates like former governor Jon Corzine can spend almost $100 million running for office if they spend their own money.

Campaign finance rules are obsolete. With the Internet, candidates can raise money from tens of thousands of small donors. Campaign finance restrictions should be lifted entirely so that personally wealthy candidates do not dominate our political process anymore and there is a level playing field for all candidates.

There are a couple of other issues to consider: can a legislative body that has 43% more millionaires than the country as a whole really be attuned to the needs of the average voter? When 10% of Congress is worth more than $50 million, do they really understand the impact of increased taxes and spending on working families? Or does their stratospheric wealth insulate them from any ability to empathize with their middle-class fellow citizens? And finally, given the vast investment portfolios of many of the wealthiest members, should they recuse themselves from votes that would help their investments?

At the other end of the spectrum, you can also see who are the poorest members of Congress. Click on the "Net Worth" column on the left-hand side. Select a year and the chamber that you wish—or all members of Congress—and click on "poorest." Those with the lowest net worth (as calculated by OpenSecrets) are:

POOREST MEMBERS OF THE SENATE

Senate Member	Average Net Worth
Deborah Stabenow (D-MI)	$ 0
Mark Pryor	$ 8,500
Jim DeMint	$ 40,501
Russ Feingold	$ 83,001
Bernie Sanders (I-VT)	$105,003

Source: Center For Responsive Politics, opensecrets.org, http://www.opensecrets.org/pfds/overview.php?type=W&year=2009&filter=H

A number of House members have a negative net worth and at least ten have a net worth of $0.

POOREST MEMBERS OF THE HOUSE

House Member	Average Net Worth
Laura Richards (D-CA)	−251,498
Nydia Velazquez (D-NY)	−159,499
Louis B. Gohmet (R-TX)	−150,001
Gregory Meeks	−87,500

Source: http://www.opensecrets.org/pfds/overview.php?type=W&filter=H&sort=A&ptysort=A&year=2009[31]

Executive Branch

The net worth of the highest level employees in the executive branch is also available in that section. Click on "Executive" and choose "Richest."

Hillary Clinton was the richest member of the executive branch in 2009, with an average net worth of $31,243,506. Next was Rahm Emanuel, former White House chief of staff, with an average of $10,995,042. President Barack Obama was number five with an average net worth of $4,960,505 as calculated by OpenSecrets. Vice President Joe Biden is number sixteen, with an average net worth of $89,512.[32]

In 2008, United States Ambassador to the UN Susan Rice was the richest member of the executive branch. There is no 2009 disclosure for her in the database.

REVIEWING FINANCIAL DISCLOSURE REPORTS

You should still be in the "Net Worth" section. To look at individual disclosure forms that are reprinted on opensecrets.org, go to the small screen on the right and type in a last name. As a case study, we'll look at Democratic congressman Maurice Hinchey of New York. His financial disclosure statement, earmarks, wife's occupation, and travel data provide an insight into how vague and inadequate the reporting requirments are, how they need to be changed, and exactly why we need to keep track of these folks. It's not that Congressman Hinchey has clearly violated the rules, it's that the rules are meant to leave the voters with insufficient information to monitor their representative and make important voting decisions.

To get to copies of Congressman Hinchey's disclosure statements and summaries of his financial data, go to the right side of the "Personal Finances Overview" page to the search box. Fill in the first three letters of the member's name—in this case, HIN. Click and it will bring you to the Maurice Hinchey page.

Click on 2009 for the most recent disclosure information. You will see that Hinchey's net worth for that year ranged from a low of $407,017 to a high of $1,080,000, ranking 224th in the House. The reason for this wide variation is that the congressional rules do not require disclosure of the exact value of an asset—only a category.

Below his net worth, you can click on "Assets" and see a description of each one. In 2009, his assets included cash and mutual funds, but his biggest holdings were two properties in Saugerties, New York, his hometown—one on Partition Street and the other on Echo Hill.

The history of Hinchey's reporting of the value and ownership of these properties reveals why there needs to be regular audits, to ask obvious questions and verify the information provided by members of Congress. The first time that Congressman Hinchey listed the two properties as assets was in 2004. His initial filing failed to include the Partition Street property, but he wrote a letter of explanation and filed an amended form.[33] At the time, the Partition Street property was valued at $15,001 to $50,000, and the Echo Hill property was valued at 0. Both properties have realized a stratosphoric increase in value. Here's why—

HINCHEY'S EARMARK: HELPING HIMSELF?

In 2010, Maurice Hinchey sponsored an earmark for $800,000 to the Department of the Interior for water and wastewater infrastructure improvements in the Town of Saugerties.[34] In a 2009 press release announcing the grant, Hinchey took credit for helping the town in its new economic development project, Partition Street Project: "Congressman Used Position on House Appropriations Subcommittee on Interior to Obtain Funds, Which Will Help Promote Economic Growth in the Village" and called the project "critical to the village's commercial future, providing adequate wastewater service to more than 30 retail businesses. . . ."[35] The press release specifically mentioned a portion of Partition Street that would be involved in the infrastructure upgrade.

This upset a number of people in Hinchey's district. Why? Because Hinchey owns a quarter of the land that is to be developed in the Partition Street Project. He and town officials have changed their tune on the reach of the earmark. Although no one corrected the 2009 press release, now Hinchey and the town deny that the earmark will in any way benefit the land owned by Hinchey.[36] The earmark may or may not have benefited Hinchey and raised the value of his Partition Street property, but something sure did. Between 2004 and 2009, his own disclosure forms reflect an increase in the value of the property from $15,001–$50,000 in 2004 to

$250,001–$500,000 in 2009. And this in one of the most economically depressed parts of the nation!

During the last campaign, Congressman Hinchey became a little touchy when the issue of Partition Street was raised. When questioned about a possible conflict of interest, he told the reporter to "shut up" and then jabbed him in the chest and shoved him.[37] Hinchey has repeatedly denied any personal gain from the earmark, and it is impossible, at this time, to determine if that is true. But the entire Partition Street Project and Hinchey's involvement in it demonstrate the need for ethical reforms. We need to know who members of Congress are in business with and what the nature of any such businesses are. And, of course, we need to ban earmarks so there's no opportunity for self-dealing by any congressmen.

We have no idea how Mr. Hinchey came up with the funds—he may have a very simple and legal explanation. His disclosures, however, do not provide any answers and underscore the need for oversight of all Congressional filings.

Both properties were purchased in 2004, when Hinchey showed cash assets of $1,000–$15,000.[38] Yet, somehow, that year, he was able to buy real estate with a combined value of from $30,000–$100,000. And within a year, the properties had drastically increased their value. The Partition Street plot surged to more than five times its original value:

PARTITION STREET PROPERTY VALUATION AND TRANSACTION

2004 purchased @ 15,001–50,000, March 1, 2004[39]

2005 disclosed value 100,001–250,000[40]

2006 disclosed value 100,001–250,000[41]

2007 disclosed value 250,001–500,000[42]

2008 disclosed value 250,001–500,000[43]

2009 disclosed value 250,001–500,000[44]

The Echo Hill property also had a substantial increase in value. In just one year, it more than doubled its value. Two years later, it doubled again:

ECHO HILL PROPERTY VALUATION AND TRANSACTIONS 2004–2009

2004 purchased @ 15,001–50,000, May 15, 2004

2004 sold @ 50,001–100,000, December 20, 2004[45]

2004 capital gain: 5,000–15,000, December 20, 2004[46]

2005 disclosed value: 50,001–100.000[47]

2006 disclosed value: 100,001–250,000[48]

2007 disclosed value: 100,001–250,000[49]

2008 disclosed value: 100,001–250,000[50]

2009 disclosed value: 100,001–250,000[51]

Source: opensecrets.org, http://www.opensecrets.org/pfds/CIDsummary.php?CID=N00001222&year=2009

So what's wrong with this picture?

Well, first of all, the 2004 disclosure form reports both the purchase and sale of the Echo Hill property before the end of 2004. In addition, the report indicates a value of "NONE" for the Echo Hill property in December 2004 and a capital gain from the sale of between $5,000 and $15,000.[52] So, according to all of the statements filed and certified as true, the entire property was sold and a substantial gain was made in 2004. Had only a portion of the property been sold, there would have been a remaining value that should have been reported on the disclosure form. There was none.

So why did Congressman Hinchey continue to list the property as an asset on every disclosure statement from 2005 to 2009? Voters will have to ask him because there is no obvious explanation.

The 2004 report suggests that the property was flipped in less than seven months from the time of purchase, but nevertheless generated a substantial profit. It was not even held long enough to qualify for a capital gains tax instead of ordinary income tax. Because of the absurd rules of reporting, we do not know the actual price of either the purchase or the sale. But we do know that he sold it for between a gain of $5,000–15,000. Not bad for a short-term holding.

Congressman Hinchey's financial statements, like those of many other members of Congress, make it obvious that reform is needed. Until recently, no one's been watching, but it's time for us to take on that job.

Note: Members of Congress are not required to disclose the value of their personal residences or any mortgages attached to them.

Let's see what else is available. Of course, you can look back at the summaries starting in 2004 and at his actual filings since 1998.

By clicking on "Transactions," we can see all of the mutual funds that he bought and sold in 2009. He sold funds in the range of $33,000 to $145,000, and he bought other funds.

Finally, we can look at "Travel." Congressman Hinchey went on two trips sponsored by the Aspen Institute—one to Amman, Jordan, and the other to Dubrovnik, Croatia, for about a week on each one.

Hinchey lists no gifts and no honoraria.

After viewing Congressman Hinchey's 2009 disclosure, what questions are raised? What do we learn about him?

After checking all of the available disclosures, it's clear that Congressman Hinchey likes to travel. Throughout his Congressional career, he's had the opportunity to see the world—for free, of course. His wife accompanied him on a few of the trips.

From 1998 through 2009, he's been on fifty trips—about four each year. Forty of the trips were to foreign countries. He's visited the following places:

Ft. Meyers, Florida	Israel
Naples, Florida (3)	Athens, Greece
Miami, Florida	Rome, Italy
Memphis, Tennessee	Baden-Baden, Germany
Newport, Rhode Island	Havana, Cuba
St. Louis, Missouri	Egypt
Zion National Park, Utah	Vancouver, B.C.
Alaska	Jordan
Cancún, Mexico	Grand Cayman
Punta Mia, Mexico	Germany
Costa Rica	St. Petersburg, Russia
Liberia	Helsinki, Finland
Honduras	Prague, Czech Republic
Montego Bay, Jamaica	Madrid
Madrid, Spain	Lichtenstein
Moscow	China
Vienna, Austria	Brataslava, Slovakia
Hamburg, Germany	Budapest, Hungary
Taipei, Taiwan (3)	Kazakhstan
Beirut, Lebanon	India
Frankfurt, Germany (2)	Amman, Jordan
Berlin, Germany	Dubrovnik, Croatia
Düsseldorf, Germany	

Source: Maurice Hinchey financial disclosure statements 1998-2009, at http://www.opensecrets.org/pfds/CIDsummary.php?CID=N00001222&year=2007

CONGRESSIONAL SPOUSES

There is another area that needs reform and emerges from a review of another of Congressman Hinchey's disclosures. We need to know much more about the business activities of spouses of members and how much money they make. More and more Congressional spouses are working in areas regulated by Congress. Many are suddenly invited to join lucrative corporate boards once their spouses are elected. Right now, all that is required is a disclosure of who the spouse works for and that they are paid "more than a thousand dollars."

Hinchey reveals that, in 2009, his wife was paid more than $1,000 by Patricia Lynch Associates and DKC Government Affairs, both Albany, New York, lobbying firms.[53] The wife's name was not disclosed. But a Google search indicates that in 2006, Hinchey married Allison Lee, who had worked in his district office. After they married, she became a lobbyist in Albany with one of the most powerful firms in the New York capital. More recently, she left to head up the lobbying arm of DKC.

One of Lee's clients was a Landsman Association from Texas that was trying to buy up land /or leases in anticipation of drilling for natural gas in shale in New York. Hinchey testified that the federal government, not states like New York, should regulate the drilling at a time when New York's governor was considering a moratorium on drilling. When questioned about his wife's work, he claimed that he did not know that she was lobbying on the issue.[54]

Is ignorance bliss?

Regardless of whether there are potential conflict of interest issues, and it is not clear that is the case here, voters have a right to know exactly who a member's spouse is working for, who spouses' partners are, what exactly they are working on. It's becoming a trend.

Once Barack Obama was elected to the Senate, Michelle Obama was invited on a corporate board in Chicago. Former senator Chris Dodd's wife, Jackie Clegg, had the same good fortune. Once her husband ascended into leadership positions in the health and banking committees, corporations with business or potential business before these committees suddenly sought out Ms. Clegg, who had no office, employees, or even a business phone. It's been quite profitable. Since her marriage to Dodd, her income has quadrupled, as she has been appointed to well-paid positions on boards of corporations that do business in the financial, insurance, health care services, and housing fields—almost all of which had concerns that fall under the jurisdiction of committees where her husband yields influence.

These board appointments, along with valuable stock that came with it, suddenly turned the Dodds into comfortable millionaires.

For example, in 2007, Clegg disclosed stock assets from the various boards of $530,000–$1,353 million.[55]

There are members who disclose a spouse's position and salary, even when it is for an institution that seeks money from Congress. Chuck Schumer, for example, reports that his wife works for the City University of New York, which obviously lobbies for federal money. Others should follow his example.

THERE'S MORE OUT THERE!

There's lots more information available, but here are a few important things to look at:

Donor look-up on opensecrets.org.

Go to the home page, click on politicians, click on Congress. The last item in the left-hand column is the donor look-up.

Also, check out the Sunlight Foundation at http://sunlightfoundation .com/. They have numerous projects dedicated to transparency and open government.

And try CREW: citizensforethics.org. They are ethical watchdogs who litigate on transparency and corruption issues.

There's much to be done. Join us in this journey of necessity.

ETHICAL REFORMS THAT ARE NEEDED IMMEDIATELY

We've described just some of the many abuses that are commonplace in Congress today. There's no question that there is a need for serious reforms—and now is the time to demand them.

We've made some proposals in the past that we'll repeat here and we've added a few new ones:

1. *Establish an independent Office of Congressional Ethics*, with a full-time staff and prosecutorial powers to receive and investigate complaints, initiate its own investigations, subpoena documents, compel

testimony, and monitor and carry a mandate to randomly audit all financial disclosure filings by members of Congress and lobbyists.

WHY: because currently there is no regular monitoring or any other serious oversight of the mandatory financial disclosure forms. Members simply file their disclosure statements and no one ever checks to see if they are accurate—or if they even make sense. There should be random audits. A review by us of many of them raise many questions. Someone needs to look at them.

In the rare instances when a complaint is filed against a member by an outside party, it is reviewed in secret without any explanation to the public of how the conclusion was reached that there was no violation, which is the usual resolution.

To instill any kind of public confidence, the entire process must be open and transparent, and there have to be serious penalties—including, when warranted, criminal prosecutions. Right now, the process is an absurd whitewash. For example, the House Ethics Committee recently found Congressman Charles Rangel guilty of eleven counts of violations, including failing to report income on a rental property, filing inaccurate financial disclosure statements, using a rent-stabilized apartment as a campaign office, and improper solicitation of charitable contributions for a public policy center named in his honor. The punishment: a censure vote on the House floor and a recommendation that he pay the IRS for his delinquent taxes. A slap on the wrist!

And even then, seventy-seven House members voted against the resolution. The House and the Senate ethics committees have conclusively demonstrated that they are incapable of policing the behavior of the members of Congress. A full-time, well-staffed, and empowered Office of Congressional Ethics is a vital necessity. Until it is created, there will be no real reform of Congressional ethics.

2. *A ban on all earmarks*

WHY: earmarks are increasingly used as bait for bribes. Between 25 and 50% of the campaign chest of the typical incumbent senator comes from campaign contributions from lobbyists and employees of companies who receive earmarks. Earmarks are also used by some members to feather their own nests and increase the value of property they own. As noted above, concerns of this sort have been raised in connection with Congressman Hinchey and, as we reported in our previous book, *2010: Take Back America—A Battle Plan*, similar questions have attached to earmarks made by Senator Harry Reid that appear to have increased the value of his property.

3. *A ban on lobbying by members of the immediate family* of any member of Congress.

WHY: the potential for conflict of interest is obvious. It's a way to funnel money to families of members from companies that might be seeking favors.

4. *A prohibition against any immediate family member accepting employment or serving on the corporate board of any corporation that hires a lobbyist or is, in any way, affected by federal legislation or regulation, or receives federal funds.*

WHY: again, it's a way to funnel money to the families of members of Congress who might be voting on legislation that is important to the company.

5. *Stop the revolving door: a ban on all members of Congress and all Congressional staff members from lobbying Congress for five years from their last date of service or employment or from working for any company or firm that performs lobbying services.*

WHY: because staff and former members should not be able to use their inside knowledge and information for personal benefit. The current bans on lobbying have two defects: they do not cover a long enough period of time after leaving Congress and they do not ban working for lobbying firms. Many ex-members and former staffers work as "consultants" or "public relations advisors," avoiding direct lobbying to comply with the restriction, but, in fact, making their inside information available to their clients.

6. *Require disclosure of all partners of members of Congress and their immediate families—in real estate deals or any other business. Prohibit partnerships with anyone who is employed by or is a director of any company doing business with Congress, seeking or getting federal funds, or lobbying Congress.*

WHY: it is impossible to tell who members might own property jointly with but it is important to know. Chris Dodd, for example, disclosed that he owned one-third of an Irish "cottage," without disclosing that his partner was a stand-in for a man for whom he got a presidential pardon and an owner of a company that sought and received funds from Congress.

7. *A ban on all free travel—including that provided by not-for-profit organizations and "think tanks."*

WHY: these trips are nothing but boondoogles. If the foundations that sponsor them are so interested in providing information to members of Congress, they can meet in Washington and avoid any travel costs. They don't have to go to Honolulu on the sands of Waikiki Beach to get educated.

8. *Require full and accurate disclosure of the actual value of all income and assets of all members and their spouses at the time of each filing.*

WHY: there is no rational reason for the current range of value used by Congress and the executive branch. The only reason for it is to keep us from knowing the exact value.

9. *Include all personal residences in disclosure of assets and all mortgages in disclosure of liabilities.*

WHY: all real estate, including all homes, should be listed. There is no rationale for the exclusion.

10. *Require that all financial disclosure statements be permanently available on each member's website.*

WHY: the voters have a right to see this information.

11. *No work, no pay. If a member is not present for more than ten consecutive workdays and does not provide a doctor's letter, he or she should not be paid.*

WHY: for $174,000 a year, we expect them to at least show up.

12. *Disclosure of all appointments with members of Congress on their government website, along with a notation about the purpose of the meeting.*

WHY: so we can tell how much of their time is spent with donors and lobbyists and on campaign matters.

13. *Prohibit private charities founded by members from receiving contributions from corporations that do business with, seek favors from, or receive money from the federal government.*

WHY: some current members have set up private charities that receive money from businesses that seek favors from the government. The money is often distributed in the member's community to enhance their image as generous to the community.

This is another backdoor payoff.
We also need:

• Full online publication of committee votes

• Full online publication of financial disclosure forms

• Full online publication of member car lease data and/or purchase with federal funds

- Full online publication of all government-sponsored travel

- Full online publication of all ethics complaints and all actions by the Ethics Committee

- Full online disclosure of any special assistance for repayment of student loans for members or staffers in Congress.

  Only by enacting these rules can we have an open and honest Congress. Tell your member to support them—right now!!!

PART SIX

THE NEW LEADERS

The elections of 2010 brought to light a new set of national leaders. Toiling well outside the spotlight of establishment media attention, these young men and women turned around the Obama program, blunted his momentum, defeated his congressmen, and laid the basis for an American recovery. They deserve our appreciation, respect, and praise.

The bold, new force on the scene of American politics in 2010 was the Tea Party. It isn't one organization. It is a term used by thousands of small groups around the country to describe themselves. They vary in size, power, ideology, and orientation. But they all agree on trimming the size of government.

It all started with Rick Santelli's rant. Rick, an on-air editor for CNBC Business News, was reporting live from the floor of the Chicago Board of Trade at the time. He first joined CNBC in 1999, and his reporting focuses primarily on "interest rates, foreign exchange, and the Federal Reserve."[1]

But it was his Rant Heard Round the World on February 19, 2009, that will earn him a place in U.S. history:[2]

RICK'S RANT

SANTELLI: This is America! How many of you people want to pay for your neighbor's mortgage that has an extra bathroom and can't pay their bills? Raise their hand.

(Booing)

President Obama, are you listening?

TRADER: How 'bout we all stop paying our mortgage? It's a moral hazard.

SANTELLI: Don't get scared, Joe. They're already scaring you. You know, Cuba used to have mansions and a relatively decent economy. They moved from the individual to the collective. Now, they're driving '54 Chevys, maybe the last great car to come out of Detroit.

KERNEN: They're driving them on water, too, which is a little strange to watch.

SANTELLI: There you go.

REBECCA QUICK: Wow. Wilbur, you get people fired up.

SANTELLI: We're thinking of having a Chicago Tea Party in July. All you capitalists that want to show up to Lake Michigan, I'm gonna start organizing.

(Whistling, cheering)

The rant spawned a movement when it fell on carefully listening ears.

There is no one leader of the Tea Party movement. It is far too diverse and disconnected. But there is great unity in the Tea Party because of a common set of beliefs centered around the need for free markets, low taxes, and less government.

There are no leaders, but there are two founders, and they deserve our appreciation: Jenny Beth Martin and Mark Meckler.

Jenny Beth Martin

How emblematic of the Tea Party is the fact that its founder—and still one of its leaders—went through a painful bankruptcy only very recently. After her husband closed his business, Jenny Beth relates how "we went from a husband working and stay at home mom family to an unemployed family to a [two]-parent working from home family."[3]

They made ends meet by "cleaning houses and repairing computers."[4] They couldn't help noticing that all those around them were also suffering and that only the government was doing well. She "began to blog about what we were going through financially. So many others are facing a difficult time due to the recession and I wanted to show that you can keep what matters most: faith in God, love of family. All the other things are truly the icing on the cake of life. They are truly things. Things that can be lost or broken, sold or given away." [5]

This is the woman who had a lot to do with changing America! She heard Rick Santelli rant on CNBC about "government bailouts." [6] She says "it truly changed my life." [7]

Jenny Beth focused her formidable organizing skills, her even temperament, and her techno-savvy on organizing a force that would change her country. In 2009, the Tea Party movement was born when she "co-hosted the Atlanta Tea Party on February 27, 2009 at the Georgia State Capitol in the pouring rain." [8]

There are more than 5,000 groups that call themselves part of the Tea Party movement and Jenny Beth's attitude is: the more the better! About 3,000 are loosely affiliated in the Tea Party Patriots organization Jenny Beth Martin cofounded (with Mark Meckler). They "meet" every Monday in a conference call where they discuss current affairs and vote—online—about whether to take certain positions or adopt various initiatives.

We both have participated in these calls and are amazed by Jenny Beth's cool, calm presence as she presides over them. At one point, a participant asked Dick a question about abortion. Before he could answer, Martin stepped in and reminded the questioner that "we are only focused on economic and financial issues. Social issues are outside of our framework." [9]

Martin, a total political novice, has fashioned a national pressure group that changed American politics. She has developed an organization that can summon millions to the streets and match the best the union/Democratic Party machines can offer.

Best of all, she and Mark have not let Tea Party Patriots become encrusted with bureaucracy and controlled by financial donors. With their mammoth organization, they have only seven employees and a monthly budget of only about $40,000. "You can't buy us because we don't take money" might as well be their motto.

Think of Europe, where the leader of a grassroots movement would likely be a self-aggrandizing politician, seeking money, fame, and power in a narcissistic mania. Then think of Jenny Beth Martin—a regular person (her blog is jenuinejen)—angered by government handouts and fighting not for the government to do more, but for it to do less. And there you have the difference between the U.S. and Europe.

For further information about Tea Party Patriots, go to their website: www.teapartypatriots.org.

Mark Meckler

Rick's rant also inspired Jenny Beth's cofounder—at the other end of the nation—Mark Meckler. Galvanized to action, Mark attended what theunion.com called a "hastily organized Tea Party on the steps of the Capitol in Sacramento." [10]

Mark went with his wife and two children. "I wanted to show the kids what the First Amendment was all about," Meckler said. "We brought pre-made signs. At first, no one was there. The police came over to give us a hard time—we didn't know we needed a permit." Eventually, 150 people came. Meckler called it "astounding." [11]

"It was liberating to feel there were other people out there. People from all walks of life, both political parties, pro-choice, pro-life, Prop. 8 supporters and gay-rights activists," Meckler said. "It was magic—it was something I'd never seen in politics. That really jacked me up." [12]

A Southern California lawyer, Meckler moved to Nevada County, California, in 1993. "I was always into the art scene and music—in college, I was a punk rock DJ," he recounts. But he makes clear that he grew up with "cowboy ethics" from his father, who "had this underlying, tremendous love of America and raised (me) as a very strong patriot." [13]

He was the owner of Cafe Mekka (*not* Mecca!), until he sold it in 1997 and started MekTek Industries, which manufactured snow-skiing equipment. He "stumbled into" Internet marketing law. Theunion.com notes that "Meckler's expertise in Internet-based marketing perfectly positioned him to facilitate the explosive growth of the Tea Party movement through social networking tools like Twitter and Facebook." [14]

Meckler became a catalyst for the Tea Party movement. In December 2009, he organized a "die-in" on Capitol Hill to protest Obama's health care policies.

He is creative, articulate, and charismatic. His networking skills have helped to build the movement, and his political savvy has helped to guide it into the force that it has become.

"I think Ronald Reagan would have loved the Tea Party," Mark says.[15]

Right on!

The Tea Party is unique for its almost total absence of financing. During the 2010 campaign, Dick addressed a gathering of 4,000 Tea Party people in Richmond, Virginia. Every single person in the room (including Dick) was there as a volunteer. The speakers, the organizers, the MC, the security guards, everybody! No movement quite like it has ever happened.

But politics needs money to succeed, and two courageous men, the brothers Koch, have stepped forward to lend their fortunes to save the country that made it possible for them to succeed, and we should all be grateful.

Charles and David Koch

Conservatives, patriots, and lovers of freedom are deeply indebted to Charles and David Koch (and David's wife, Julia). Their financial generosity let us equal the fund-raising machine the Democrats have put together.

But there is one key difference: the Democrats' money came directly or indirectly from us, the taxpayers, while the conservative efforts were all privately funded.

The Democrats drew on donations from lobbyists for earmarks of taxpayer-funded projects, funds from public employee unions docked from the taxpayer-funded paychecks of their members, and donations from others seeking favors from the Obama White House. Conservatives had David and Charles Koch and their privately amassed fortune.

NPR reports that in the past thirty years, the Kochs have donated "more than $100 million" to "dozens of political organizations, many of which are trying to steer the country in a more libertarian direction," including the Cato Institute and the Mercatus Center at George Mason University in Virginia.[16]

More important has been the Koch brothers' role in forming and helping to fund Americans for Prosperity (AFP)—a key driving force behind the drive that led to victory in 2010. AFP, with millions of members and chapters in most states, fueled much of the grassroots organizing that drew voters to conservative causes. And, without their targeted advertising, we could not have won in 2010.

AFP—and American Crossroads, led by Karl Rove and Ed Gillespie—stepped in where the Republican National Committee (RNC) failed. The RNC was so absorbed by its own overhead that it could spare little for the 2010 campaign. We were astonished to learn that as of July 2010, the RNC had raised $106 million for the 2010 election cycle and had spent $100 million of it! On what? Building a direct mail base in the era of the Internet and God knows what else.

But AFP, Rove, and Gillespie stepped in and saved the day. And the Koch brothers were a big part of what made that possible.

Politics is, of course, not the only venue for their generosity. Jane Mayer, a left-wing reporter, did a hit piece on them in *The New Yorker*, but had to note that David Koch "donated a hundred million dollars to modernize Lincoln Center's New York State Theatre building, which now bears his name. He has given twenty million to the American Museum of Natural History, whose dinosaur wing is named for him. This spring, after noticing the decrepit state of the fountains outside the Metropolitan Museum of Art, Koch pledged at least ten million dollars for their renovation. He is a trustee of the museum, perhaps the most coveted social prize in the city, and serves on the board of Memorial Sloan-Kettering Cancer Center, where, after he donated more than forty million dollars, an endowed chair and a research center were named for him." [17]

The New Yorker reports that the annual revenues of Koch Industries "are estimated to be a hundred billion dollars." It notes that the Kochs operate "oil refineries in Alaska, Texas, and Minnesota, and control some four thousand miles of pipeline. Koch Industries owns Brawny paper towels, Dixie cups, Georgia-Pacific lumber, Stainmaster carpet, and Lycra, among other products." [18]

Frank Rich, writing in the *New York Times*, erroneously reported that the Kochs are "the sugar daddies who are bankrolling . . . America's ostensibly spontaneous and leaderless populist uprising." [19] Mr. Rich, whose skills as a political observer have never quite equaled his abilities as a drama critic, is misinformed. The Kochs help to fund AFP, which is quite independent of the Tea Party Patriots organization. The efforts of Martin, Meckler, and their colleagues are not bankrolled! They are exactly a "spontaneous and leaderless populist uprising." And that is why they are both so remarkable and so outside the realm of Mr. Rich's comprehension.

But it took a unique talent to be able to channel the Koch resources—and those of many others—into concrete political action. That's where Tim Phillips came in.

Tim Phillips

It is not easy to coordinate an organization of 1.6 million members with chapters in thirty-two states. But Tim Phillips, president of Americans for Prosperity (AFP), showed such organizational talents in 2010 that he was able to mobilize and harness his group's energy to bring critical mass to bear in crucial states at exactly the right time. Like a chessmaster competing on one hundred boards at once, he directed the AFP's human and financial resources with precision and flair.

Phillips's warm-up for the 2010 election was the 2009 AFP drive against ObamaCare. Sponsoring more than three hundred "hands off my health care" bus rallies and town hall meetings, he tapped into and helped fan the massive backlash against Obama's program and its arrogant Democratic Congressional sponsors.

And, at about the same time, AFP organized eighty-two events in "cost of hot air" tours aimed at defeating the cap and trade legislation.

In a movement of amateurs, Tim was the rare political veteran. For twenty-four years, he has been a strategist working at all levels of politics. In 1998, *Campaigns & Elections* magazine named him a "rising star in politics." In 2010, he rose!

For more information, go to www.americansforprosperity.org.

Or watch this clip on YouTube: http://www.youtube.com/AforP#p/u/22/mqD1nAdNl-0

FoxNews

But all the organization and funding in the world would not have worked its magic if the liberal, left-wing media continued its domination of news in this country. The fact that it has not been able to do so is attributable to the genius of two men: Rupert Murdoch and Roger Ailes. Their courage and confidence led them to craft a truly independent voice, a dissonant note from the harmonized liberal chorus that is the mainstream media.

It was not an easy journey. Murdoch and Ailes had to force their way onto cable systems throughout the nation until the attractiveness of their product made their exclusion unthinkable.

Some have accused them of conservative bias. If that appears to be the case to some people, it is only because of the backdrop of liberalism that dominates the three networks and the two other cable news stations. Impartial rating services have consistently found that FoxNews offers more balance in its news coverage than any of the other outlets.

FoxNews is really like Radio Free Europe, beaming its signal to those who seek the truth and who are not hypnotized by the uni-think coverage of the mainstream media.

Newsmax.com, another new voice empowering conservatism, has also broken the monopoly of the establishment media. Its online coverage, e-mailings, magazine, and access to conservative activists did a lot to catalyze the 2010 victories. If there is, indeed, a "vast right-wing conspiracy" as Hillary charged, then Newsmax.com is its spinal cord.

Bill O'Reilly

Fox would not have succeeded without its star: Bill O'Reilly.

In a media world dominated by softball interviews (see Larry King on CNN), O'Reilly carved out his own niche by a zero tolerance for baloney (or any of its synonyms). When he says "the spin stops here," he means it and does not hesitate to cut guests down to size or to debate their opinions.

In his shows, he creates a kind of tension as he challenges his guests and his audience to think along with him and to defend their views in the face of his often harsh cross-examination.

But O'Reilly is, at heart, a journalist. He is an equal opportunity opponent of hypocrisy whether from the left or the right. He is a populist, not a conservative. A vigorous proponent of American values, he styles himself more as a "culture warrior" than as a partisan political figure.

Bill's uniqueness is his ability to stay outside the political process and think like an outsider. When you are making big bucks, lionized in society, fêted as a celebrity, the hardest thing to do is to keep looking at things as if you had none of these advantages, and think like a regular person. O'Reilly's head is never turned by fame. He keeps squarely focused on the original values that shaped his life. That is his strength.

But Glenn Beck and Sean Hannity have stepped out to provide the on-air voice of political conservatism.

Glenn Beck

Too often political movements exist only in the present, preoccupied by the daily struggles they face in their battle to prevail. But the genius of Glenn Beck is to put our efforts in their historical context, analyzing their constitutional roots and their political antecedents. While some dwell in the two-dimensional world of today, Beck adds the third dimension of history, providing depth and perspective to our debates.

Indeed, Beck explains how to marry the social conservatives with the free market economic libertarians. He examines the moral dimension of what some treat as purely financial questions. For example, while some oppose America's headlong rush into colossal debt on economic grounds, Beck objects to the "unhealthy relationships" debt causes. Examine America's inability to leverage its economic relationship with China to promote human rights or to curb North Korea as examples. We are so much in the People's Republic's debt that we are helpless to affect their behavior.

Using his pulpit on FoxNews and the vast audience he has built through his six *New York Times* bestselling books, he has given conservatism a new voice and added vigor. He doesn't just state his opinions and fight for them, he explains them, teaching us as a professor would, replete with chalkboard, readings, and even homework.

His time slot on FoxNews—from 5 to 6 P.M. ET—is not prime time in television land. But Beck has become so popular that he attracts an audience that parallels the prime-time viewers in size and intensity.

But, in 2010, he played a very special role as a political leader, attracting, organizing, and then addressing a throng of more than one hundred thousand activists in Washington, D.C., on September 12, right as the fall elections were heating up. The ripples from the splash he made on that day only gained in strength as they helped to wash away the Democratic establishment eight weeks later.

We will need Beck's continuing leadership as we face the budget struggles of 2011 and the elections of 2012. He is a potent new force on the political scene.

Already there when Beck arrived was Sean Hannity, whose constant battles for conservative causes have animated FoxNews for its entire history.

Sean Hannity

Sean is like a compass that always points north. Sean always points right toward true conservatism whether it be in the battles for economic freedom, national security, justice, or values. He reliably tells us where right is. Even if we don't always want to go there, it is important to know where conservatism is on each political question.

Unlike a lot of on-air commentators, Sean doesn't need to examine talking points or feeds from the national party to know where true conservatism points. He just looks within himself. His own values system is so attuned to the political compass of our time that he doesn't need to reason out his position. It springs from within him.

For those who have known him since he started at FoxNews, the amazing thing is how little fame and success have changed him. He is neither self-centered nor narcissistic. His values not only determine his politics, but his personal conduct as well.

He did not compromise or equivocate in the face of the national lurch to the left in 2008. From the moment the ballots were counted, he called himself the leader of the "conservative opposition in exile" and, like the fallen monarch of a nation the Nazis had overrun, waited patiently until the moment for his return arrived.

And when it came, Sean Hannity continued his conservatism. Sean's strength lies in the fact that he is a conservative, not a Republican. His priority is ideological, not partisan. Like any compass, it is his consistency that makes him so valuable.

Some of the leaders of the 2010 surge have been working in the vineyards for some time, but now their moment has come. One such is David N. Bossie, the head of Citizens United.

David N. Bossie

Not all the blows for liberty were struck on Election Day of 2010. Earlier in that historic year, Citizens United, headed by conservative movement leader David N. Bossie, won its landmark case, *Citizens United v. Federal Election Commission*. The case freed much political speech from the shackles imposed on us by the McCain-Feingold legislation. It allowed small businesses, corporations, and unions to spend on political messaging, paving the way for much of the independent expenditures on both sides that shaped the 2010 election.

The case began with a film, *Hillary the Movie*, produced by David, directed by Alan Peterson, that featured Dick. Under the McCain-Feingold campaign finance legislation, Citizens United was prohibited from broadcasting *Hillary the Movie* on Video on Demand, because then-Senator Hillary Clinton was gearing up for a presidential run.

Consequently, Bossie and Citizens United sued the Federal Elections Commission (FEC) and began their long trek through the federal courts in search of their freedom of speech. After adverse rulings at the District Court, they persevered—and the private, small, individual donations on which they rely made their perseverance possible. The Supreme Court accepted their case.

Initially, Citizens United was just seeking the right to broadcast its films and advertisements without being subjected to fines from the FEC. But the Court, after hearing the case in the spring of 2009, withheld a verdict and called for reargument in the fall term on the broader question of the constitutionality of the McCain-Feingold law's restrictions on political speech. The decision, early in 2010, struck down most of its prohibitions on corporate political speech by a 5–4 decision. Their empowerment of groups of Americans to fight for their freedoms so outraged President Obama that he used his State of the Union address in January 2010 to criticize the decision—with the Justices sitting right in front of him unable to comment.

Bossie's victory for free speech was heard around the nation and catalyzed much of the dynamic that swept the Democrats from control of the House later last year.

Citizens United was founded in 1988 and Bossie became its president in 2001. With more than 500,000 members and supporters, it is a key force for conservatism. Its films, television ads, web ads, op-eds, policy papers, newsletters, grassroots organizing, and PAC donations have made it a tremendous power for good.

Particularly its films. Alive to the new opportunities for political advocacy films afford, Bossie has produced seventeen full-length movies since 2004. These include:

- *Battle for America*, which attacks Obama's programs and policies and calls for a grassroots effort to reverse the damage he has inflicted. It is inspired by our most recent book, *2010: Take Back America—A Battle Plan.*

- *Generation Zero*, a probing look at how the deterioration of our values sparked the financial and economic crisis.

- *Nine Days That Changed the World*, narrated by Newt and Callista Gingrich, about Pope John Paul II's pilgrimage to Poland in 1979 and the fall of communism.

- *America at Risk*, also narrated by the Gingrichs, critiques the failures of the Obama administration in the battle against terrorism.

- *Fire from the Heartland* focuses on women in the conservative movement.

- *Ronald Reagan: Rendezvous with Destiny* is an award-winning celebration of his life and achievements.

To order any of these films, go to www.citizensunited.org.

David Bossie, the man behind the movies, has led an extraordinary life. Born in Boston, David has served for over twenty years as a volunteer firefighter in Montgomery County, Maryland, where he lives. Often sleeping on a bunk bed in the firehouse, he has saved many lives and risked his own frequently. Facing out-of-control blazes proved to be good training for the Washington, D.C., political wars.

He and his wife, Susan, have shown strength, courage, love, and commitment in raising their four children, Isabella, Griffin, Lily Campbell, and Margaret Reagan—particularly Griffin, who was born with a narrowed aorta and holes in his heart and at six months suffered a brain aneurysm. After six costly, life-endangering surgeries, he is now living a healthy, happy life. He may have had a hole in his heart, but the Bossies have none in theirs.

Obama thought he had it all figured out when he proposed his health care changes. He got the drug companies on board, the American Medical Association's endorsement, and backing from the insurance industry. The elderly? He figured that when he bought the American Association of Retired Persons (AARP)—by cutting subsidies to the Medicare Advantage Program, which gave AARP's Medigap policies strong competition—he would bring along the elderly. He figured wrong. He didn't figure on Jim Martin and the 60 Plus Association.

Jim Martin

The head of 60 Plus, the organization of the elderly that really fights for their interests, Jim has only one defect. He looks just like Ted Turner. Not even Jane Fonda could tell them apart! But their politics are as different as their looks are similar. Jim is an articulate, able leader who galvanized America's seniors into the battering ram that crashed in the door of the Democratic fortress in Washington.

With support from 5.5 million seniors, 60 Plus made a vast difference in the health care debate and, with their grassroots organizing and independent expenditures, in the outcome of the 2010 elections.

It wasn't Martin's first contribution to freedom. It was Jim who coined the phrase "death tax" to describe the inheritance tax championed by liberals. It was his persistent battling that led to its repeal in 2001 and held it down when Obama brought it back again last year.

Born in 1936, he and his wife, Mary Lou, have seven children and fifteen grandchildren. They live in Arlington, Virginia. Jim served two tours in the U.S. Marines (1953–58) and still has the fitness and swagger of a member of the Corps. He swims a mile a day, pitches for a nationally ranked over-65 Maryland softball team, and plays basketball in two leagues—the over-60 and 65 Saints and Sinners teams.

For guidance on how to age—and fight those who would oppress the elderly—go to www.60plus.org!

CONCLUSION

But it is not the leaders who will prevail in the next two years—it is their followers! The overthrow of the Obama-dominated House of Representatives in 2010 would never have happened without the involvement of millions of ordinary Americans, united, not by hope of personal gain, but by a patriotic abhorrence of what the president is doing to our country.

We are determined not to leave a legacy of debt to our children!

We are determined to keep the best health care system in the world alive, available, and free of government control and rationing.

We are determined to end the policy of punishing success and to reward those who create jobs and build America.

We are determined to let our manufacturing industry continue to lead the world without imposing ideological shackles upon it.

We are determined to let workers make their own decisions, by secret ballot, on whether or not to form unions.

We are determined to end earmarking and the corruption it spawns in Washington.

We are determined to use our majority in the House to reform it, change it, open it up, and restore it to the spirit of our Constitution.

We are determined to free state and local government from the control of public employee unions and to return the power of local self-government to the people.

We are determined to wage and win the war on terror and will not be hobbled by the shibboleths and myths pushed by our liberal president.

We do what our founders did. We pledge our "lives, our fortunes, and our sacred honor" to this task!

ACKNOWLEDGMENTS

We would like to acknowledge the great work of our editor, Adam Bellow. He really brought new insights to us and we are grateful.

Morgan Buehler, who has worked with us on several past books, was, as usual, an invaluable help in researching and getting the endnotes right.

Economist Barry Elias guided us through the trickier waters of economic policy and deserves our deepest thanks.

And thanks also to Ryan Ellis of Americans for Tax Reform for his help in wrestling with the dynamics of federal budget making.

Tom Gallagher, Irma Cruz, and Maureen Maxwell, as ever, deserve a great vote of appreciation for their wonderful help.

We would also like to thank Jim Dugan for his excellent editing, spotting errors others missed.

Stan Pottinger, our agent and close friend, made this book possible and we thank him deeply.

Thanks also to the folks at Center for Responsive Politics for their website opensecrets.org. Their work renders transparent the deepest secrets of Washington, D.C. They deserve our thanks and your—and our—financial support.

And to those at HarperCollins who made this book happen: Jonathan Burnham, Kathy Schneider, Kathryn Whitenight, our thanks as well.

NOTES

INTRODUCTION

1 Tony Blair, *A Journey: My Political Life* (New York: Knopf, 2010), p. 7.

PART ONE

1 Presidential Approval Index: "Daily Presidential Tracking Poll," RasmussenReports .com, December 24, 1010, http://www.rasmussenreports.com/public_content/politics/ obama_administration/daily_presidential_tracking_poll.

2 The Zogby Poll: "Trends Over Time," Zogby.com, http://www.zogby.com/features/ featuredtables.cfm?ID=171.

3 "shellacking": "After 'Shellacking,' Obama Laments Disconnect with Voters," MSNBC .com, November 3, 2010, http://www.msnbc.msn.com/id/39987154/ns/politics-decision _2010/.

4 Comparison of Favorable Personal Ratings: Jeffrey M. Jones, "Historical Favorability Ratings of Presidents," Gallup.com, July 29, 2003, http://www.gallup.com/poll/8938/ historical-favorability-ratings-presidents.aspx.

5 Pollster John Zogby: E-mail to author from John Zogby, November 19, 2010.

6 "I neglected some things": Michael D. Shear, "Obama Blames Himself for Tone in Washington," *New York Times*, November 15, 2010, http://thecaucus.blogs.nyimes .com/2010/11/15/obama-blames-himself-for-tone-in-washington/.

7 A McLaughlin & Associates: Jim McLaughlin and John McLaughlin, "The 2010 Midterm Election—What Really Happened and Why," National Post-Election Survey, McLaughlin online.com, November 17, 2010.

8 The recession ended: "National Income and Product Accounts Table," BEA.gov, November 23, 2010, http://www.bea.gov/national/nipaweb/TableView.asp?SelectedTable=1&View Series=NO&Java=no&Request3Place=N&3Place=N&FromView=YES&Freq=Qtr& FirstYear=1990&LastYear=1992&3Place=N&Update=Update&JavaBox=no#.

9 and the fourth quarter: Ibid.

10 11.5 million new jobs: "The Unemployment Situation January 1994," bls.gov, February 4, 1994, http://www.bls.gov/news.release/history/empsit_020494.txt.

11 According to the Rasmussen: "57% Favor Repeal of Health Care Law," RasmussenReports .com, November 22, 2010, http://www.rasmussenreports.com/public_content/politics/ current_events/healthcare/november_2010/57_favor_repeal_of_health_care_law.

12 Ideology of American Voters: Lydia Saad, " 'Conservatives' Are Single-Largest Ideological Group," Gallup.com, June 15, 2009, http://www.gallup.com/poll/120857/conservatives -single-largest-ideological-group.aspx. Jim McLaughlin and John McLaughlin, "National Post-Election Survey—A Conservative Landslide," McLaughlinOnline.com, November 5, 2010.

13 16,500 new agents: Paul Collins, "Griffith Targets Issues, 10 Percent Pay Cut," Martinsville Bulletin, November 21, 2010, http://www.martinsvillebulletin.com/article .cfm?ID=26283.

14 According to the Rasmussen: Michael Barone, "Card Check: Good for Unions, Bad for America," RasmussenReports.com, March 21, 2009, http://www.rasmussenreports.com/ public_content/political_commentary/commentary_by_michael_barone/card_check_ good_for_unions_bad_for_america.

15 But when asked: "53% Say EPA Should Not Regulate Greenhouse Gases Without Congress' OK," RasmussenReports.com, December 9, 2009, http://www.rasmussenreports .com/public_content/politics/current_events/environment_energy/53_say_epa_ should_not_regulate_greenhouse_gases_without_congress_ok.

16 About half . . . a week or more: Survey by Opinion Research, August 21, 2010.

17 Although he led: "Republican Presidential Primary," RealClearPolitics.com, http://www .realclearpolitics.com/epolls/2012/president/us/republican_presidential_primary-1452 .html.

18 "the former . . . of our time": Grace-Marie Turner, "The Failure of RomneyCare," Wall Street Journal, March 16, 2010, http://online.wsj.com/article/SB100014240527487036253 04575115691871093652.html.

19 "ultimate conservative plan": Ibid.

20 "Both have an individual": Ibid.

21 "our plan is working": Ibid.

22 While 97% of his: Ibid.

23 Like Obama . . . average: Ibid.

24 A study by the: Ibid.

25 "Many patients are insured": Ibid.

26 "we didn't do what": Ibid.

27 But the requirement: Ibid.

28 "the disaster of": Michael Graham, "Mitt's Bad Medicine," Boston Herald, November 18, 2010, http://www.bostonherald.com/news/opinion/op_ed/view.bg?articleid=1297196& srvc=home&position=emailed.

29 "created under Romeycare": Ibid.

30 "Before Romneycare, you": Ibid.

31 36–51 unfavorable: "November 22, 2010—American Voters Could Deny Obama Reelection, Quinnipiac University National Poll Finds; President Tied with Romney, Huckabee but Leads Palin," Quinnipiac.edu, November 22, 2010, http://www.quinnipiac.edu/x1295.xml?ReleaseID=1538.

32 54–33 favorable: Ibid.

33 59% of likely voters: Dan Balz and Jon Cohen, "Post-ABC Poll: Sarah Palin Lags Obama in Theoretical 2012 Presidential Election," *The Washington Post,* December 17, 2010, http://www.washingtonpost.com/wp-dyn/content/article/2010/12/17/AR2010121701512.html

34 The realclearpolitics: "Republican Presidential Primary," RealClearPolitics.org, http://www.realclearpolitics.com/epolls/2012/president/us/republican_presidential_primary-1452.html.

35 He runs second: Ibid.

36 41–25 in the November: "November 22, 2010—American Voters Could Deny Obama Reelection, Quinnipiac University National Poll Finds; President Tied with Romney, Huckabee but Leads Palin."

37 "Oh no . . . of change": Conversation between Dick Morris and Mike Huckabee in 1993.

38 "everyone makes . . . and 1970s": "Gov. Huckabee Failed to Factor Cop Killer Clemmons' Prison Violence," *Seattle Times*, October 18, 2010, http://www.thenewstribune.com/2010/10/18/1386375/gov-huckabee-failed-to-factor.html.

39 The former Speaker: "Republican Presidential Primary."

40 The November 22: "November 22, 2010—American Voters Could Deny Obama Reelection, Quinnipiac University National Poll Finds; President Tied with Romney, Huckabee but Leads Palin."

41 Who can forget: William M. Welch, "Democrats Seize on Gingrich's Negatives," *USA Today*, March 18, 1996, http://www.usatoday.com/news/index/budget/nbud026.htm.

42 "In February . . . end the NMMP": "Minnesota Murabalitionists," LinkedResources.com, http://blogs.linkedresources.com/blogview.php?blogger=act4mn&topic=murabalitionist.

43 "Imagine a program": Dick Morris and Eileen McGann, *Catastrophe* (New York: HarperCollins, 2009).

44 "commitment to streamlining": Michelle Millhollon, "State's Bond Rating Upgraded Again," 2theadvocate.com, October 10, 2009, http://www.2theadvocate.com/news/63908172.html.

45 "Are you under": Robert Paul Reyes, "Funny Video: Michele Bachmann Makes Chris Matthews Look Like Jackass," Newsblaze.com, November 3, 2010, http://newsblaze.com/story/20101103094810reye.nb/topstory.html.

46 "how's that tingly": Ibid.

PART TWO

1 According to them: "Cycle Dating Committee, National Bureau of Economic Research," NBER.org, September 20, 2010, http://www.nber.org/cycles/sept2010.html.

2 "My husband . . . reality": "The New Normal: What to Expect of Our Economy," CBS News, September 26, 2010, http://celebrifi.com/gossip/The-New-Normal-What-to -Expect-of-Our-Economy-3567493.html.

3 Since Obama took: "A-1. Employment States of the Civilian Noninstitutional Population 16 years and over, 1970 to date," BLS.gov, http://www.bls.gov/web/empsit/cpseea1.pdf.

4 Job Loss in the Recession: Phil Gramm, "Echoes of the Great Depression," *Wall Street Journal*, October 1, 2010, p A-19.

5 GDP is still below: Ibid.

6 Many leading economists: "Gross Domestic Income Shows More Sluggish Recovery," CalculatedRiskBlog.com, May 27, 2010, http://www.calculatedriskblog.com/2010/05/ gross-domestic-income-shows-more.html.

7 "is only 1.2%": Ibid.

8 "suggests the recovery": Ibid.

9 16% of our economy: "National Health Expenditures 2008 Highlights," Centers for Medicare and Medicaid Services, http://www.cms.gov/NationalHealthExpendData/ downloads/highlights.pdf.

10 11% of the economy: "Value Added by Industry as a Percentage of Gross Domestic Product," BEA.gov, September 30, 2010, http://www.bea.gov/industry/gpotables/gpo_ action.cfm.

11 The energy sector: "Gross Domestic Income Shows More Sluggish Recovery."

12 21% of the economy: "Value Added by Industry as a Percentage of Gross Domestic Product."

13 Cuts in Spending versus Cuts in Deficit: "Political Tracking Crosstabs," Rasmussen Reports.com, December 8, 2010, http://www.rasmussenreports.com/platinum/political _tracking_crosstabs/december_2010/crosstabs_reducing_federal_deficit_december _7_8_2010.http://www.rasmussenreports.com/platinum/political_tracking_crosstabs/ december_2010/crosstabs_reducing_federal_deficit_december_7_8_2010.

14 Government Spending as Percentage of GDP: http://www.usgovernmentspending.com. Specific government data sources used by this website: http://usgovernmentspending .blogspot.com/2009/03/table-of-data-sources-by-year.html.

15 In 2007, the United: "Factbook 2010: Economic, Environmental and Social Statistics," OECD-iLibrary.org, http://www.oecd-ilibrary.org/sites/factbook-2010-en/10/01/01/ index.html?contentType=&itemId=/content/chapter/factbook-2010-75-en&container ItemId=/content/serial/18147364&accessItemIds=&mimeType=text/html.

16 In 2007, the United: Ibid.

17 In the 219 years: 1. "Presidential Oaths of Office," http://memory.loc.gov/ammem/ pihtml/pioaths.html. 2. USGovernmentSpending.com, http://www.usgovernment

spending.com. 3. USDebtClock.org, http://www.usdebtclock.org/. 4. TreasuryDirect
.gov, http://www.treasurydirect.gov.

18 Increase in National Debt: "Time Series Chart of US Government Spending," USGovern
mentSpending.com, http://www.usgovernmentdebt.us/downchart_gs.php?year=1792_
2014&view=1&expand=&units=b&fy=fy11&chart=H0-fed&bar=0&stack=1&size=m
&title=&state=US&color=c&local=s.

19 2008 2,983: "Historical Budget Data," CBO.gov, http://www.cbo.gov/ftpdocs/108xx/
doc10871/AppendixF.shtml#1097333.

20 2009 3,519: "The Spending Outlook," CBO.gov, http://www.cbo.gov/ftpdocs/108xx/
doc10871/Chapter3.shtml#1119832.

21 2010 3,524: Ibid.

22 2011 3,650: Ibid.

23 U.S. Government Spending by Function: "Historical Budget Data," and "The Spending
Outlook."

24 First he said: Tara Weiss, "Obama's Stimulus Plan Promises New Jobs," MSNBC.com,
January 16, 2009, http://www.msnbc.msn.com/id/28695368/ns/business-careers/.

25 Then, he amended: "Obama Speaks at Energy Department," *Washington Post*, February 5,
2009, http://projects.washingtonpost.com/obama-speeches/speech/36/.

26 Under Obama, our: "A-1. Employment Status of the Civilian Noninstitutional Population
16 Years and Over, 1970 to Date."

27 Obama's Stimulus Spending List: Susan Ferrechio, "After a Flurry of Stimulus Spending,
Questionable Projects Pile Up," *Washington Examiner*, November 3, 2009.

28 Fully 85% of the: http://www.recovery.gov/Pages/home.aspx.

29 The Fed Slashes Interest Rates: "Daily Treasury Yield Curve Rates," Treasury.gov, http://
www.treasury.gov/resource-center/data-chart-center/interest-rates/Pages/TextView
.aspx?data=yieldAll.

30 Banks flocked . . . the economy: a. "Factors Affecting Reserve Balances, FederalReserve
.gov, December 9, 2010, http://www.federalreserve.gov/releases/h41/Current/.
b. "Factors Affecting Reserve Balances, FederalReserve.gov, July 5, 2010, http://www
.federalreserve.gov/releases/h41/20070705/.
c. "Aggregate Reserves of Depository Institutions and the Monetary Base," FederalReserve
.gov, December 9, 2010, http://www.federalreserve.gov/releases/h3/current/h3.htm.
d. "Money Stock Measures," FederalReserve.gov, December 9, 2010, http://www.federal
reserve.gov/releases/h6/current/h6.htm.
e. "St. Louis Adjusted Monetary Base," StLouisFed.org, December 10, 2010, http://
research.stlouisfed.org/fred2/data/AMBNS.txt.

31 The money supply: Ibid.

32 "to take away the": N. Gregory Mankiw, "How to Avoid Recession? Let the Fed Work," *New
York Times*, December 23, 2007, http://www.nytimes.com/2007/12/23/business/23view
.html?ex=1356066000&en=3337604c8708710a&ei=5090&partner=rssuserland&emc
=rss.

33 According to the: Sara Murray, "Middle Class Slams Breaks On Spending," *Wall Street Journal*, October 6, 2010, p A4.

34 Cuts in Consumer Spending, 2007–09: Ibid.

35 The only increases: Ibid.

36 The savings rate rose: "Flow of Funds Accounts of the United States," Federal Reserve, December 9, 2010, http://www.federalreserve.gov/releases/z1/Current/z1.pdf.

37 Since the middle: "Vital Signs," *Wall Street Journal*, October 8, 2010, A1.

38 "nonfinancial companies": Justin Lahart, "U.S. Firms Build Up Record Cash Piles," *Wall Street Journal*, June 10, 2010, http://online.wsj.com/article/SB10001424052748704312104575298652567988246.html.

39 "Consumers are unsettled": Justin Lahart, "Layoffs Ease But Hiring Sluggish" *Wall Street Journal*, October 8, 2010, p A2.

40 "the problem . . . is that": Ibid.

41 "If taxpayers get refunds": Dick Morris and Eileen McGann, *Catastrophe* (New York: HarperCollins, 2009).

42 Massive stimulus spending: "Barack Obama-San," *Wall Street Journal*, December 16, 2008, http://online.wsj.com/article/SB122938932478509075.html.

43 He sent out $100: Martin Feldstein, "The Tax Rebate Was a Flop. Obama's Stimulus Plan Won't Work Either," *Wall Street Journal*, August 6, 2008.

44 When he . . . going down: "Civilian Unemployment Rate," StLouisFed.org, December 3, 2010, http://research.stlouisfed.org/fred2/data/UNRATE.txt.

45 When you add: "Table A-15. Alternative Measures of Labor Underutilization," BLS.gov, December 3, 2010, http://www.bls.gov/news.release/empsit.t15.htm.

46 U.S. Growth Rate Compared: Gramm, "Echoes of the Great Depression."

47 "You never want": Gerald F. Seib, "In Crisis, opportunity for Obama," *Wall Street Journal*, November 21, 2008, http://online.wsj.com/article/SB122721278056345271.html.

48 While, by definition: Robert Frank, "U.S. Economy is Increasingly Tied to the Rich," *Wall Street Journal*, August 5, 2010, http://blogs.wsj.com/wealth/2010/08/05/us-economy-is-increasingly-tied-to-the-rich/.

49 consumer spending generates: "Table 1.1.5. Gross Domestic Product," BEA.gov, December 22, 2010, http://www.bea.gov/national/nipaweb/TableView.asp?SelectedTable=5&Freq=Qtr&FirstYear=2008&LastYear=2010.

50 A Rasmussen Reports poll: "51% Favor Extending Bush Tax Cuts for the Wealthy," RasmussenReports.com, September 13, 2010, http://www.rasmussenreports.com/public_content/business/taxes/september_2010/51_favor_extending_bush_tax_cuts_for_the_wealthy.

51 10% of our GDP: "US Federal Deficit as Percent of GDP," USGovernmentSpending.com, http://www.usgovernmentspending.com/federal_deficit_chart.html.

52 Obama's defenders say: Brian Riedl, "Achieve a Balanced Federal Budget Through Spending Restraint," Heritage.org, November 8, 2010, http://www.heritage.org/Research/Commentary/2010/11/Achieve-a-Balanced-Federal-Budget-Through-Spending-Restraint.

53 $713 billion by the time: "Time Series Chart of US Government Spending," USGovern mentSpending.com, http://www.usgovernmentspending.com/downchart_gs.php?chart =&year=2008_2012&units=b.

54 The budget deficit: Ibid.

55 $150 billion per month: "Quarterly Data Release," Treasury.gov, http://www.treasury .gov/resource-center/data-chart-center/quarterly-refunding/Documents/Quarterly datarelease.xls.

56 $60 trillion of goods: "Gross Domestic Product," World Bank, World Development Indi- cators, http://www.google.com/publicdata?ds=wb-wdi&met=ny_gdp_mktp_cd&tdim =true&dl=en&hl=en&q=global+gdp.

57 $58.9 trillion: Mike Hewitt, "Growth of Global Money Supply," MonetaryCurrent.com, January 12, 2009, http://www.monetarycurrent.com/commentaries/52-analysis/256 -growth-of-global-money-supply.html.

58 $40 trillion: "The Global Debt Clock," Economist.com, http://www.economist.com/ content/global_debt_clock.

59 Private companies, banks: Ibid.

60 How Much We Would Have to Pay: "Average Interest Rates," October 31, 2010, Treasury Direct.gov, http://www.treasurydirect.gov/govt/rates/pd/avg/2010/2010_10.htm.

61 The Commission would only: Mike Sorohan, "Panel Report Recommends Cutting Mort- gage Interest Deduction," MortgageBankers.org, http://www.mortgagebankers.org/ tools/FullStory.aspx?ArticleId=18707.

62 The most important: "2005–2009 American Community Survey 5-Year Estimates," Census.gov, http://factfinder.census.gov/servlet/ACSSAFFFacts?_submenuId=factsheet _1&_sse=on.

63 In 2010, it saved: Stephen Clark, "Proposal to Limit or Eliminate Tax Deduction for Homes is Unpopular, Could Raise Billions," FoxNews.com, November 11, 2010, http:// www.foxnews.com/politics/2010/11/11/proposal-limit-eliminate-tax-deduction-homes -unpopular-raise-trillions/.

64 4.6% for a thirty-year fixed: "Today's Rates," WellsFargo.com, December 24, 2010, https:// www.wellsfargo.com/mortgage/rates/.

65 Home ownership has fallen: Hubble Smith, "Brookings Fellow Calls to Cut, or Kill, Mortgage Interest Tax Deduction," November 28, 2010, http://www.lvrj.com/business/ brookings-fellow-calls-to-cut-or-kill-mortgage-interest-tax-deduction-110930674 .html.

66 "A rollback of the mortgage": Sorohan, "Panel Report Recommends Cutting Mortgage Interest Deduction."

67 The construction of 100 homes: Caroline Sutton, "Makes No Sense to Target Mortgage Interest Deduction," Citizen-Times.com, December 8, 2010, http://www.citizen-times .com/article/20101208/OPINION02/101207036/1007/COLUMNISTS.

68 "could critically erode home": "End to the American Dream," MemphisDailyNews.com, December 7, 2010, http://blog.memphisdailynews.com/?p=1325.

69 "housing prices . . . their mortgage": Linda Chavez, "Scandalous Suggestion from Debt Commission," PostChronicle.com, December 7, 2010, http://www.postchronicle.com/commentary/article_212336879.shtml.

70 "This would . . . tax policy": Ibid.

71 $304 billion a year: http://www.givingusa.org/press_releases/gusa/gusa060910.pdf.

72 $35 billion a year: Ibid.

73 The Commission would: Stephanie Strom, "Nonprofits Fear Losing Tax Benefit," *New York Times*, December 2, 2010, http://www.nytimes.com/2010/12/03/business/03charity.html?src=busln.

74 "wealthy givers are more": Sandra Block, "Tax Uncertainty Could Hurt Charitable Giving," *USA Today*, November 12, 2010, http://www.usatoday.com/money/perfi/basics/2010-11-11-charitable-contributions-taxes_N.htm.

75 "People give because they": Ibid.

76 Obama's Commission also recommended: "Ten Facts About Claiming the Child Tax Credit," IRS.gov, http://www.irs.gov/newsroom/article/0,,id=106182,00.html.

77 Right now, employers: "Social Security," NYC.gov, http://www.nyc.gov/html/opa/html/taxes/socialsecurity.shtml.

78 Now, Obama's deficit: Justin Bryan, "Individual Income Tax Returns, 2008," IRS.gov, http://www.irs.gov/pub/irs-soi/08inreturnsbul.pdf.

79 From 1983 to 1988: Jeremy Weltmer, "Grover Norquist Outlines Recommendations to the Obama Debt Commission," ATR.gov, July 27, 2010, http://www.atr.org/grover-norquist-outlines-recommendations-obama-debt-a5252.

80 In fact, spending rose: Ibid.

81 When President Ronald: Ibid.

82 And when Reagan: Ibid.

83 And when Clinton: Ibid.

84 The Americans for Tax Reform: Ibid.

PART THREE

1 "America decided to put": "Election Night in America; Republicans Win House; Democrats Keep Senate," CNN.com, November 2, 2010, http://transcripts.cnn.com/TRANSCRIPTS/1011/02/se.05.html.

2 In the *New York*: Matt Bai, "Debt-Busting Issue May Force Obama Off Fence," *New York Times*, December 1, 2010, p A22.

3 "Mr. Obama . . . plan": Ibid.

4 "A rising tide": "400—Remarks in Heber Springs, Arkansas, at the Dedication of Greers Ferry Dam," October 3, 1963, http://www.presidency.ucsb.edu/ws/index.php?pid=9455.

5 "The best social": QuoteDB.com, http://www.quotedb.com/quotes/3253.

6 Budget Deficits Under Reagan: "Time Series Chart of US Government Spending," US GovernmentSpending.com, http://www.usgovernmentspending.com/downchart_gs .php?chart=G0-total&year=1900_2014&units=p.

7 Three-quarters of the money: Michael Ettlinger and Michael Linden, "A Thousand Cuts," AmericanProgress.org, September 21, 2010, http://www.americanprogress.org/ issues/2010/09/thousand_cuts.html.

8 We spend $2 billion: Ibid.

9 We could save $3.6 billion: Ibid.

10 Cut their grants by 10%: Ibid.

11 We should sell off: Ibid.

12 Roll back the cost: Ibid.

13 Cut spending for the: Ibid.

14 15% cut in Army: Ibid.

15 20% cut in our: Ibid.

16 The National Infrastructure: Ibid.

17 Build America Bonds: Ibid.

18 We now spend about: Ibid.

19 Federal pensions are all: Ibid.

20 We should cut: Ibid.

21 Grants to states: Ibid.

22 Cut it by $1.2: Ibid.

23 Eliminate this left-wing: Ibid.

24 If we kill Obama's: Ibid.

25 Cut out Obama's: Ibid.

26 A 10% cut would: Ibid.

27 Special Aid to District: Ibid.

28 A Clinton-era: Ibid.

29 Obama plans to spend: Ibid.

30 "according to the Bureau": E-mail from Ryan Ellis, October 2010.

31 Repeal the Davis-Bacon Act: Weltmer, "Grover Norquist Outlines Recommendations to the Obama Debt Commission."

32 Sell off government assets: Ibid.

33 "President Bush, who": Mattie Corrao, "Conservatives Should Support Defense Spending Cuts," DailyCaller.com, October 8, 2010, http://dailycaller.com/2010/10/07/conservatives -should-support-defense-spending-cuts/.

34 "redirecting those [savings]": Ibid.

35 Weapon's We Don't Need: Ibid.

36 Defense Department Civilian: Ibid.

37 As noted, during Obama's: "US Welfare Spending," USGovernmentSpending.com, http://www.usgovernmentspending.com/.

38 Indiana governor—and possible: Mitch Daniels, "Hoosiers and Health Savings Accounts," *Wall Street Journal*, March 1, 2010, http://online.wsj.com/article/SB10001424052 748704231304575091600470293066.html.

39 "In 2009 . . . state": Ibid.

40 New York, for example: "Medicaid and State Funded Coverage Income Eligibility Limits for Low-Income Adults, 2009," StateHealthFacts.org, http://www.statehealthfacts.org/comparereport.jsp?rep=54&cat=4.

41 A Rasmussen Reports poll: "Most Voters Continue to Say No to Higher Taxes, More Government Spending," RasmussenReports.com, November 7, 2010, http://www.rasmussenreports.com/public_content/business/taxes/november_2010/most_voters_continue_to_say_no_to_higher_taxes_more_government_spending.

42 "Democrats who supported": Michael D. Tanner, "What Republicans Can—And Can't—Do about ObamaCare " *New York Post*, November 7, 2010.

43 ObamaCare would bring huge: Henry J. Aaron, Ph.D., "The Midterm Elections—High Stakes for Health Policy," *New England Journal of Medicine*, October 28, 2010, http://www.nejm.org/doi/pdf/10.1056/NEJMp1011213.

44 "contains 64 specific": Ibid.

45 "at least $50 billion": "DeMint Predicts 'A Very Intense Showdown' If Obama Opposes GOP Efforts to Defund Health Reform," ThinkProgress.org, November 3, 2010, http://wonkroom.thinkprogress.org/2010/11/03/demint-defund-showdown/.

46 The only actual: Aaron, "The Midterm Elections—High Stakes for Health Policy."

47 "without large additional": Ibid.

48 "If [ObamaCare] opponents: Ibid.

49 "the number . . . any school": Robert Pear, "G.O.P. to Fight Health Law with Purse Strings," *New York Times*, November 6, 2010, http://www.nytimes.com/2010/11/07/health/policy/07health.html?_r=1&scp=1&sq=ObamaCare%20new%20york%20times%20robert%20pear&st=cse.

50 "House Republicans could": Ibid.

51 "They'll get not one": Daniel Foster, "GOP Majority Will 'Chip Away,' Defund ObamaCare," NationalReview.com, September 21, 2010, http://www.nationalreview.com/corner/247192/gop-majority-will-chip-away-defund-ObamaCare-daniel-foster.

52 "If all of ObamaCare": Robert Pear, "G.O.P. to Fight Health Law with Purse Strings."

53 The IRS says: Michael D. Tanner, "What Republicans Can—And Can't—Do about ObamaCare."

54 "IRS could have to hire": "Ways and Means Republicans' Report: Democrats' Health Care Bill Contains Massive Expansion of IRS's Power," House.gov, March 18, 2010, http://republicans.waysandmeans.house.gov/News/DocumentSingle.aspx?DocumentID=176997.

55 This expansion would add: "Internal Revenue Service," Wikipedia.org, http://en.wikipedia.org/wiki/Internal_Revenue_Service.

56 The Ways and Means: "Ways and Means Republicans' Report: Democrats' Health Care Bill Contains Massive Expansion of IRS's Power."

57 "minimum essential coverage": "Summary of New Health Reform Law," KFF.org, http://www.kff.org/healthreform/upload/8061.pdf.

58 After all, an American: "Taxation in the United States," Wikipedia.org, http://en.wikipedia.org/wiki/Taxation_in_the_United_States.

59 Required Premium Payments Under Obamacare: "Summary of New Health Reform Law."

60 According to pollster: John Zogby, postelection survey, November 4, 2010.

61 The ObamaCare legislation: Merrill Goozner, "Republicans Throw the Gauntlet on Health Care Reform," TheFiscalTimes.com, November 8, 2010, http://www.thefiscal times.com/Issues/Health-Care/2010/11/08/Republicans-Set-on-Defunding-Health -Bill.aspx.

62 "Medicare will cover": Robert Pear, "Obama Returns to End-of-Life Plan that Caused Stir," New York Times, December 25, 2010, http://www.nytimes.com/2010/12/26/us/politics/26death.html?_r=1&emc=eta1.

63 "Under the rule": Ibid.

64 "Democratic Senator Ron Wyden": Tanner, "What Republicans Can—And Can't—Do about ObamaCare."

65 "Should Congress block": Ken Terry, "Republicans Could Cripple Healthcare Reform by 'Defunding' It," bnet.com, October 29, 2010, http://www.bnet.com/blog/healthcare -business/how-republicans-could-cripple-healthcare-reform-by-8220defunding -8221-it/2007.

66 "if a large number": Ibid.

67 A study by no less: "Night of the Living Death Tax," Wall Street Journal, March 31, 2009, http://online.wsj.com/article/SB123846422014872229.html.

68 A 2009 study by: Curtis Dubay, "Economic Case Against the Death Tax," Heritage.org, July 20, 2010, http://www.heritage.org/research/reports/2010/07/the-economic-case -against-the-death-tax.

69 The report said: Ibid.

70 "families often must sell": Ibid.

71 "currently, the heirs": Ibid.

72 In 2008, it yielded: Ibid.

73 Bryan Real, president: Kevin McKeough, "Small-Biz Owners Say They Can't Get Loans; Banks Say Few are Borrowing; They're Both Right," ChicagoBusiness.com, Octber 11, 2010, http://www.chicagobusiness.com/article/20101009/ISSUE02/310099997/small-biz -owners-say-they-can-8217-t-get-loans-banks-say-few-are-borrowing-they-8217-re -both-right.

74 The National Small: Ibid.

75 The Federal Deposit: Ibid.

76 According to the Federal: Ibid.

77 "it seems clear": Ibid.

78 The National Federation: Ibid.

79 Barlow Research Associates: Ibid.

80 Chase made $2.1: Ibid.

81 The Census Bureau: Scott Shane, "Small Business Job Creation Numbers for Politicians," SmallBizTrends.com, July 26, 2010, http://smallbiztrends.com/2010/07/the-ideal-small-business-job-creation-numbers-for-politicians.html.

82 two-thirds of all loans: Massimo Calabresi, "Collateral Damage: The Death of a Small Town Bank," *Time*, November 7, 2010, http://www.time.com/time/magazine/article/0,9171,2026914,00.html.

83 Big banks: Rob Cox and Rolfe Winkler, "Community Banks Don't Need Another Obama Sop," Reuters.com, February 1, 2010, http://blogs.reuters.com/columns/2010/02/01/community-banks-dont-need-another-obama-sop/.

84 In the third quarter: Ibid.

85 "seize ... these companies": David S. Huntington, "Summary of Dodd-Frank Financial Regulation Legislation," Harvard.edu, July 7, 2010, http://blogs.law.harvard.edu/corpgov/2010/07/07/summary-of-dodd-frank-financial-regulation-legislation/.

86 The FDIC can move: Ibid.

87 "responsible for the failed": Ibid.

88 "shareholders ... do not": Ibid.

89 In 2010, 143: Elizabeth Warren, "When Bankers Make Windfall Profits from the FDIC," Reuters.com, November 11, 2010, http://blogs.reuters.com/felix-salmon/2010/11/11/when-bankers-make-windfall-profits-from-the-fdic/.

90 But the FDIC's: Calabresi, "Collateral Damage: The Death of a Small Town Bank."

91 "we see federal": Interview with West Virginia bank officer, September 1, 2010, in Charleston, WV.

92 *Time* magazine tells the: Calabresi, "Collateral Damage: The Death of a Small Town Bank."

93 *Time* notes that: Ibid.

94 "A lot of people": Ibid.

95 The FDIC decimated: Ibid.

96 "got a sewer": Ibid.

97 By 2005, it held: Ibid.

98 "not and work": Ibid.

99 Now, under the new: Ibid.

100 The banks had: David Moberg, "Too Important to Fail," InTheseTimes.com, February 24, 2010, http://www.inthesetimes.com/article/5581/too_important_to_fail/.

101 A philanthropist, Kelly: Ibid.

102 FBOP got into trouble: Ibid.

103 But then TARP: Ibid.

104 "FDIC invoked": Ibid.

105 "As the . . . deadline": Ibid.

106 "the FDIC lost": Warren, "When Bankers Make Windfall Profits from the FDIC."

107 "It certainly looks as": Ibid.

108 "community banks don't need": Cox and Winkler, "Community Banks Don't Need Another Obama Sop."

109 Most of the subprime: Associated Press, "Will Subprime Mess Ripple Through Economy?" MSNBC.com, March 13, 2007, http://www.msnbc.msn.com/id/17584725.

110 "one reason community": T.A. Frank and Phillip Longman, "Too Small to Fail," WashingtonMonthly.com, http://www.washingtonmonthly.com/features/2008/0811.longman.html.

111 the EPA announced on Christmas: Associated Press, "EPA Moving Unilaterally to Limit Greenhouse Gases," Businessweek.com, December 24, 2010, http://www.businessweek.com/ap/financialnews/D9KA9NN80.htm.

112 "to regulate greenhouse": "Sensenbrenner Plans to Keep Pelosi-Devised Global Warming Panel," FoxNews.com, November 8, 2010, http://www.foxnews.com/search-results/search?q=EPA+regulations&submit=Search.

113 "The tactic . . . the issue": Phil Kerpen, "Standing Up to the EPA's Power Grab," FoxNews.com, September 14, 2010, http://www.foxnews.com/opinion/2010/09/14/phil-kerpen-senate-epa-carol-browner-harry-reid-jay-rockefeller-global-warming/.

114 "I would . . . rule changes": Ibid.

115 "Obama will try": "Chicago Climate Exchange to Shut Down Emissions Trading," Forbes.com, November 17, 2010, http://billionaires.forbes.com/article/0fddcdD8rMbxh?q=Aaron+Smith.

116 "best available technology": "Examiner Editorial: New EPA Regs Would Kill Jobs, Stall Economy," WasthingtonExaminer.com, November 11, 2010, http://www.washingtonexaminer.com/opinion/New-EPA-regs-would-kill-jobs_-stall-economy-1531812-107341498.html.

117 "University of . . . get started": Ibid.

118 The EPA regulation: Ibid.

119 Change in American Energy Sources: "Net Generation by Energy Source: Total (All Sectors)," eia.doe.gov, November 15, 2010, http://www.eia.doe.gov/cneaf/electricity/epm/table1_1.html.

120 EPA also wants to: Brian M. Johnson, "EPA Regulation of Carbon Will Harm US Economy," ATR.org, January 25, 2010, http://www.atr.org/epa-regulation-carbon-harm-economy-a4438#.

121 The Heritage Foundation: "Waxman's Global Warming Plan that will Save our Economy," Heritage.org, January 15, 2010, http://blog.heritage.org/2009/01/15/waxmans-global-warming-plan-that-will-save-our-economy/.

122 Gasoline prices will rise: Brett Vassey, "'Cap' Industrial Competitiveness and 'Trade' Domestic Manufacturing Jobs Abroad," Townhall.com, http://townhall.com/columnists/

BrettVassey/2009/10/05/"cap"_industrial_competitiveness_and_"trade"_domestic_manufacturing_jobs_abroad/page/full/.

123 Manufacturing by Country: "What are the Top Manufacturing Countries?" wise GEEK.com, http://www.wisegeek.com/what-are-the-top-manufacturing-countries .htm.

124 The U.S. has lost: Richard Deitz and James Orr, "A Leaner, More Skilled U.S. Manufacturing Workforce," NY.FBR.org, February 2006, http://www.ny.frb.org/research/current_issues/ci12-2.pdf.

125 "inflation averaged 3.7%": http://www.cato-at-liberty.org/a-wall-street-journal-column -understates-the-size-of-u-s-manufacturing/

126 "automation in my": Author interview with Dr. Tim Nerenz on September 25, 2010.

127 Dr. Nerenz points: Ibid.

128 "manufacturers are making": Vassey, "'Cap' Industrial Competitiveness and 'Trade' Domestic Manufacturing Jobs Abroad."

129 U.S. Coal Exports to China: Elizabeth Rosenthal, "The West's Love-Hate Relationship with Coal," *International Herald Tribune*, November 23, 2010, p. A-1.

130 "rejected claims that": Kim Chipman and Simon Lomax, "EPA Issues Carbon Guidance to Help States Enforce Rules," Bloomberg.com, November 10, 2010, http://www.bloom berg.com/news/2010-11-10/epa-set-to-release-guidance-on-new-u-s-carbon-rules -advocacy-group-says.html.

131 "Such an unstable": Ibid.

132 "card check was": "Back Door Card Check," *Wall Street Journal*, September 14, 2010, http://online.wsj.com/article/SB10001424052748703597204575483882585485368 .html.

133 "the labor . . . secret ballots": Ibid.

134 In Arizona and Utah: "Union Card Checkmate," *Wall Street Journal*, November 9, 2010, http://online.wsj.com/article/SB10001424052748704353504575596790376536822 .html?mod=googlenews_wsj.

135 After peaking in 1979: Jerry White, "UAW Membership Continues to Plummet," WSWS .org, April 2010, http://www.wsws.org/articles/2010/apr2010/uawm-a01.shtml.

136 The impact of unionization: James Sherk, "What Unions Do: How Labor Unions Affect Jobs and the Economy," Heritage.org, May 21, 2009, http://www.heritage.org/Research/ Reports/2009/05/What-Unions-Do-How-Labor-Unions-Affect-Jobs-and-the-Economy #_ftn20.

137 "one study found": Ibid.

138 Since the late: Ibid.

139 A consulting firm: Anne Layne-Farrar, "An Empirical Assessment of the Employee Free Choice Act: The Economic Implications," March 3, 2009,http://thetruthaboutefca.com/ media/docs/efcaStudy_layneFarrar.pdf.

140 Earmarks cost us: "TCS FY2010 Earmark Analysis: Apples-to-Apples Increase in Earmark Totals," GovExec.com, http://www.govexec.com/pdfs/041210rb1.pdf.

141 As soon as the: Brian Stelter, "A New Test is Proposed in Licensing Radio and TV," *New York Times*, December 2, 2010, http://www.nytimes.com/2010/12/03/business/media/03fcc.html?src=busln.

142 "a renewed commitment": Ibid.

143 "is more localism": Ibid.

144 "Mr. Copps said": Ibid.

145 "determine the extent": Ibid.

146 "It's a pretty": "Congressman Blasts FCC Over Proposed Media Regulations," FoxNews .com, December 7, 2010, http://www.foxnews.com/politics/2010/12/07/congressman -blasts-fcc-commissioner-proposed-media-regulations/.

147 "I hope": Ibid.

148 "Although your concern": Ibid.

149 "liberals are planning": Dick Morris and Eileen McGann, *Fleeced* (New York: Harper-Collins, 2008), p. 77.

150 "big telecommunications firms have slowed": David Eldridge, "New FCC Plan to Oversee Internet Draws GOP Fire," *Washington Times*, December 1, 2010, "http://www.washington times.com/news/2010/dec/1/new-fcc-plan-to-oversee-internet-draws-gop-fire/.

151 "big telecommunications firms counter": Ibid.

152 "critics see the net": Ibid.

153 "imposing net neutrality": Ibid.

154 "We stand at": Theodore Roosevelt, "We Stand at Armageddon, and We Battle for the Lord," http://www.cooperativeindividualism.org/roosevelt-theodore_on-the-land-ques tion.html.

155 In 2010, states: Adam B. Schaeffer, "They Spent WHAT? The Real Cost of Public Schools," CATO.org, March 10, 2010, http://www.cato.org/pub_display.php?pub_id=11432.

156 State and Local Government Deficit: "Total Budgeted Government Revenue," http:// www.usgovernmentrevenue.com.

157 Incoming Speaker John: "August 10, 2010 Republican Leadership Press Conference," GOP.gov, August 10, 2010, http://www.gop.gov/media-events/10/08/10/august-10-2010 -republican.

158 There are $2.8 trillion: Elisse B. Walter, "Securities and Exchange Commission Field Hearing on the State of the Municipal Securities Market," SEC.gov, September 21, 2010, http://www.sec.gov/spotlight/municipalsecurities/092110transcript.txt.

159 In 2009, there were: Ibid.

160 Increase in the Cost of Insuring Against State Default: "State Default Risk and a Com-parison to Sovereign Debt," SeekingAlpha.com, July 1, 2010, http://seekingalpha.com/article/212825-state-default-risk-and-a-comparison-to-sovereign-debt?source=feed.

161 On November 18: Michael Anerio and Stu Woo, "California Bond Woe Bodes Ill For States," *Wall Street Journal*, November 18, 2010, p. A-1.

162 "The tax-exempt": Ibid.

163 After seven months: Ibid.

164 On average, these: "Total Budgeted Government Spending," USGovernmentSpending .com, http://www.usgovernmentspending.com/#usgs30.2a.

165 "In my 49 years": Bob Lewis and Dena Porter, Bloomberg.com, March 15, 2010, http:// www.businessweek.com/ap/financialnews/D9EF4LH00.htm.

166 But McDonnell managed: Ibid.

167 In New Jersey: Associated Press, "New Jersey Legislature Passes Christie's Budget," FoxNews.com, June 29, 2010, http://www.foxnews.com/politics/2010/06/29/new-jersey -legislature-passes-christies-budget/.

168 While only 7%: "Union Members Summary," BLS.gov, January 22, 2010, http://www.bls .gov/news.release/union2.nr0.htm.

169 The unions are about: "Margaret Thatcher on Socialism," Snopes.com, http://www .snopes.com/politics/quotes/thatcher.asp.

170 In California, for example: "52% in California Say Public Employee Unions Significantly Strain Budget," RasmussenReports.com, March 21, 2010, http://www.rasmussenreports .com/public_content/politics/general_state_surveys/california/52_in_california_say_ public_employee_unions_significantly_strain_budget.

171 In 1975, President: Frank Van Riper, "Ford to New York: Drop Dead," NYDailyNews.com, October 30, 1975, http://www.nydailynews.com/features/bronxisburning/battle-for -the-city/Ford-to-New-York-Drop-Dead.html.

172 Education (35%): Schaeffer, "They Spend WHAT? The Real Cost of Public Schools."

173 One-third of all: Sam Dillon, "With Turnover High, Schools Fight for Teachers," *New York Times*, August 27, 2007.

174 In the past: John Stossel, "Stupid in America: How Lack of Choice Cheats Our Kids Out of a Good Education," ABC News, January 13, 2006.

175 "it took years to fire": Ibid.

176 After six years: Ibid.

177 Every day, Klein: Ibid.

178 The *New York Post*: Yoav Gonen, Kelly Magee, and Kevin Sheehan, "Custodian Probed for Using School Funds to Renovate 10 Houses," *New York Post*, November 6, 2010, http:// www.nypost.com/p/news/local/queens/custodian_mopping_up_PSlJB5h2UN2jB8ob0s J77K#ixzz14onIdk7s.

179 In 2007, the *Kalamazoo*: Julie Mack, "Cost-Cutters Target Teacher Benefits," *Kalamazoo Gazette*, June 3, 2007, http://blog.mlive.com/kalamazoo_gazette_extra/2007/06/cost cutters_target_teacher_ben.html.

180 Over a five-year: David Wegbreit, "Grand Rapids Public School Contracts Transportation to Save," STOnline.com, November 1, 2007, http://stnonline.com/resources/operations/ related-regular-transportation-articles/1720-grand-rapids-public-schools-contracts -transportation-to-save.

181 Elsewhere, the Clarenceville: Karen Smith, "Clarenceville, Michigan Picketers Protest Privatization," CommonDreams.org, July 18, 2010, http://www.commondreams.org/ headline/2010/07/18-2.

182 Cost Per Pupil of Public and Private Schools: Schaeffer, "They Spend WHAT? The Real Cost of Public Schools."

183 With average per pupil: Jennifer Cohen, "Examining the Data: State Per Pupil Expenditures and State Graduation Rates," NewAmerica.net, September 16, 2010, "http://edmoney.newamerica.net/blogposts/2010/examining_the_data_state_per_pupil_expenditures_and_state_graduation_rates-36914.

184 the lower average: 2010 Charter School Survey, Center for Education Reform.

185 Hobbled by its teachers: Cohen, "Examining the Data: State Per Pupil Expenditures and State Graduation Rates." http://edmoney.newamerica.net/blogposts/2010/examining_the_data_state_per_pupil_expenditures_and_state_graduation_rates-36914.

186 Charter School Enrollment by State: "Number of Public Charter Schools & Student, 2009–2010," PublicCharters.org, September 3, 2009, http://www.publiccharters.org/enrollment.

187 School Choice Programs: "Choice Options State by State," EdReform.com, http://www.edreform.com/School_Choices/Choice_Programs/?Choice_Options_State_by_State.

188 16 million new patients: Devon Herrick, "Medicaid Expansion will Bankrupt the States," NCPA.org, October 25, 2010, http://www.ncpa.org/pdfs/ba729.pdf.

189 Washington will pick: Ibid.

190 In Texas, for example: Ibid.

191 Increases in State Medicaid Spending Due to Obamacare: Ibid.

PART FOUR

1 2010 House Democratic Seats That Switched to Republican: "House Lineup 112th Congress," House.gov, http://www.house.gov/daily/112ElectionStats.htm.

2 Voted with Democrats: "110 Congress Senate Members Voting with their Parties," http://projects.washingtonpost.com/congress/110/senate/party-voters/.

3 64% of the voters: "Election 2012: Nebraska Senate," RasmussenReports.com, December 29, 2009, http://www.rasmussenreports.com/public_content/politics/elections/election_2012/nebraska/election_2012_nebraska_senate.

4 He points to the: "Ben Nelson Calls for Bipartisan Camp David Fiscal Summit, Full Tax Cut Extension," HuffingtonPost.com, September 29, 2010, http://www.huffingtonpost.com/2010/09/29/nelson-calls-for-bipartis_n_743481.html.

5 "Nelson and his wife": Manu Raju, "Ben Nelson Tries to Repair Damage at Home," Politico.com, January 14, 2010, http://www.politico.com/news/stories/0110/31488.html.

6 "I'm perfectly prepared": Harold Meyerson, "Ben Nelson, the Nebraska Narcissist, is at it Again," Washington Post, April 27, 2010, http://voices.washingtonpost.com/postpartisan/2010/04/ben_nelson_the_nebraska_narcis.html.

7 The American Insurance: David Goldman and Tami Luhby, "Where Your Money is Going," CNNMoney.com, http://money.cnn.com/news/storysupplement/economy/aig/index.html.

8 "the goal of the provision": Tom Petruno, "Report: Warren Buffett Loses Bid to Weaken Senate Bill Derivatives Regulation," *Los Angeles Times*, April 26, 2010, http://latimesblogs .latimes.com/money_co/2010/04/buffett-berkshire-derivatives-bill-senate-collateral .html.

9 "extensively uses derivatives": Ibid.

10 "Nelson's most recent": Brady Dennis and Lori Montgomery, "Suspicion Greets Democrat's Stated Reason for Opposing Financial Overhaul Bill," *Washington Post*, April 29, 2010, http://www.washingtonpost.com/wp-dyn/content/article/2010/04/28/AR2010042 805807.html?hpid=topnews.

11 "Berkshire Hathaway": Ibid.

12 "protested that he was": Meyerson, "Ben Nelson, the Nebraska Narcissist, is at it Again."

13 "I mean," the president said: "Obama's Interview with Progressive Bloggers (FULL TRANSCRIPT)," HuffingtonPost.com, October 27, 2010, http://www.huffingtonpost .com/2010/10/27/obamas-interview-with-progressive-bloggers_n_775112.html.

14 A Rasmussen Reports: "Election 2012: Nebraska Senate," RasmussenReports.com, December 29, 2009, http://www.rasmussenreports.com/public_content/politics/elections/ election_2012/nebraska/election_2012_nebraska_senate.

15 89% of the time: "110th Congress Senate members Voting with their Parties," *Washington Post*, http://projects.washingtonpost.com/congress/110/senate/party-voters/.

16 "Well, I think . . . Thank you, Alexis": "Senator Jon Tester on Drilling Bill," FoxNews .com, July 18, 2008, http://www.foxnews.com/story/0,2933,386041,00.html.

17 "A pioneer in ethics": Tester.Senate.gov, http://tester.senate.gov/.

18 Tester, who sponsored: "111th Congress Earmarks," OpenSecrets.org, http://www .opensecrets.org/earmarks/index.php?type=SC&cycle=2009.

19 Tester's Earmarks and Donations: "Jon Tester: Earmarks (Fiscal Year 2010)," Open Secrets.org, http://www.opensecrets.org/politicians/earmarks.php?cid=N00027605& cycle=2010.

20 91% of the time: "110th Congress Senate Members Voting with their Parties," *Washington Post*, http://projects.washingtonpost.com/congress/110/senate/party-voters/.

21 "Jim Webb went to the": David Paul Kuhn, "Jim Webb: Why Reagan Dems Still Matter," RealClearPolitics.com, November 8, 2010, http://www.realclearpolitics.com/ articles/2010/11/08/jim_webb_why_reagan_dems_still_matter_107875.html.

22 "Democratic leaders broadly": Ibid.

23 " 'I've been . . . business people' ": Ibid.

24 "His criticism [of the]": Ibid.

25 He's gotten $129: "111th Congress Earmarks," http://www.opensecrets.org/earmarks/ index.php?type=SC&cycle=2009.

26 $9.6 million: "James Webb," OpenSecrets.org, http://www.opensecrets.org/politicians/ summary.php?cid=N00028058&cycle=2010.

27 Jim Webb: Earmarks for Campaign Contributions: "James Webb: Earmarks (Fiscal Year 2010,)" http://www.opensecrets.org/politicians/earmarks.php?cid=N00028058&cycle=2010.

28 "still sorting that out": Kuhn, "Jim Webb: Why Reagan Dems Still Matter."

29 And thus the native: *The Tragedy of Hamlet, Prince of Denmark* (Washington Square Press, ed., 1992, Folger Shakespeare Library).

30 96% of the time: "110th Congress Senate Members Voting with their Parties," *Washington Post*, http://projects.washingtonpost.com/congress/110/senate/party-voters/.

31 Sherrod Brown is the: William Hershey, "Sherrod Brown Among Most Liberal," DaytonDailyNews.com, March 3, 2010, http://www.daytondailynews.com/news/politics/magazine-sherrod-brown-among-most-liberal-576852.html.

32 "need to speed": "Sherrod Brown: 'The Stimulus Package was Not a Failure,'" RightOhio.com, July 10, 2009, http://www.rightohio.com/tag/sherrod-brown/page/2/.

33 "So eager was Brown": "Brown Likely to Lose in 2012," November 17, 2010, http://www.theintelligencer.net/page/content.detail/id/548941/Brown-Likely-To-Lose-in-2012.html?nav=511.

34 "we must craft": Ibid.

35 "tax breaks for": Sherrod Brown, "How to Fight Tea Party's Faux Populism," *USA Today*, October 3, 2010, http://www.usatoday.com/news/opinion/forum/2010-10-04-column04_ST1_N.htm.

36 According to William: Ibid.

37 General Motors employs: "General Motors," Wikipedia.org, http://en.wikipedia.org/wiki/General_Motors.

38 68,000 of them: "Number of GM Employees in the US," NumberOf.net, http://www.numberof.net/number-of-gm-employees-in-the-us/.

39 donated $5,000: Eamon Javers, "General Motors Now Making Political Donations," CNBC.com, September 22, 2010, http://www.cnbc.com/id/39308274/General_Motors_Now_Making_Political_Donations.

40 "ACORN provided contributions": "GOP Congressional Report Accuses ACORN of Political Corruption, Widespread Fraud," FoxNews.com, July 23, 2009, http://www.foxnews.com/politics/2009/07/23/gop-congressional-report-accuses-acorn-political-corruption-widespread-fraud/.

41 Brown spent $121: "Sherrod Brown: Earmarks (Fiscal Year 2010)," OpenSecrets.org, http://www.opensecrets.org/politicians/earmarks.php?cid=N00003535&cycle=2010.

42 $12.6 million: Ibid.

43 Sherrod Brown: Earmarks for Campaign Contributions: Ibid.

44 95% of the time: "110th Congress Senate Members Voting with their Parties," *Washington Post*, http://projects.washingtonpost.com/congress/110/senate/party-voters/.

45 He was barred: "Casey Tapped for Dem Convention," ABCNews.com, August 13, 2008, http://blogs.abcnews.com/politicalradar/2008/08/casey-tapped-fo.html.

46 Junior endorsed Obama: "Robert P. Casey," WhoRunsGov.com, http://www.whoruns gov.com/Profiles/Robert_P._Casey.

47 Junior only backs: David Freddoso, "He's Not His Father's Pro-Life Democrat," National Review.com, September 12, 2007, http://www.nationalreview.com/articles/222136/hes -not-his-fathers-pro-life-democrat/david-freddoso.

48 "He voted against": "U.S. Senate Roll Call Votes 110th Congress—1st Session," Senate .gov, http://senate.gov/legislative/LIS/roll_call_lists/roll_call_vote_cfm.cfm?congress= 110&session=1&vote=00379.

49 Junior was one: Dustin Hockensmith, "Sen. Bob Casey Jr. Taking Heat for Vote in Sup- port of ACORN," *Patriot-News*, September 15, 2009, http://www.pennlive.com/midstate/ index.ssf/2009/09/sen_bob_casey_jr_taking_heat_f.html.

50 Casey's spokesman said: Ibid.

51 Despite having attended: "Bob Casey on Education," OnTheIssues.org, http://www.on theissues.org/senate/Bob_Casey.htm.

52 Even though tort: Peter Hamby, "Tort Reform Could Save $54 Billion, Report Says," CNN .com, October 12, 2009, http://politicalticker.blogs.cnn.com/2009/10/12/tort-reform -could-save-54-million-report-says/#more-7282.

53 "office has released": Steven Ertlet, "Senate Democrats Nelson, Casey Backing Down on Abortion, Health Care Battle," LifeNews.com, November 17, 2009, http://www.lifenews .com/2009/11/17/nat-5670/.

54 "thinks that health": Ibid.

55 "the comments": Ibid.

56 he has sponsored: "Bob Casey: Earmarks (Fiscal Year 2010)," OpenSecrets.org, http:// www.opensecrets.org/politicians/earmarks.php?cid=N00027503&cycle=2010.

57 $20.2 million: "Bob Casey," OpenSecrets.org, http://www.opensecrets.org/politicians/ summary.php?cid=N00027503&cycle=2010.

58 Bob Casey: Earmarks for Campaign Contributions: "Bob Casey: Earmarks (Fiscal Year 2010)."

59 84% of the time: "110th Congress Senate Members Voting with their Parties," *Washington Post*, http://projects.washingtonpost.com/congress/110/senate/party-voters/.

60 "wrapped around this": "Upset with Washington? McCaskill Doesn't See what the Fuss is all About," MOGOP.org, July 19, 2010, http://www.mogop.org/2010/07/ 4164/.

61 "I certainly . . . choices": Doug Powers, "Claire McCaskill: Missouri Voters Too Stupid to Realize What's Good for Them," MichelleMalkin.com, August 5, 2010, http://michelle malkin.com/2010/08/05/claire-mccaskill-missouri-voters-too-stupid-to-realize-whats -good-for-them/.

62 "declared that Democrat": "Vulnerable McCaskill Doubles-Down on Support for Liberal Agenda, Votes for Reid for Senate's Top Spot," MOGOP.org, November 16, 2010, http:// www.mogop.org/2010/11/4930/.

63 She says that: Stephanie Williams, "One Man's Sexual Assault is Claire McCaskill's Love Pat," Examiner.com, November 18, 2010, http://www.examiner.com/conservative-in -kansas-city/one-man-s-sexual-assault-is-claire-mccaskill-s-love-pat.

64 "that the public": Ibid.

65 "everybody needs to take": "Senator Claire McCaskill in Sedalia, Missouri—May 27, 2009—Part 1," May 27, 2009, http://leftword.blogdig.net/archives/articles/May2009/27/ Senator_Claire_McCaskill_in_Sedalia_Missouri_May_27_2009_part_1.html.

66 "compared terrorists to violent": "McCaskill Scolds Missourians for Opposition to Terrorists in the U.S.," MOGOP.org, June 11, 2009, http://www.mogop.org/2009/06/ 1152/.

67 "Terrorism prosecutions in this": "Terror Trial Trouble," Republican.Senate.gov, May 22, 2009, http://republican.senate.gov/public/index.cfm?FuseAction=Blogs.Detail&Blog_ ID=00033572-51ea-4a39-8fa9-8e0e5785a977&Month=5&Year=2009.

68 "Environmental Protection Agency": "2010 Missouri General Assembly," SierraClub.org, March 31, 2010, http://missouri.sierraclub.org/legis/showbills.asp.

69 she told FoxNews.com: "Graham, McCaskill Discuss Lame Duck," FoxNews.com, No- vember 28, 2010, http://fns.blogs.foxnews.com/2010/11/28/graham-mccaskill-discuss -lame-duck/.

70 "whenever Mom got": "McCaskill Turns Her Back on the 2nd Amendment," MOGOP .org, May 13, 2009, http://www.mogop.org/2009/05/1048/.

71 "Dad was shooting": Ibid.

72 "She said she would": Jo Mannies, "McCaskill Criticizes Israel, Emphasizes Support for Gun-Rights and China Hub at Forum," St. Louis Beacon, June 1, 2010, http://www.stl beacon.org/content/view/102770/314/.

73 she voted no: "Senator Claire McCaskill," VoteSmart.org, http://www.votesmart.org/ voting_category.php?can_id=2109.

74 "no one will ever": Jo Mannies, "Mo GOP Challenges McCaskill's Comments in Favor of Gun Rights," St. Louis Beacon, June 2, 2010, http://www.stlbeacon.org/index.php?Itemid =314&id=102810&option=com_content&task=view.

75 "this country continues": Ibid.

76 "guns are not": Ibid.

77 "is valued at up to": "More Democrat Tax Hypocrisy: Claire McCaskill Double Standard on Tax Shelters," MOGOP.org, March 6, 2010, http://www.mogop.org/2009/03/903/.

78 "Like Warren Buffett": "McCaskill Blames Husband for Bermuda Tax Shelter," MOGOP .org, May 5, 2009, http://www.mogop.org/2009/05/975/.

79 "assets of my family": Ibid.

80 "There is absolutely": Angie C. Marek, "Republicans Make McCaskill's Husband, Wealth Major Campaign Issue," USNews.com, October 20, 2006, http://www.usnews.com/ usnews/politics/campaign_diary/missouri/archive/2006/10/republicans_make_mc caskills_hu.htm.

81 "profits come from": David Cay Johnston and Joseph B. Tester, "Bermuda Move Allows Insurers to Avoid taxes," *New York Times*, March 6, 2000, http://www.nytimes.com/2000/03/06/business/bermuda-move-allows-insurers-to-avoid-taxes.html

82 53% disapproval rating: "Vulnerable McCaskill Doubles-Down on Support for Liberal Agenda, Votes for Reid for Senate's Top Spot,"

83 "reiterated her support": "On this Week, McCaskill Promises Unpopular Public Option," MOGOP.org, October 26, 2009, http://www.mogop.org/2009/10/1598/.

84 "I have gone": Shannon Bream, "Senate Democrats View 2012 with Trepidation," FoxNews.com, November 22, 2010, http://politics.blogs.foxnews.com/2010/11/22/senate-democrats-view-2012-trepidation.

85 96% of the time: "110th Congress Senate Members Voting with their Parties," *Washington Post*, http://projects.washingtonpost.com/congress/110/senate/party-voters/.

86 "listed numerous investments": Associated Press, "Sens. Ted Kennedy, Herb Kohl Among Wealthiest Members of Congress," FoxNews.com, June 14, 2007, Amhttp://www.foxnews.com/story/0,2933,282676,00.html.

87 He authored 69: "Herb Kohl: Earmarks (Fiscal Year 2010)," OpenSecrets.org, http://www.opensecrets.org/politicians/earmarks.php?cid=N00004309&cycle=2010.

88 "by playing the earmark": "Herb Kohl's Turn to Give Up Earmarks," *Wisconsin State Journal*, November 17, 2010, http://host.madison.com/wsj/news/opinion/editorial/article_468e03b6-f2a2-11df-a8f4-001cc4c002e0.html.

89 And consider some of the: "Herb Kohl: Earmarks (Fiscal Year 2010)."

90 "a meaningful but": "Leahy Builds Coalition Urging Temporary Boost in Dairy Price Supports," Leahy.Senate.gov, July 15, 2009, http://leahy.senate.gov/press/press_releases/release/?id=622c4a03-2f6d-46ed-aef7-6e8ddbb85b6a.

91 96% of the time: "110th Congress Senate Members Voting with their Parties," *Washington Post*, http://projects.washingtonpost.com/congress/110/senate/party-voters/.

92 Then she went through: Deborah White, "Profile of Sen. Jeff Bingaman of New Mexico," About.com, http://usliberals.about.com/od/liberalpersonalprofiles/p/SenBingaman.htm.

93 "Global Crossing's adventures": Richard S. Dunham, "Washington Outlook," Business Week.com, February 11, 2002, http://www.businessweek.com/magazine/content/02_06/c3769068.htm.

94 In 1998, Global Crossing: Ibid.

95 "They came out of": Ibid.

96 "in 1999, Global Crossing": Ibid.

97 92% of the time: "110th Congress Senate Members Voting with their Parties," *Washington Post*, http://projects.washingtonpost.com/congress/110/senate/party-voters/.

98 While 12.4% of the: "Projected Future Growth of the Older Population," AoA.gov, http://www.aoa.gov/aoaroot/aging_statistics/future_growth/future_growth.aspx#state.

99 "I have to quota": Interview by Dick Morris on September 18, 2010.

100 With the elderly: Ibid.

101 "what we are seeing": Nathan Crabbe, "Sen. Bill Nelson Lashes out at White House Staff," *Gainesville Sun*, November 19, 2010, http://www.gainesville.com/article/20101119/ARTICLES/101119287/-1/news?Title=Sen-Bill-Nelson-lashes-out-at-White-House-staff.

102 "the president cannot": Ibid.

103 "the White House staff": Ibid.

104 "put part of the": Ibid.

105 Bill Nelson: Earmarks for Campaign Contributions: "Bill Nelson: Earmarks (Fiscal Year 2010)," OpenSecrets.org, http://www.opensecrets.org/politicians/earmarks.php?cid=N00009926&cycle=2010.

106 In all, Nelson: Ibid.

107 "said Florida has benefited": "Sen.-Elect Marce Rubio, Sen. Bill Nelson Disagree on Earmarks," TheStateColumn.com, November 16, 2010, http://www.thestatecolumn.com/articles/sen-elect-marco-rubio-sen-bill-nelson-disagree-on-earmarks/.

108 "pleaded guilty to felony": "Bill Nelson," SourceWatch.org, http://www.sourcewatch.org/index.php?title=Bill_Nelson#Riscorp_scandal:_illegal_campaign_contributions.

109 $80,000: Ibid.

110 "Sen. Nelson has": Ibid.

111 95% of the time: "110th Congress Senate Members Voting with their Parties," *Washington Post*, http://projects.washingtonpost.com/congress/110/senate/party-voters/.

112 The recent IPO: John Crawley, "GM Seeks Easing of Executive Pay Restrictions," ABCNews.com, November 10, 2010, http://abcnews.go.com/Business/wireStory?id=12364303.

113 In 2010, we paid: "Deborah Ann Stabenow," OpenSecrets.org, http://www.opensecrets.org/politicians/earmarks.php?cid=N00004118&cycle=2010.

114 $12.4 million her: "Deborah Ann Stabenow," OpenSecrets.org, http://www.opensecrets.org/politicians/summary.php?cid=N00004118&cycle=2010.

115 Debbie Stabenow Earmarks for Donations: "Deborah Ann Stabenow: Earmarks (Fiscal Year 2010)," OpenSecrets.org, http://www.opensecrets.org/politicians/earmarks.php?cid=N00004118&cycle=2010.

116 Stabenow added insult: Javers, "General Motors Now Making Political Donations."

117 In the months before: "Manchin Scandal Growing in West Virginia," TalkingSides.com, September 23, 2010, http://www.talkingsides.com/blogs/2010/09/23/manchin-scandal-growing-in-west-virginia.

118 In a second probe: Ibid.

119 After a public: Vicki Smith, "Ex-WVU Employees Sue Over Unearned Degree Scandal," MySanAntonio.com, December 7, 2010, http://www.centredaily.com/2010/12/07/2386078/ex-wvu-employees-sue-over-unearned.html.

120 96% of the time: "110th Congress Senate Members Voting with their Parties," *Washington Post*, http://projects.washingtonpost.com/congress/110/senate/party-voters/.

121 On July 21: Terry Hurlbut, "Menendez Tried to Wangle Special Favor for Politically Connected Bank," Examiner.com, February 9, 2010, http://www.examiner.com/essex-county

-conservative-in-newark/menendez-tried-to-wangle-special-favor-for-politically
-connected-bank.

122 The senator neglected: Ibid.

123 "received more than": Terry Hurlbut, "First BankAmericano Scandal Breaks Wide Open," Examiner.com, February 10, 2010, http://www.examiner.com/essex-county -conservative-in-newark/first-bankamericano-scandal-breaks-wide-open.

124 "'cease and desist'": Ibid.

125 Menendez's friends, contributors: David Kocieniewski and Ray Rivera, "Waterfront Project Reflects 2 Images of a Senator," New York Times, October 29, 2006, http://www.ny times.com/2006/10/29/nyregion/29menendez.html?sq=robert%20menendez&st=cse& scp=12&pagewanted=all.

126 "the first major": Ibid.

127 "more than $250,000": Ibid.

128 "perhaps no one": Ibid.

129 Menendez got Scarinci: Ibid.

130 "a fierce recall": Ibid.

131 During Menendez's campaign: Ibid.

132 "subpoenaed the records": Ibid.

133 "wrote a letter to": Randy Bergmann, "Menendez's 'Constituent Service,'" October 16, 2006, http://rbergmann.blogspot.com/2006/10/menendezs-constituent-service.html.

134 "guilty by geography": Kocieniewski and Rivera, "Waterfront Project Reflects 2 Images of a Senator."

135 Menendez is up to: "Robert Menendez: Earmarks (Fiscal Year 2010)," OpenSecrets.org, http://www.opensecrets.org/politicians/earmarks.php?cid=N00000699&cycle=2010.

136 Robert Menendez: Earmarks for Campaign Contributions: Ibid.

137 Consider the $250,000: Ibid.

138 Or the $200,000: Ibid.

139 Or the $200,000: Ibid.

140 The money Menendez: "Robert Menendez: Earmarks (Fiscal Year 2010)," OpenSecrets.org, http://www.opensecrets.org/politicians/earmarks.php?cid=N00000699&cycle=2010.

141 After the capture of: Aaron Blake, "Emmer Concedes, Redistricting Battlefield Set," Washington Post, December 8, 2010, http://voices.washingtonpost.com/thefix/governors/ emmer-concedes-gop-holds-29-20.html.

142 Gains and Losses in House Seats, 2012: Monica Davey, "Winners and Losers in Reapportionment," New York Times, September 27, 2010, http://thecaucus.blogs.nytimes .com/2010/09/27/winners-and-losers-in-reapportionment-are-predicted/.

143 Among the states: Blake, "Emmer Concedes, Redistricting Battlefield Set."

144 Among those that will: Ibid.

145 Arizona: Sean Trende, "A Preview of 2012 Redistricting," RealClearPolitics.com, November 11, 2010, http://www.realclearpolitics.com/articles/2010/11/11/a_preview_of_2012_ redistricting_107924.html.

146 Since Republicans get: Ibid.

147 "A bookstore owner": Patrick McGreevy, "California Begins a New Era in Redistricting," *Los Angeles Times*, November 18, 2010, http://articles.latimes.com/2010/nov/18/local/la -me-redistricting-20101119.

148 "These two changes": Ibid.

149 "heavily Republican Atlanta": Trende, "A Preview of 2012 Redistricting."

150 a Democratic one: Ibid.

151 the Republicans will suffer: Ibid.

152 Trende thinks a: Ibid.

153 The Republicans have: Ibid.

154 Nevada gains a seat: Ibid.

155 New Jersey loses: Ibid.

156 If New York: Ibid.

157 Republicans got 55%: Ibid.

158 Ohio will lose: Ibid.

159 South Carolina gains: Ibid.

160 In 2001, Republicans: Ibid.

161 Utah gets a new: Ibid.

162 Washington State's new: Ibid.

163 Patty Murray's negative: E-mail to Dick Morris from Robert Savino, aide to Dino Rossi, sent on October 18, 2010.

164 Murray's ad: Ibid.

165 "the hobgoblin of little": "Self-Reliance," EmersonCentral.com, http://www.emerson central.com/selfreliance.htm.

166 John Zogby's post election: "Zogby Interactive: Late Deciding Voters May Have Prevented Greater Democrat Losses," Zogby.com, November 8, 2010, http://zogby.com/news/Read News.cfm?ID=1916.

167 15% of single: Ibid.

168 (who voted Democrat): Ibid.

PART FIVE

1 In the late: Sir Francis Bacon, *Religious Meditations,* "Of Heresies," 1597.

2 The final health care: John Tamny, "Health Care: 16% of GDP," Forbes.com, February 1, 2010, http://www.forbes.com/2010/01/31/health-care-gdp-reform-opinions-columnists -john-tamny.html.

3 The average Senate: Christopher Beam, "Paper Weight," Slate.com, August 20, 2009, http://www.slate.com/id/2225820/.

4 "I love these": Paul Blumenthal, "Rep. Conyers: Don't Read the Bill," SunlightFoundation .com, July 27, 2010, http://blog.sunlightfoundation.com/taxonomy/term/John -Conyers/.

5 Moore: "How could": "Fahrenheit 9/11 Trailer," YouTube.com, http://www.youtube .com/watch?v=2Zf2nCiBJLo.

6 John McCain was: Brian Montopoll, "Tallying the Health Care Bill's Giveaways," CBS News.com, December 21, 2009, http://www.cbsnews.com/8301-503544_162-6006838 -503544.html.

7 The "Cornhusker . . . Connecticut: Ibid.

8 In early March: Mary E. O'Leary, "Dodd Sees Mood Shift in Health Care Debate," *New Haven Register,* March 9, 2010.

9 According to Rasmussen: "Health Care Law," RasmussenReports.com, December 20, 2010, http://www.rasmussenreports.com/public_content/politics/current_events/ healthcare/health_care_law.

10 "I think that": Mike Allen, "David Axelrod: Reform Will Get More Popular," Politico.com, September 12, 2010, http://www.politico.com/news/stories/0910/42023 .html.

11 In 2010, the industry: "Health Professionals: Lobbying, 2010," OpenSecrets.org, http:// www.opensecrets.org/industries/lobbying.php?cycle=2010&ind=H01.

12 Campaign Contributions from Lobbyists, 2010: "Lobbyists: Top Recipients," Open Secrets.org, http://www.opensecrets.org/industries/recips.php?ind=K02&cycle=2010 &recipdetail=S&mem=Y&sortorder=U; http://www.opensecrets.org/industries/recips .php?ind=K02&cycle=2010&recipdetail=H&mem=Y&sortorder=U.

13 There are, however: Stephen J. Dubner, "New York Congressman Anthony Weiner Answers Your Questions," *New York Times,* May 21, 2009, http://freakonomics.blogs .nytimes.com/2009/05/21/new-york-congressman-anthony-weiner-answers-your -questions/.

14 In a ranking of all: Lydia Saad, "Congress Ranks Last in Confidence in Institutions," Gallup.com, July 22, 2010, http://www.gallup.com/poll/141512/congress-ranks-last -confidence-institutions.aspx.

15 According to both: Jeffrey M. Jones, "Obama's Approval Rating Lowest Yet, Congress' Declines," Gallup.com, March 18, 2010, http://www.gallup.com/poll/126809/obama -approval-rating-lowest-yet-congress-declines.aspx.

16 39% approval rating: Saad, "Congress Ranks Last in Confidence in Institutions."

17 In April 2010: "Obama's Job Approval Rating Stagnant," UPI.com, April 23, 2010, http:// www.upi.com/Top_News/US/2010/04/23/Obamas-job-approval-rating-stagnant/UPI -43451272027845/.

18 which made massive: "Health Professionals: Top Recipients," OpenSecrets.org, http:// www.opensecrets.org/industries/recips.php?cycle=2010&ind=H01.

19 The leadership of both: "Health Professionals: Money to Congress," OpenSecrets.org, http://www.opensecrets.org/industries/summary.php?ind=H01&cycle=2010&recip detail=S&mem=Y.

20 Former senator Blanche: Ibid.

21 Of course, all: "Health Professionals: Top Recipients," OpenSecrets.org, http://www
.opensecrets.org/industries/recips.php?ind=H01&cycle=2008&recipdetail=P&mem=
N&sortorder=U.

22 Roll Call 1: "Final Vote Results for Roll Call 1," Clerk.House.gov, January 12, 2010, http://
clerk.house.gov/evs/2010/roll001.xml.

23 Roll Call 2: "Final Vote Results for Roll Call 2," Clerk.House.gov, January 13, 2010, http://
clerk.house.gov/evs/2010/roll002.xml.

24 Roll Call 3: "Final Vote Results for Roll Call 3," Clerk.House.gov, January 12, 2010, http://
clerk.house.gov/evs/2010/roll003.xml.

25 Roll Call 4: "Final Vote Results for Roll Call 4," Clerk.House.gov, January 13, 2010, http://
clerk.house.gov/evs/2010/roll004.xml.

26 Roll Call 5: "Final Vote Results for Roll Call 5," Clerk.House.gov, January 13, 2010, http://
clerk.house.gov/evs/2010/roll005.xml.

27 In fact, 237: $645,503: Erika Lovley, "237 Millionaires in Congress," Politico.com, No-
vember 6, 2009, http://www.politico.com/news/stories/1109/29235.html.

28 Whereas about 1%: Ibid.

29 But most of them: William Danko and Thomas J. Stanley, "The Millionaire Next Door:
The Surprising Secrets of American's Wealthy," New York Times, http://www.nytimes
.com/books/first/s/stanley-millionaire.html.

30 Darrell Issa . . . $58,436,537: "Net Worth," OpenSecrets.org, http://www.opensecrets
.org/pfds/overview.php.

31 Poorest Members of the House: "Net Worth, 2009," OpenSecrets.org, http://www
.opensecrets.org/pfds/overview.php?type=W&year=2009&filter=H&sort=A.

32 Hillary Clinton was: "Net Worth, 2009," OpenSecrets.org, http://www.opensecrets.org/
pfds/overview.php?type=W&year=2009&filter=E.

33 The first time: Maurice D. Hinchey, "Congress of the United States," June 14, 2005, http://
pfds.opensecrets.org/N00001222_2004_A.pdf.

34 In 2010, Maurice: "Maurice Hinchey: Earmarks (Fiscal Year 2010)," OpenSecrets
.org, http://www.opensecrets.org/politicians/earmarks.php?cid=N00001222&cycle=
2010.

35 In a 2009 press: "Hinchey Stresses His Lack of Involvement in Saugerties Development,"
DailyFreeman.com, May 21, 2010, http://www.dailyfreeman.com/articles/2010/05/21/
news/doc4bf60ccc73723880294024.txt?viewmode=3.

36 This upset a number: Ibid.

37 During the last: Julia Reischel, "Beat the Press," WatershedPost.com, October 19, 2010,
http://www.watershedpost.com/2010/beat-press.

38 Both properties: "Financial Disclosure Statement for Calendar Year 2004," OpenSecrets
.org, http://pfds.opensecrets.org/N00001222_2004.pdf.

39 2004: "Disclosure Statement," OpenSecrets.org, June 14, 2005, http://pfds.opensecrets
.org/N00001222_2004_A.pdf.

40 2005: "Financial Disclosure Statement for Calendar Year 2005," OpenSecrets.org, http://pfds.opensecrets.org/N00001222_2005.pdf.

41 2006: "Financial Disclosure Statement for Calendar Year 2006," OpenSecrets.org, http://pfds.opensecrets.org/N00001222_2006.pdf.

42 2007: "Financial Disclosure Statement for Calendar Year 2007," OpenSecrets.org, http://pfds.opensecrets.org/N00001222_2007.pdf.

43 2008: "Financial Disclosure Statement for Calendar Year 2008," OpenSecrets.org, http://pfds.opensecrets.org/N00001222_2008.pdf.

44 2009: "Financial Disclosure Statement for Calendar Year 2009," OpenSecrets.org, http://pfds.opensecrets.org/N00001222_2009.pdf.

45 2004 sold: "Maurice Hinchey (D-NY), 2004," OpenSecrets.org, http://www.opensecrets.org/pfds/CIDsummary.php?CID=N00001222&year=2004.

46 2004 capital gain: "Financial Disclosure Statement for Calendar Year 2004."

47 2005 disclosed value: "Maurice Hinchey (D-NY), 2005," OpenSecrets.org, http://www.opensecrets.org/pfds/CIDsummary.php?CID=N00001222&year=2005.

48 2006 disclosed value: "Maurice Hinchey (D-NY), 2006," OpenSecrets.org, http://www.opensecrets.org/pfds/CIDsummary.php?CID=N00001222&year=2006.

49 2007 disclosed value: "Maurice Hinchey (D-NY), 2007," OpenSecrets.org, http://www.opensecrets.org/pfds/CIDsummary.php?CID=N00001222&year=2007.

50 2008 disclosed value: "Maurice Hinchey (D-NY), 2008," OpenSecrets.org, http://www.opensecrets.org/pfds/CIDsummary.php?CID=N00001222&year=2008.

51 2009 disclosed value: "Maurice Hinchey (D-NY), 2009," OpenSecrets.org, http://www.opensecrets.org/pfds/CIDsummary.php?CID=N00001222&year=2009.

52 Well, first of all: Financial Disclosure Statement for Calendar Year 2004."

53 Hinchey reveals that: "Maurice Hinchey (D-NY), 2009."

54 When questioned about: Allison Sickle, "Congressman Denies Knowing His Wife Lobbied for Landman Group," DCBureau.org, April 7, 2010, http://dcbureau.org/20100407358/Natural-Resources-News-Service/hinchey-denies-knowing-his-wife-lobbied-for-landman-group.html.

55 For example, in: "Christopher J. Dodd (D-Conn), 2007," OpenSecrets.org, http://www.opensecrets.org/pfds/CIDsummary.php?CID=N00000581&year=2007.

PART SIX

1 "interest rates": "Rick Santelli," CNBC.com, http://www.cnbc.com/id/15837966.

2 his Rant: For the video go to: http://www.cnbc.com/id/15840232?video=1039849853 Full Transcript: http://freedomeden.blogspot.com/2009/02/rick-santelli-tea-party.html.

3 "We went from a": Jenny Beth Martin, "Boy, Has My Life Changed or Maybe Not," JenuineJen.com, June 15, 2010, http://jenuinejen.com/.

4 "cleaning houses": Ibid.

5   "began to blog": Ibid.

6   "government bailouts": Ibid.

7   "it truly changed": Ibid.

8   "co-hosted the": Ibid.

9   "we are only": Conference call with Tea Party Patriots.

10 "hastily organized": Liz Tellar, "Local Lawyer Emerges as Face of Tea Party move-
    ment," TheUnion.com, February 27, 2010, http://www.theunion.com/article/20100227/
    NEWS/100229809.

11 "I wanted to show": Ibid.

12 "It was liberating": Ibid.

13 "I was always": Ibid.

14 "Meckler's expertise in": Ibid.

15 "I think Ronald": Ibid.

16 NPR reports that: "The Brothers Koch: Rich, Political and Playing to Win," NPR.org,
    August 26, 2010, http://www.npr.org/templates/story/story.php?storyId=129425186.

17 "donated a hundred": Jamie Mayer, "Covert Operations," *New Yorker*, August 30, 2010,
    http://www.newyorker.com/reporting/2010/08/30/100830fa_fact_mayer.

18 *The New Yorker*: Ibid.

19 "the sugar daddies": Fank Rich, "The Billionaires Bankrolling the Tea Party," *New York
    Times*, August 28, 2010, http://www.nytimes.com/2010/08/29/opinion/29rich.htm.